I0093809

Inside ISI

**The story and involvement of the ISI in
Afghan Jihad, Taliban, Al-Qaeda, 9/11,
Osama bin Laden, 26/11 and
the Future of Al-Qaeda**

Inside ISI

The story and involvement of the ISI in
Afghan Jihad, Taliban, Al-Qaeda, 9/11,
Osama bin Laden, 26/11 and
The Future of Al-Qaeda

by

S K Datta

(Established 1870)

United Service Institution of India
New Delhi

Vij Books India Pvt Ltd
New Delhi (India)

Published by

Vij Books India Pvt Ltd
(Publishers, Distributors & Importers)
2/19, Ansari Road
Delhi – 110 002
Phones: 91-11-43596460, 91-11-47340674
Fax: 91-11-47340674
e-mail: vijbooks@rediffmail.com

Copyright © 2014, United Service Institution of India, New Delhi

Paperback Edition 2015

All rights reserved.

No part of this book may be reproduced, stored in a retrieval system, transmitted or utilised in any form or by any means, electronic, mechanical, photocopying, recording or otherwise, without the prior permission of the copyright owner. Application for such permission should be addressed to the publisher.

The views expressed in the book are of the author and not necessarily those of the USI or publishers.

CONTENTS

PREFACE

This book is dedicated to the victims of terrorism and intelligence and law enforcement agencies of all the countries of the world. Thousands of them have laid down their lives fighting terrorists. To uphold the democratic and secular fabric of India and combating terrorism, every year more than a thousand police personnel lay down their lives. Thousands of civilians, men, women and children are killed in India by foreign terrorists to create a climate of terror for promotion of their political agenda. India's 26/11 was committed in November 2008, an incident of such kind was never witnessed before. More such brutal and lethal attacks are likely to happen in India and elsewhere.

The book is relevant to those who wished to know why and how terrorism shifted from West Asia to South and Southeast Asia and Africa. This significant shift needs to be studied in depth for policy formulation and future strategy. The book will reveal that the so called Islamic Terrorism is traceable to Pakistan from concept to reality. Pakistan as a state and not Pakistanis, has provided the platform for outward and inward march of jihadis. For this to happen the ISI has been playing the principal role. Thus, the focus in this book is on ISI as an instrument of spreading jihadi culture in Pakistan and elsewhere.

Terrorist attacks are always unexpected and dramatic. Each attack is a benchmark of lethality and brutality. The future attacks are likely to be more destructive and lethal. Even depleted uranium mixed with RDX can cause havoc in any city of the world. Such a situation is a possibility. Experts dealing with the subject agree on this possibility. In 2000, Tariq Ali with his wide knowledge of inside happenings in Pakistan said that 'it is no secret that the fundamentalists have penetrated the army on every level. What distinguishes them from the old-style religious groups is that they want to seize state power and for that they need the army.'[1] In the event of that happening the nuclear button will be in the hands of the fundamentalists, a danger that is looming large in the horizon. The nuclear weapon of Pakistan today, thanks to US-China participation in Afghan jihad, was possible due to US indulgence and China's clandestine help to Pakistan. The bomb was ready in 1988 during Gen Zia's time. This was given to 'empower those bent on global jihad.'[2]

The danger of world wide jihadi terrorism will continue unless the world takes notice of states sponsoring and supporting such acts of terrorism. The tidal wave jihadi terrorism has to be understood. The Islamic scholars have to reinterpret jihad in the context of the present globalized world, if the clash of civilization is to be avoided.

The central focus of this book is on terrorism in the name of Islam that originated from Pakistan from concept to reality. The reality is that in this all the leading players of the world were deeply involved for reasons of immediate benefits and short sightedness. The terrible consequences are clearly visible now.

Khaled Ahmed , a thinker and a journalist of repute of Pakistan, wrote in the year before 9/11 that 'Pakistan is a threat to global terrorism as it sponsors international terrorism, internal chaos based on armed militancy, violation of human rights, religious fanaticism, drug smuggling and irredentism associated with all pan-Islamic movements'.[3]

The work is the result of many years of hard work on data collection and their interpretation. My previous career background and investigation of cases of terrorism gave me the benefit of culling out the core areas of concern. Reading books on Pakistan by Pakistani writers have helped me in understanding the political, social, ethnic and economic dynamics of Pakistan.

My wife Krishna, my son Amit and daughter Sushmita have helped me in every possible way. I also thank Vivek Das, Madan

---

1 Tariq Ali, *On the Abyss*, HarperCollins, 2000, p27.

2 Adrian Levy& Catherine Scott-Clark, *Deception*, Atlantic Books, London, 2007, p1

3 *The Friday Times,* March –April 28, 2000.

Kumar, Renu Gupta and Rajat Gupta who helped me in typing the manuscript. I must convey my gratitude to USI and Col V K Singh for encouraging me to write this book. Some footnotes are not complete in detail which I regret. This has however, been compensated by including fairly detailed bibliography. One or two cases have been repeated in more than on chapter. This is unavoidable as the intention is to seek international co-operation in solving such old cases as they have possible ramifications in US homeland security.

The humanity must be saved from a 'final confrontation' which jihadis are looking for creation of Islamic Ummah. This is the critical area of study of this book.

Let me quote from a great master.

> *There is only one caste,*
>
> *the caste of humanity.*
>
> *There is only one religion,*
>
> *The religion of love.*
>
> *There is only one language,*
>
> *the language of heart.*

Let me now end with a soul stirring prophetic utterance of Jonathan Swift (1667-1745) which inspired me to write this book.

'We have enough religion to hate, but not enough to love each other.'

– S.K. DATTA

The ISI of Pakistan

The ISI is the real ruler of Pakistan

- Steven Emerson

You look for the ISI, you find al Qaeda; you look for al Qaeda; you end up finding the ISI.

- Henry Levis

Introduction

Generals of Pakistan and the ISI chiefs, retired and serving, have great admiration for the Inter-Services Intelligence (ISI). One of them described the ISI as the 'most dreaded organization of South Asia'. For Pakistanis South Asia means India. This sadism dominates the character of this infamous institution, which was created by an Australian born British Major General Robert Cawthome of Pakistan Army in 1948. This was the parting gift of the British forces to the Pakistanis. He was so favourite of the Pakistani generals that he was subsequently posted as Australian High Commissioner to Pakistan where he developed unique close relationship with Ishkinder Mirza and Gen. Ayub, who were responsible for derailment of democracy in Pakistan from the very beginning of creation of Pakistan.

Unique institution with no accountability

This unique institution, the kind of which is not seen anywhere in the world, is not accountable to anyone except the army of Pakistan.

Unlike democracies, the ISI combines the role of internal and external intelligence agencies. It wears the twin mask of the FBI and CIA rolled into one in Pakistani-style. It is more than two-in-one. It has developed an independent space to function outside the government control. Pursuing the institutional interest of the army, the ISI during Gen Zia's time, successfully neutralised the Intelligence Bureau, an organ of the British creation in undivided India. ISI often plays dirty games to neutralise other competing agencies like the Intelligence Bureau. The ISI taped the conversation between daughter of Zia with someone. The tape recovered from the IB, was shown and played back before Zia. The IB was then under the charge of Zia's selected Prime Minister Mohammed Khan Junejo. He was selected as he was a Sindhi and the Sindhi card was used to tone down their feelings as Sindhis were angry for hanging Bhutto in a sham trial. Junejo was gradually showing his independence and demanded action against Lt. Gen. Akthar Abdur Rehman and Lt. Gen. Hamid Gul for Ojhri fire that destroyed American gifted arms including Stinger missiles on 10 April 1988. Two birds were killed with one stone. Junejo was dismissed and the IB was downgraded.

To add to Junejo's misfortune, Arnold Raphel the US Ambassador to Pakistan provided Junejo with a complete inventory of the $ 130 million worth of stockpile that was blown up in the fire. Junejo was kept in the dark of the ISI's stockpile of arms and ammunition in Ojhri camp. Such leakage of information to a civilian Prime Minister enraged Zia. After all, the ISI was not to be under the domination of a civilian Prime Minister. That remained so even after restoration of democracy following Gen. Zia's mysterious death.

Protection of institutional interest

The ISI's primary role is to protect the institutional interest of the Pakistan Army. For this, it has to make the army relevant to political dynamics of Pakistan and decide on policy doctrines on India, Afghanistan, Bangladesh, Nepal and other neighbouring countries. India and Afghanistan Policy is solely dictated by the army and the ISI and not by politicians or the foreign office even during the civilian rule. Benazir Bhutto had to wait for a long period to become the second elected Prime Minister of Pakistan. She agreed to toe the army and the ISI line on Afghanistan and the Indian issue on the basis of army and ISI's demand. After Gen. Zia's death the long delayed general election was held in Pakistan in 1998. Benazir Bhutto's party got 92 seats out of 215 seats in National Assembly, but clearly emerged as the largest single party to be called to form the government. She had to wait for a long period as the ISI again tried to knit together a coalition of defeated parties. President Ishaq Khan, a Zia protégé, gave time for such a coalition to emerge.

The US aid of $ 600 million was dependent on her confirmation as the Prime Minister. A lot of negotiations were carried out through intermediaries and Benazir agreed 'not to rock the boat'; respect the army; keep away from nuclear issue and appoint Sahabzada Yakub Khan as the Foreign Minister. Punjab should remain under the control of Nawaz Sharif. She had to agree as she was dealing 'with killers'.[1]

Steven Emerson is an investigator-cum-journalist. He had visited Pakistan in 1994. He writes: "The fundamentalists had never had a very popular following, although their doctrine pervaded the Inter-Services Intelligence Directorate, the ISI, which is the real ruler of Pakistan." Every Pakistani knows this. The fundamental doctrine as said by Steven is Jihad. Gen (Retd) Mohammad Musa believed that in 1965 war 'the real motivating force for the super performance of the armed forces was their spirit of jihad.' In the final analysis he argued that 'Islam and the concept of Gazi or Shaheed provides the motivation ....and this concept must be nurtured and preserved.'[2]

Gen Chisti, who spearheaded the 1977 coup on behalf of Gen Zia-ul Haq, was a close associate of Zia. Subsequently, he had to part ways with Gen Zia. Thereafter, he was hounded by the ISI, facing a variety of harassments like intimidation, wiretapping and surveillance. Such was the fate of other dissenting generals.[3] Gen Ghulam Jilani Khan, who served and survived while serving

---

1   Adrian Levy & Catherine Scott-Clark, *Deception*, Atlantic Books, London, p188.

2   Musa Mohammad, *My Version, India Pakistan War 1965*, ABC Publishuing House, New Delhi, p111.

3   Tirmazi Brigadier Syed A.I., *Profiles of Intelligence*, Combined Printers, Guardi Trust Building, Lahore, p337. Also see Chist's book *Betrayals of Another Kind*.

Zulfikar Ali Bhutto and Gen Zia in the ISI, too was apprehensive of being under ISI's surveillance when he became the Governor of the Punjab province. Who can prove this more than what former Governor of Sindh Daupoto had said. He was an Air Marshal and posted as Governor of Sindh by Gen Musharraf. He said that while he was Governor of Sindh, the real orders were given by Corps Commander of Karachi.[4]

Protection of ideological frontiers of Pakistan

Gen. Musharraf has often said that the Army of Pakistan has the responsibility to protect the ideological frontiers of Pakistan. The ideological frontiers of Pakistan are nothing but the mask of sustaining the outdated concept of the 'two-nation theory'. Any discussion on two nation theory by any one in Pakistan can lead to penal action under section 153-A of the Pakistan Penal Code. Zia too often said on this ideological state of Pakistan. He once said "Pakistan is like Israel. Take out Judaism from Israel and it will collapse like a house of cards. Take Islam out of Pakistan and make it secular state, it would collapse." It is often said that for perpetuation of the army rule in one form or other, Pakistan army and the ISI need Pakistan and not otherwise. For protection of so-called ideological frontiers, the Pakistanis are made to believe that India is her permanent enemy. Major General Durrani, who became a dove after retirement, made a frank confession that he had joined Pakistan Army as he had genuinely believed that 'a dead Indian is the best Indian.' The army and the ISI thrive on this psychosis of fear of a secular ideology of India. Thus, a friendly Indo-Pak relationship is a threat to army and ISI as these institutions would become irrelevant and they would face the prospect of downsizing of their strength with reduction of budgetary support. As it is, Pakistan's defence expenditure is to the tune of 5 to 6 percent of the GDP as against 2.5 percent of India.

The truth of the matter is that Pakistan can never be a plural and democratic state unless Pakistan army and the ISI are deprived of their dominant role enabling the civil society to grow to shape the destiny of the country. "This thinking of protecting the ideological frontier lowered the threshold of senior army dons to interfere in

---

4   *The Friday Times*, July 7-13, 2000.

domestic political arena."[5]

Out of this typical projection of so-called frontiers of Pakistan ideology, the army and the ISI, which are inter-linked, encourages the birth of the idea of expansion of ideological frontiers to neighbouring countries like Afghanistan, India, Nepal and Bangladesh. For this to happen, the ISI started building up ideological pockets of influence in the neighbouring states and beyond. Russian President Putin took an unusual step to write to President Musharraf to stop providing 'material and trained mercenaries to Chechnya rebels in September 2000 and prevent Taliban from making armed intrusions into Tajikistan and other Central Asian countries. Previously Russia had accused Pakistan of giving platform to anti-Russian Chechen by providing training camps for guerrillas. Even a Pakistani was arrested in Russia recruiting people for training in Pakistan.[6] This is a dangerous threat and the threat is clearly visible and real.

Structure of ISI

The Structure of ISI has evolved over the years. The details of the organisational chart are secret. It is said to have manpower strength of 25,000 men and officers, drawn from various services on the basis of their aptitude, ideological bearings and physical stamina. Its higher posts always remain with the officers drawn from the army. The Director General of ISI has always been drawn from the rank of a serving army officer barring a brief period when Benazir Bhutto appointed a retired Lt. Gen. Shamsur Rehman Kallu replacing Gen Hamid Gul. This appointment caused a rift between the COAS Gen. Mirza Aslam Beg and Benazir Bhutto. Immediately after dismissal of Benazir Bhutto's government, Lt Gen (Retd) Shamsur Kallu was replaced by Gen Mohammed Assad Durrani as DG by President Ghulam Ishaq Khan. As history would reveal, even the civilian Presidents always acted as per the wishes of the COAS/ISI. There was informal sharing of power between them. Both of them were products of Zia's regime.

---

5 Manirruzzaman Takiledar, Military withdrawal from politics: A comprehensive study, Cambridge, Massachusetts, Ballinger Publishing Co, 1987, p10.

6 *Indian Express*, September 26, 2000, Dadan Upadhya reporting from Moscow.

When Nawaz Sharif became Prime Minister, he brought in Lt Gen Javed Nasir as DG ISI reportedly on the advice of IB Chief Brig Imtiaz Khan. The duo remained close to Nawaz Sharif throughout. Lt Gen. Javed Nasir intensified operations in Kashmir and elsewhere in the world like Bosnia and South East Asia. Soon Pakistan was brought close to being designated as a terrorist sponsored state by the USA. In a write up in Dawn, a respected daily of Pakistan, some revelations have since come to light. Dr. Maleeha Lodhi said that he was dismissed from the army as he was associated with some adventures in policies and actions of ISI, which was opposed by the US. Gen. Nasir filed a petition in October 2002 in the anti-terrorism court in Lahore that he was a prominent member of Tabligi Jammat and would not compromise in the interest of Islam and Pakistan. He even supported airlifting of sophisticated anti-tank guided missiles to Bosnia. In the petition he hinted at the role he had played to revive the Sikh separatism in the Punjab in India.[7]

Further revelations came from another knowledgeable analyst Khaled Ahmed who wrote that Nasir had been participating Tabligi Jammat's programme in Malaysia and Indonesia. The Jammat was promoting the jihadi culture[8]. The most damaging story was that he was contributing money for purchase of arms for aborted coup led by Major General Zaheer ul Islam Abbasi in 1995. Nasir was to play a decisive role in the final hour of the coup. The first act of Musharraf, when he came to power, was to release Abbasi from jail. If ever Dawood is handed over to India he would expose to the world the real face of the ISI. That is the real reason why Pakistan will never hand him over to India.

Soon after dismissal of Nawaz Sharif's government, President Ghulam Ishaq Khan appointed Lt Gen Javed Ashraf Qazi as DG ISI in April 1993 with the concurrence of COAS. This move brought ISI under the control of GHQ completely. After Lt Gen. Qazi's retirement, the post was given to Lt Gen Nassim Rana. He too was replaced when Nawaz Sharif came to power for the second time. He appointed Lt. Gen. Ziauddin as ISI Chief. Lt. Gen. Ziauddin

---

7   *Dawn*, 12 Jan 2003.

8   *The Friday Times*, November 2002.

was from Corps of Engineers and had no control on ISI and did not maintain good relationship with the COAS. After Gen Musharraf's coup on 12 October 1999, the ISI chief was put under detention. He was replaced by Gen Mahmud Ahmed who was close to Musharraf and was also considered a hawk. He, by accident or by design, was in the USA when Al Qaeda operatives crashed landmark buildings by hijacking four civilian planes on 11 September 2001. He too was replaced after 9/11, possibly on the US pressure as there were reasons to believe that he was close to some hardliner elements including Al Qaeda and Taliban.

The organizational chart of ISI can be constructed on the basis of released information by the former ISI operatives and otherwise. Graphically it reads as follows:

DG (ISI)

DDG- External	DDG- Internal	DDG Special Wings
JIB	JCIB	The Defence Services
JSIB	JIA	Intelligence Academy
JIM		Military Liaison Section
JIN		(MLS)
JIT		

Joint Signal Intelligence Bureau (JSIB) collects intercepts of neighbouring countries. Officers and men are generally drawn from Army Signal Corps. It has detachments at Lahore, Karachi and Peshawar. It has three sections namely, monitoring, photo and wireless communication. It runs a chain of intercept stations all along the Indo-Pak border. It runs clandestine radio stations, static and mobile, from Indian soil. As per some estimates such stations may be more than 200. It is headed by a Director Technical under the overall control of a DDG. The detachment centres are under the control of three Deputy Directors.

Joint Counter Intelligence Bureau (JCIB): It is responsible for counter intelligence operations within Pakistan, which works under Deputy Director General and is assisted by four Directors. Under it, there is a Inter Service Security Section (ISSS) which keeps surveillance on ISI staff.

Joint Intelligence Miscellaneous (JIM): Espionage activities abroad by engaging agents and also carries out offensive intelligence operations. The Director who heads this organisation functions under a DDG. This unit was in charge of clandestine procurement of equipment and items of machinery required for enrichment of uranium and other sophisticated items.

Joint Intelligence North (JIN): This is India, Kashmir and Afghan oriented unit. It provides training, weapons, funds, psy-war publications to militants and also inducts non-Kashmiris for proxy war in Kashmir and elsewhere. It is headed by a Director who is under control of DDG.

Joint Intelligence for Administration: Looking after administration, budget. It is headed by a Director (Administration) and works under a DDG.

Special Wings: These are some special wings. Two of them need to be mentioned. The Defence Service Intelligence Academy provides training to ISI cadres. The Military Liaison Section otherwise called MLS, maintains Liaisons with all civilian security agencies, Para-Military organizations, Federal Investigation Agency and the Passport and Immigration Directorate.

Legal Back-up: The lack of legal back-up of ISI was raised in Najam Sethi's case of his illegal detention by ISI. Ordinarily, a person arrested and detained is required to be produced before a magistrate within twenty four hours. Najam Sethi, the respected editor of The Friday Times, was detained for a long duration without production before a magistrate. He was picked up on the night on May 8, 1999 from his residence by ISI. On a petition filed by his wife, the Lahore High Court was informed that Sethi was in the custody of ISI which was investigating his suspected links with a hostile "Intelligence Agency" (read India) under Article 199(3) of the Pakistan Constitution. Thus, the Lahore High Court has no power to interfere with the affairs of the Army, as the ISI is headed by a Director General from the Army.

The defence rightly said ISI has no such legal cover as it was neither a branch of the army nor was it established under the Pakistan's Army Act. Faced with this situation, the Lahore High Court gave a peculiar judgement in support of ISI. It said "the detainee is in the custody of the ISI, a Corps of Intelligence, manned by the army personnel and headed by a serving Lt Gen of the Pakistan Army. The custody of the detainee is with the army officers of the ISI in their capacity as members of the armed forces of the Pakistan. In the absence of any jurisdictional defect of the action being coram-non-judice or void the writ of habeas corpus simpliciter is not maintainable under Clause 3 of 1973 Constitution of the Islamic Republic of Pakistan".

Now the ISI of Pakistan has received a legal cover for illegal acts like investigation and detention of civilians. The judgement has other implications. Army officers heading any civilian organization with a back-up support of any army personnel can claim similar privileged position under the Army Act or under Article 199 (3) of the Constitution. The Intelligence Bureau of Pakistan and India have no power to arrest or investigate a case. If Pakistan army manages to stuff IB of Pakistan with army officers, which it has done over the years in substantial strength, the IB can as well claim a privileged position and may get a supportive cover from the Hon'ble court of Pakistan. For fear of army and ISI such fundamental questions of law can never be settled, unless Pakistan becomes a truly democratic country.

In Najam Sethi's case, the Lahore High Court has strengthened the ISI in its notorious internal operations. CIA, RAW, MI6 or any other external intelligence organizations have no internal role to play. What High Court failed to elicit from the Government was to know as to how an external intelligence agency is tasked to play a different role in the internal affairs of the country with powers of investigation and detention which was not in the original scheme.

CIA-ISI relationship

Gen Ayub cultivated Allen Dulles CIA chief before and during his presidency. Senior John Foster Dulles was the US Secretary of State. During the Afghan jihad sponsored by the US, the ISI officers were sent to CIA's training camp at Fort Bragg. This training centre is used to train US Delta Force, also called Green Beret. Delta Force also used CIA's training camp Peary. This centre is used for training of spies, infiltrators and covert operations. The ISI trainees were sent to this centre. They were taught use of explosives, firing of various weapons and para-military operations.[9]

Green Barets and US Navy Seals instructed key Pakistani officers and senior mujahideen in infiltration techniques and ways of capturing weapons from behind enemy lines. Mujahideen and the ISI profitably used these techniques for worldwide terrorist acts. Tariq Ali described Pakistan army as 'one of the Pentagons's spoilt child'.[10] Pakistan was the condom, the Americans need to enter Afghanistan, to resist the Russians in Afghanistan.[11]

The anti-US stance of Pakistan was evident from the very beginning of creation of Pakistan. The US was blackmailed to fund Pakistan by using the Islamic card of danger. US still believe that Pakistan can be engaged by doling funds and arms. One stray remark of Gen Zia as president of Pakistan sparked a mob raid on US embassy in Islamabad and then US president thanked Zia for controlling the situation. Pentagon and the CIA were out of tune. It is believed that they still hold the age-old view that the Pakistan army and the ISI could be tamed. Jihadi supporters are in the army and the ISI at all levels. The problem can not be solved by adopting an ostrich like pose. The US has a view that Pakistan's military is their last bet to save Pakistan from disintegration. Democracy in Pakistan did not develop as the Pakistan army intervened every now and then. A powerful politician is a threat to generals.

---

9   P Johan & Cooly.

10   On the Abyss, Harper Collins.

11   Ibid.

Destabilization strategy

The thrust area of the ISI is to destabilise the neighbouring countries. It destabilised Afghanistan by pushing through the Islamic ideology through its surrogate the Taliban. The two decade long proxy war was fought on Afghan soil by the ISI overtly and covertly on the strength of jihad. This has been discussed in the chapter on Afghan jihad. Names of several Pak army generals came to surface when they fought against the Northern Alliance along with the Taliban which was its own creation. Ahmed Shah Masood embarrassed Pakistan by revealing that he had hundreds of Pakistani prisoners including 17 from Pakistan army. Pakistan called them as all relieved from service and could have gone to Afghanistan on their own.[12] Pakistan's army and the ISI sustained the hated Taliban regime by providing money, manpower and supplies. In the midst of the US-led 'war on terror' the Commander-in-Chief of the Taliban army Jalaluddin Haqqani visited Peshawar for consultation and recruitment of jihadis. This could not have happened without the ISI's support system. The last consignment of arms from Pakistan reached Afghanistan on 8 October 2001 despite of UN sanctions.

ISI-Taiban-Al-Qaeda nexus

Almost all the 9/11 suicide squad members had transited through Pakistan for consultation, briefing with Al Qaeda operative chiefs like Mohammed Atef, Abu Zubaidah and others. In 1999, Hambali, an Al Qaeda Southeast Asia point-man, had visited Karachi to work out the plan to blast the US installations in Singapore. The 'White Paper' of the Singaporean government brings out these meticulous details. Was it possible for suicide bombers of 9/11 and Hambali to visit and discuss with Al Qaeda leadership in Karachi and elsewhere without a valid visa and a nod from the ISI? After all the ISI is credited with total surveillance and wiretapping capability. All phone calls from India to Pakistan are monitored and people receiving calls from India are questioned and their antecedents are thoroughly checked. A year before 9/11 a Pakistani intellectual and writer said very categorically that Saudi born terrorist Osama bin

---

12 Khaled Ahmed, Fundamental Plans, on the Abyss, Harper Collins.

Laden maintained close contacts with the ISI.[13]

The authors of the book called 'Cell' cite an interesting case of close relationship between Bin Laden and the ISI just before 9/11. Max, a code name of a Bin Laden operative, was recruited by Saif Rahman, the son of the blind cleric Omar Abdel Rahman serving lifetime imprisonment in the USA. After recruitment he was trained in an Al-Qaeda camp by Saif al-Adel, who was one of the top commanders of Bin Laden group. He had to undergo through a tough course of selection of targets for which the target was to be video taped and a note sent to higher leadership for detailed planning. Once the plan was drawn up, a separate bombing group used to be sent for the act of bombing the selected target. This was true in case of major Al-Qaeda operations. Max was not keen to do this type of task. He decided to quit and settle down in America. This motivated him to approach the US consulate in Peshawar. He had several meetings with officers of the US in Peshawar, who decided to obtain clearance from US. FBI, under O' Neil, could not obtain clearance due to delay in the system. In the meantime the ever watchful ISI visited his home to enquire why he had visited the US consulate. That exposed him with the Pakistanis and possibly with Al-Qaeda as the 'ISI had extensive contacts with Bin Laden group'.[14]

The ISI maintained its operational offices in Kabul, Kandahar, Herat and other sensitive areas in Afghanistan to keep a tight hold on the Taliban. When things went wrong in Afghanistan like destruction of the Buddha statues in Bamiyan, Pakistan army and Musharraf undertook make believe damage control exercises to distance itself from this barbaric acts of vandalism by expressing regrets of its inability to tame the Taliban regime. If that was the regime character how then till 9/11 General Musharraf was pleading with the world powers to recognize the Taliban regime on the basis of 'ground reality' theory? Even after 9/11 Gen Musharraf in his first address to the nation said: "We are trying our best to come out of this critical situation without any damage to Afghanistan and the Taliban. This is my earnest endeavour and with the blessings of Allah, I will continue

---

13 Tariq Ali, On the Abyss, Harper Collins, Delhi 2000, p28.

14 The Cell, Miller, Stone and Mitchell, HYPERION, New York, pp280-281.

to seek such a way out......What I would like to know (from the US) is how do we save Afghanistan and the Taliban". And lastly he said "may Allah be with us in our endeavours". Musharraf tried his best to delay US-led coalition attack on the Taliban and Al Qaeda by proposing farcical initiatives like holding discussion with the Taliban Chief Mulla Omar. The ISI Chief visited Kandahar. Other religious teams were also sent. These tricks did not fool anyone. After Bangladesh defeat, the Pakistani military establishment boasted having expanded its ideological frontiers to Afghanistan to secure strategic depth against India.

When the US-led attack was mounted in Afghanistan, Gen Musharraf called for a brief and short war. When that did not happen he called for Ramazan ceasefire. His main concern was to rescue Pakistani soldiers and officers trapped in Afghanistan. He did succeed by pleading with the US. On several occasions he announced death and survival of Osama bin Laden. It was another trick to fool the US. The daring raid on the Indian Parliament was organised by the Jaish-e-Mohammed and Lashker-e-Toiba, who work in tandem with the ISI, to divert attention from the US-led war on terror in Afghanistan. All the suicide attackers of Indian parliament were from Pakistan. Before that on 1 October 2001 Kashmir State Assembly was attacked in the same manner. There was a design and strategy behind these attacks.

The ISI is still toying with the idea of destabilization of Afghanistan. It is now relying on Sirajuddin Haqqani and Gulbuddin Hekmatyar of Hizb-e-Islami fame. During 1979-89 Afghan Jihad Hekmatyar was promoted by the ISI as he was proving more loyal than the King. Now the remnants of Al Qaeda, the Taliban and Haqqani and Hekmatyar have regrouped and are organizing attacks on Kabul Government and the US-led coalition forces from bordering areas of Pakistan-Afghanistan. The ISI's game plan in Afghanistan would require close watch. Afghanistan is still on the radar screen of the ISI. After all Afghanistan, as per the thinking of the army and the ISI, is key to survival of Pakistan. At the opportune time the ISI will surely walk in covertly and overtly. This is bound to happen sooner or later. Did not Gen Musharraf try his best to prevent entry of Northern Alliance into Kabul by making all possible diplomatic efforts and open statements? After all the victory of Northern Alliance was a defeat for the ISI. On 9 September, the beloved leader of the Northern Alliance, Ahmed Shah Masood, was killed by two foreign militants of Moroccan origin who secured visa from the office of the Pakistan's High Commission in London and entered Afghanistan from Pakistan.

ISI-Omar Sheik-Al Qaeda in Daniel Pearl's murder in Karachi

A veteran journalist Henry Levy, who had previously covered Afghanistan and Bosnia, has given out startling revelations in the case of murder of Daniel Pearl in his book 'Who killed Daniel Pearl? He visited Pakistan and many other countries to find out the truth of the matter.

The main culprit Omar Sheik was sentenced to death by a court. That is not beginning or end of the mystery behind the case. Much is hidden which needs to be told to the world. Omar Sheik was born on 23 December 1973 in East London. He is a dropout from the London School of Economics. He visited Sarajevo in a convoy under Asad Khan for rendering relief by an entity called the Third World Relief Agency which had links with the fundamentalist groups in Bosnia. Reaching there he came in contact with Abdul Rauf, a Pakistani combat veteran of Kashmir and a member of Harkat-ul-Mujahideen (HUM). Rauf gave a letter of recommendation to London branch of HUM for him to get training in Afghanistan. To facilitate that Rauf told Maulana Ismail, the Imam of Clifton mosque in London, to recruit him for Afghanistan for jihad.

Reaching Pakistan Levy found bin Laden was a hero. His images were even found on post cards. He also found two million illegal Afghans, Bangladeshis, Arabs, Somalians, Sudanese, Egyptians, and Chechens in Pakistan ready for recruitment in Al Qaeda.

Pearl was in Pakistan to find out truth behind killing of Daniel Pearl, a task assigned to him. One reason may be that a Wall Street journalist had previously procured a computer he had purchased from market which had a lot of information on Al Qaeda and the management wanted verification. Omar Sheik met Pearl in Akbar

Hotel in Rawalpindi. It is not clear how they came in contact with each other. Pearl sought to meet Mubarak Ali Shah Gilani, leader of the Jammat-ul-Fuqrah, a terrorist sect on the FBI's list of terrorist organizations. It is said that Gilani was one of the gurus of Richard Reid, a shoe bomber caught on Paris-Miami flight. Much is not known about Gilani in India. He is said to be very secretive having a network in America in different names. He has high contacts in Pakistan. In Pakistan he was known to be close to Osama bin Laden. In 1993 he was shown on a TV channel holding hand in hand with Osama in Sudan. Gilani's ideology is explained in a propaganda booklet bearing the title: "United States of Islam". In that booklet the existing Islamic states were shown in green colour. The other map the entire world was shown green in another 20 years[15]. It may be mentioned that Daniel Pearl had written an article on 'Al-Qaeda's involvement in diamond smuggling in Tanzania'. Thus, Pearl was taking all the risk visiting Pakistan and seeking to meet Gilani. Duglus Farah of the same paper *i.e.* Free Street Journal had highlighted how Al Qaeda was engaged in cash-diamond-cash transactions. It may be that Pearl too was working on the same subject of terrorist financing from Karachi and might have obtained some valuable leads for his story.

On the pretext of such a meeting Omar took Pearl to Karachi suburbs on 22 January and on 31 January 2002 he was brutally killed. Levy met several persons to find out the truth. He met Javed Iqbal Cheema, Minister of Interior of Sindh who, as the practice in Pakistan, gave hints of Indian involvement by saying that Omar made 24 calls to India including calls to 'a minister's collaborator.' If that was the truth then Indian government should have been informed to bring the criminal to justice or for confirmation of these so-called calls. This was just a cover story to fool the world. Infact, the truth is that Cheema had links with the ISI. Omar was anti-Jew and hated England. He used to make such utterances in Indian jail. For nearly 9 days Pearl was in captivity of the ISI. It is alleged he was killed by three Yemenites who were called to kill him brutally. Omar reportedly said that kidnapping was committed to get the

---

15 Adrian Levy and Catherine Scott-Clark, Deception, Pakistan, The United States and The Global Nuclear Conspiracy, Atlantic Books, 2007.

Afghan ambassador released.

The house where Pearl was killed belonged to Saud Memon, who vanished to Waziristhan, where bin Laden had landed in December 2001 to escape arrest or liquidation from US-led alliance attack in Afghanistan. He was guarded by 50 fully armed guards. Memon was found to have acted as a manager of the Al- Rashid Trust, which was under the control of Maulana Azhar Masood, chief of Jaish-e-Mohammed. Rashid Trust was publishing the Islam in Urdu, Zerb-e-Momin in Urdu, and Jaish-e-Mohammed. The theme of these publications was against Hindus, Jews and Christians akin to Al Qaeda's 1998 Fatwa.

To please America on 10 November 2002, 10 months after the murder of Pearl, the Pakistan police on US intelligence and help raided a building no 63c, 15 Commercial Street in the Defence Colony, Karachi. Incidentally at the same place Ramzi Binalshib and Khalid Sheikh Mohammed were interviewed by Yosri Fouda representing an Arab TV channel. It only proved that Al Qaeda major operatives were not in hiding in mountain areas as always claimed by Pakistani establishment. The raid resulted in the arrest of 10 Yemenis and it was said that the damaging documents and material exhibits were not seized like a computer, maps of major US cities, flying manuals. It was alleged that three sons of bin Laden namely Saad, Mohammed and Ahmed were allowed to escape.

There are more startling revelations by Levy. He learnt that the home minister of Punjab Brig. Ejaz Shah was a close friend of Musharraf and Shah was in charge of Harkat-ul-Mujahideen and the HUJI. It also came to his knowledge that Omar was in the custody of the ISI for seven days before his actual arrest shown on paper. This time was utilised to debrief him and the allegation was also made that even Musharraf spoke to Omar's father, who in return spoke to his son to avoid making any statement that could be harmful to Pakistan's national interest. Thus, Omar said nothing during the police interrogation. But by way of big mistake he told TV channels that he would be in jail for three to four years as if that were promised to him.

Levy learnt that while Omar was in jail in India, his defence was organised by the station chief of ISI in London. The defence attaché and other staff of Pakistan embassy in Delhi were in regular touch with him. On his release from Kandhahar Omar remained with a Col. of the ISI and the said Col. called the ISI chief Gen. Mahmud Ahmed. The most important point for India is that Omar, while in India, had purchased a house, the location of which has not been mentioned. If that be true, where did he get the money from?

When Omar reached Pakistan from London, he was sent to two training camps and two of his instructors were Subedar Saleem and Abdul Hafiz, both former members of SSG commando force. Omar's links with the ISI are reinforced from a news report of Dawn of 9 October that DG ISI was replaced after the FBI found links between ISI and Sheik. Omar was never arrested. He surrendered before a highly placed ISI official as he was an alleged agent of the ISI. Another reason for transfer of DG ISI may be because of a report that $100,000 were transferred to Mohammed Atta in August 2000 from a bank in UAE by a person called Mustaffa Muhammed Ahmed who came to Dubai two months earlier with a Saudi passport. On September 11, Atta sent back the unused money to same Mustafa who transferred it to a Pakistani bank and flew back to Pakistan on the same date and the same passport. On reaching he just disappeared after withdrawing the money from the bank in Pakistan. Levy and many others have reasons to believe Mustafa's real name is Omar Sheik. The Wall Street Journal had written on 10 October 2001 that the American authorities had confirmed the fact that 100,000 dollars were transferred to Mohammed Atta by Ahmed Umar Sheikh, at the request of General Ahmed Mahmood then chief of the ISI. Levy finally asserts that Al Qaeda and the ISI worked together towards the destruction of twin Towers.

There is an Indian twist to this story of money transfer to Atta. Aftab Ansari masterminded the kidnapping of Partha Pratim Burman, a business tycoon from Calcutta, now called Kolkata. It was reported that the ransom money was obtained in Hyderabad and passed on to Ansari in Dubai through Hawala route. A part of that money was given to Omar Sheik in Dubai, who transmitted the same to Atta for financing 9/11 attack. Aftab and Omar Sheik were known to each other in jail in India. Thus, in a sense Indian money was partly used in 9/11 operation by Al-Qaeda.

Levy wanted more information on Omar Sheik from Afghanistan. He met the governor of Kandahar, Gul Agha Sherzai who called a police officer Amine. From him he learnt that Omar was trained first around March 1994 where he first met Azhar. His second stay in Afghanistan was in January 2000 and he was introduced to bin Laden. They discussed Kashmir. He reportedly became involved with bin Laden's Majlis-e-Shura and was given the task in setting up logistics, like setting up a secured website for Al Qaeda and secured communication. He was subsequently allowed to work in Pakistan and was recruited as an agent of the ISI. Thus, Omar became a link between Al Qaeda and the ISI.

ISI's Kashmir operation

The ISI has special focussed attention on India. It has been attempting to replicate its Afghan Jihad strategy in Kashmir since 1989. It is significant to note that Soviet troops vacated Afghanistan in early 1989 and the ISI shifted its attention to India thereafter. Like Afghan jihad of 1979-89, the ISI has built up a Kashmir jihadi council for disbursement of fund and weapon to keep tight control of jihadis and their supporting political fronts.

During the Afghan War (1979-89) the ISI built up a strong infrastructure to sustain the proxy war. The same infrastructure is being used for targeting India. The equipment gifted by the US are being used by Jihadi groups, all based on Pakistani soil. The US communication network, gifted during the Afghan jihad, were more advanced and difficult to jam as it is secured from such dangers. Their use in J&K was detected from the very beginning. The ISI has a stockpile of Stinger missiles some of which were used during the Kargil war.

The ISI and Gen Zia were under the spell of an idea that if a superpower like Russia could be defeated by guerrillas, then why not India. The grand strategy was two pronged; maximise the cast of guerrilla war for India and bleed India white and keep the Pakistani cost of proxy war to a pittance by mobilizing and sending Jihadis across the line of control.[16]

This grand strategy based on Afghan jihad did succeed initially as India did not prepare itself for an offensive policy. Pakistan's proxy war that gradually inducted foreign guest jihadis to promote Pakistan's so called pan-Islamic agenda. Such an agenda had to be adopted for getting dispensable jihadis from the Taliban and Al Qaeda for fighting in Kashmir. 'The indigenous Kashmiri leadership had no choice but to eat out of ISI's hand! This observation was made by an ISI operative.[17] In spite of upgraded weaponry and high motivation of jihadis, India did not disintegrate.

During Gen Zia's time this proxy war was taken note of by India as revealed from a statement made by minister of state P. Chidambaram, when he told the Rajya Sabha that this was brought to the notice of Zia in 1986 and 1987 and Benazir Bhutto in December 1998 when she became the Prime Minister of Pakistan.[18] The policy to bleed India white now was to engage India by attacking Indian secular fabric by creating Hindu-Muslim divide. Incidents in Gujarat, Mumbai and elsewhere have to be examined in this light.

Osama bin Laden's name in Kashmir operation came up first with the arrest of Abbas Bhai, an Afghan, who turned Baramulla district into a safe haven for foreign jihadis. He, like many others, was trained in bin Laden camps. On 20 August 1998, the US missile attack in Afghanistan in Khost, where a bin Laden camp was located, killed a number of Harkat-ul-Mujahideen fighters who were being trained to fight in Kashmir. Khalid, a Pakistani who got injured in Kashmir was treated in Rawalpindi. He admitted that he had been trained in a bin Laden camp in Afghanistan.[19]

Many of the so-called jihadis came to fight in Kashmir for money. They sign up two-year contract and paid Rs 4 lakh, half in advance. Some of the contracted jihadis just whiled away their time.

---

16 Abu Saif, Kashmir Policy: What Went Wrong? [Dawn (internet) June 15, 2002]

17 Abu Saif, ibid.

18 *Indian Express*, dated 11August, 1989.

19 *Outlook*, September 7, 1998.

To supervise their performance the ISI used to send its own staff across the border. One ranger of the Pakistan's paramilitary force was arrested in 1998. He spilled the beans.[20]

Young school going boys were often kidnapped and sent across to Pakistan. Many parents lodged missing reports with the police. In 1998, 51 school boys were rescued by the Indian army. Some of them actually managed to escape and surrendered before the army.[21]

The jihadi out-fits namely Harkat-ul-Mujahideen, Lashker-e-Toiba, Al Badr and lately Jaish-e-Mohammed are really the extended arms of the ISI. These fanatics are the creation of the ISI. Their training programmes are remote controlled by the ISI. Ex-ISI officers are largely drawn to provide support at various levels. Gen. (Retd) Hamid Gul, a former Chief of the ISI, often used to smoke pipe with Hafiz Mohammad Saeed at Muridke, where the Lashker headquarters are located. Hamid Gul and Saeed have one converging interest *i.e.* to destabilise India at all costs. It was Hamid Gul who unleashed proxy war in J&K. For him J&K became an obsession as he had completely failed to consolidate the Afghan jihad. During his time, the Jihadi parties of Afghanistan were fighting against each other. He failed even to capture Jalalabad from Afghan Government forces of Dr. Najibullah. Gen Zia built up Hamid Gul as counter to Gen Akthar Abdur Rehman, who became popular as architect of the Afghan jihad. He stayed in the ISI for almost a decade. Gen. Hamid Gul was first made DGMI and in that capacity he was tasked by Zia to raise a survey section for reporting on political pulse of the nation. At the opportune time, Gen Akthar was replaced by Gen Gul who made a mess of Afghan jihad. In 1989, Lt Gen Hamid Gul was pursuing an independent policy of his own on Afghanistan, launching a proxy war in Kashmir and cobbling an Islamic Front called the Islamic Jamhoori Ittehad (IJI) against Benazir's PPP to fight the election in 1988 after Zia's death in an air-crash. He, out of Afghan war experience, dreamed of 'Islam's redeeming role in today's increasingly materialistic world.' In fact, by becoming DG ISI in 1987, he saw the prospect of becoming the COAS of the

---

20 Ibid.

21 Ibid.

Pakistan Army through the ISI route which failed as IJI could not capture power in Pakistan. He was removed in May 1989 which upset him. He became anti-American as he thought that Americans did not make him COAS, forgetting that he had been to America for training and discussions.

Under the ISI's guidance foreign Afghan war veterans were drawn from various countries, were sent for proxy war in Kashmir. Foreign nationals could visit and stay in Pakistan on the strength of visa. Obviously, Pakistani establishment and the ISI would know each of them by name, character and colour of their ideology. One such fighter Masud of Sudan even boasted that about 6000 foreign Mujahideen were preparing to enter into the valley. Four guest Mujahideen died in encounter.[22] In Pakistan the guerrilla groups made wide publicity of such fake achievements giving an excellent opportunity to cover up the reality of the so-called Kashmir jihad.

In 1984 the Human Rights organization confirmed this in their report. It categorically said that the flow of arms to the Islamist militants were directly linked to the CIA's creation of an Afghan pipeline for arms to the holy warriors during the anti-Soviet war of the 80's. These arms had been stockpiled and inventoried by the ISI, then passed on to the insurgents. Kashmiri militants were trained by the ISI and those who had fought the Russians in Afghanistan. There was siphoning of the weapons from the Pakistani pipeline. It is further reinforced by capturing of weapons of high order like machine guns, missiles and the like.[23]

On 26 January 1995 Governor of J&K Gen Krishna Rao was addressing a gathering at Azad Memorial Stadium at Srinagar. He was attacked with a remote controlled blast but escaped. An accused of this case Mohammad Irfan was a resident of Tanda of Pakistan. He revealed that the attack was planned by the Sialkot detachment of the ISI in tandem with Hizbul Mujahideen.

On March 20, 2000 on the eve of Bill Clinton's India visit, 36 Sikhs were massacred. Arrested accused Muhammed Suhail, a

---

22 Manoj Joshi, Kashmir: The Lost Rebellion, p104.

23 Cooly, John K., Unholy War, p235.

resident of Sialkot, was trained at the Lashker's training camp in 1997-98 and on the directions of Lashker, the massacre occurred. Presently, he is in Tihar jail.[24]

In the past and now Indo-Pak peace process is being derailed by the ISI. During President Clinton's stay in India innocent Sikhs were killed in Kashmir giving a fresh communal character of the proxy war. Even Clinton admitted in India that some elements in Pakistan establishment were averse to peace process.

Mir Mustafa, and independent MLA of the dissolved Assembly, was kidnapped in early ninety. The day he was kidnapped the militants gunned down 73 year old veteran CPI leader Abdul Sattar Ranjoor followed by killing of Mustaq Ahmed, son of a veteran kisan leader Abdul Kabir Wani. About the same time the militants killed Gulam Nabi Kullar, a Congress activist. All these killings were signal to JKLF not to enter into negotiation with government.

Mir Mustafa was apparently close to JKLF. During his election campaign he hit both the fundamentalist and colonial mentality of Delhi. The only advance hint of Mir Mustafa's fatal end came from Pakistan TV and Radio claiming that 'freedom fighters' had threatened to kill Mustafa if 10 of their associates were not released within 35 hours. In the early stage of militancy Pakistani TV and Radio channels used to provide guidelines and instructions to pro-Pak militants.[25] Mir Mustafa's gruesome murder was attributed to Hizbul Mujahideen. The role of the ISI was clear. It wanted division of pro-Azadi elements within Kashmir.

The ISI's Kashmir agenda has the backing of various fundamentalist groups around the world. Omar Bakri, an exile from Arab world living in England, presided over Al-Muhjiroun, which created a network for collection of funds and volunteers for jihad. More than 100 websites had existed in UK offering information and help for jihad in Kashmir, Chechnya and other hotspots. In 2000 a new internet emerged under the banner of 'The ultimate jihad' as reported by the Sunday Telegraph. An 18 year old Muslim student,

---

24 *Outlook*, 22 October, 2001.

25 *Times of India*, 2 April 1990.

Omar Kyam, who lived on the outskirts of London, was allegedly enticed by agents of Al Mujhiroun and flown to Islamabad capital of Pakistan, in January 2000. His father was in deep despair as his son would be sent to Kashmir to be killed.[26] This is the same way Pakistani jihadi outfits enticed boys from Kashmir. Unwilling boys were kidnapped and sent across the border. Pakistani establishment would give visas without a question being asked. For overseas jihadis the visa regime of Pakistan is porous as it was during the Afghan jihad.

ISI Operation in rest of India

The ISI has substantial network of 'assets', 'sleepers' and 'spies' in India. Assets are locals who act on behalf of Pakistan. 'Sleepers' are non-residents who infiltrate and settle down in India posing as locals with changed identity and then they marry local girls, obtain ration cards, voting rights and may even acquire passports. Spies are Pakistanis who visit India in various capacities and collect intelligence. There may be overlapping of functions. All the three are given tasks. For example sleepers are told to build up a chain of front organizations or motivate people to take revenge against other community and government for their alleged excesses. The religious cards are used to arouse their emotions for the cause of Islam. Locals then become assets for the ISI. There is a chain process. Sleepers are inducted who create assets and assets work for the ISI. In the Indian context, one chain is a module of the ISI. The handlers of these modules operate from Pakistan, Nepal or Bangladesh. Many of the sleepers and assets are jihadis trained in Pakistan and Afghanistan. As ISI and jihadi groups work in tandem, money can be contributed by way of a settled arrangement. Thus, India being a secular and plural society can be exploited by the ISI to its advantage.

The Bombay serial blasts in 1993 were the landmark achievements of the ISI. For this the Dawood's underworld outfit was profitably used. He lives in a heavily guarded palatial home in Clifton, Karachi which is a posh residential area where Benazir Bhutto had her residential accommodation. He is the key accused of the Bombay blasts case. In Pakistan he has several names like

---

26 *The Hindustan Times*, 23 May 2000, Vijay Dutt reporting from London.

Iqbal Seth 'He doubles up an ISI-backed don in exile who remote controls and empire spread across Mumbai, (Bombay) Gujarat, UP, Delhi and Dubai'. He is the ISI's main source of information from India and helps the ISI in anti-India operations. In exchange of these services he gets all advantages of the world. He is secured in Pakistan.. He and his associates also carry Pakistani passports. Whenever he is in difficulty the ISI pulls the strings. Nothing is published about him in Pakistani newspapers and journals. Dawood has delivered to Pakistan 'what it could never dream of having'. His trademark is a leather belt with a diamond studded 'D' on the buckle. Dawood has developed real estate business in Pakistan and he even reportedly gave a dollar loan to Pakistan's central bank to tide over foreign exchange crisis. 'Bhai knows too many secrets of this country. Every influential Pakistani, whether he is a politician or a military man is indebted to Bhai' said an associate. He does not pay taxes. Tiger Menon, one of the key accused of the blast cases, stays with Dawood in Karachi. He is still an important asset for the ISI to launch operations in India. Pakistan refuses to extradite him for trial.[27]

In Kanishka plane crash case Ajaib Singh Bagri was facing trial in Canada. The same Bagri was invited by Jamaat-I-Islami, Bangkok, headed then by Syed Qaisar Inba. At the request of the Pakistan Embassy in Bangkok he organised a meeting of the local Sikhs in Bangkok. The local Sikhs protested when Bagri made anti-India and anti-Hindu speeches which he delivered in a Gurudwara. The local Thai police had to intervene and restore order. Jamaat-I-Islami has branches all over the world and all of them can be utilised by the ISI for its anti-India agenda.

Can RSS chief be appointed as head of Delhi's Jama Masjid? Yes, this had happened in Pakistan. Lt Gen (retd) Javed Nasir became the president of the Pakistan's Sikh Gurudwara Prabandak Committee. He is a die-hard Tabligi Jaamat with anti-India tag on his breast. As ISI chief in the early nineties he played havoc in the Punjab and successfully organised serial blasts in Bombay in 1993. He openly said that the separatist involvement would be revived in

---

27 Ghulam Hasnain, *Outlook*, November 20, 2000.

the state of Punjab. His appointment during Nawaz Sharif regime must have happened under the ISI pressure.[28] The Sikh expatriates with separatist agenda did not protest. They in fact deliberated with the ex-ISI chief during the centenary of Khalsa in Dera Shahib and Nanka Shahib located in Pakistan. The trio promoter of Sikh militancy Ganga Singh Dhillon, Satnam Singh Panta and Surender Singh met the Pakistani Prime Minister attracting the limelight and the Indian contingent was just pushed to the background. An Imam addressed the jatha for the separatist cause.[29]

Mehfooz Ali, a resident of Multan, Pakistan, and two Bangladeshis namely Timor Ali and Mohammed Sharif were arrested in 1994 in the Chandni Chowk area of Delhi. Mehfooz claimed to be a member of a Pakistani outfit called Islamic Inquilab Mahooz of Pakistan and claimed to have been trained by Pakistan Rangers. They were sent to India as a group to organise terrorist activities in India. He entered India in January 1994 via Bangladesh and Nepal with large quantity of explosives, arms and ammunitions. Their task was to blow up buildings, railway stations and also to poison water supply. They were sentenced to five years of rigorous imprisonment under the Foreigners Act 1946 and under section 3,4,5 of the TADA in June 2000. As they had remained in jail for more than five years, the court directed their deportation.

Abu Nasir, a Bangladeshi national, was initially recruited by Lashker-e-Toiba chief Hafiz Saeed when he reportedly visited Bangladesh in 1998. Azam Cheema, launching expert of Lashker Jihadis in India, tested him. He was deputed to build ISI bases in Siliguri corridor and was also tasked to attack US installations in India. He was accompanied by foreign nationals of other countries. While he was apprehended, others managed to escape. He made startling disclosures of the ISI's role in India aided and abetted by the Lashker-e-Toiba.

The ISI is targeting India by sending Pakistani nationals as 'sleepers' like Junaid who was arrested in Hyderabad in July 1998. His cover organisation was Lashker-e-Toiba. He was tasked to recruit

---

28 'ISI focus on Punjab, *The Tribune*, April 26, 1999-PTI Islamabad.

29 *The Tribune*, April 26, 1999.

local boys for training in Pakistan and settle them in Hyderabad. He infiltrated into India in 1995 through Jammu border. He was blessed with a child in March 1998 after his marriage with a local Indian girl. Several Lashker-e-Toiba activists were arrested in Delhi, Hyderabad on the basis of the disclosure statement of Junaid. Sizeable quantity of explosives and arms were seized.[30] ISI carriers were arrested with explosives in Guwahati. These explosives were to be dispatched to different militant outfits in the Northeast for acts of subversion. Assam's DIG CID S.P. Kar made such a disclosure to the press.[31] Five Pakistanis were arrested with arms and ammunition on June 6, 1999. They entered India through Kutch border.[32] Sleepers always marry local girls for merging with the crowd. The Red Fort attack was also staged by a sleeper now resting in Tihar Jail. Hawash, a Sudanese national, was in Jaipur for a good length of time. He was recruited by Al-Safani of Al Qaeda to organise blast of the US Embassy in New Delhi. Al-Safani was also involved in USS Cole attack in 2000.

UP, a state of India has been targeted by the ISI in a big way. Salim, an ISI agent, was arrested in 1998 from Western UP. A lot of information could be obtained from his interrogation. It was learnt that one Major Fida Hussain of the ISI had visited Western UP and stayed in Sadiq Nagar for two months.

On April 16, 1997 Zakir Balik was arrested by the Meerut police. He was tasked by the ISI to take photographs of vital installations. His former wife too was arrested by the Meerut police on May 14, 1997 as she was handing over documents to an ISI agent.

Did Osama bin Laden visit India? Jayalalitha, then Chief Minister of Tamil Nadu reported in the Economic Times of 11 October, 1998 that she had received information that the Coimbatore blasts on February 14, 1998 was staged by bin Laden. This story came out of interrogation of Mir Shabir Ahmed (Indian) after his arrest on September 28, 1998 by the Tamil Nadu Police from his hide-out in Hyderabad. Osama reportedly visited India in early 1998 and met

---

30 *The Times of India*, 9/11/98.

31 *Pioneer*, 13/12/1998.

32 *Economic Times*, 7/6/1999.

with one political leader. The same leader earlier came to light when Mohd. Sharif, a top ISI agent, was arrested in the early nineties. Mir Shabir Ahmed, a resident of Tamil Nadu confessed of having undergone training at bin Laden's camp in Afghanistan along with few others. On the basis of his statement and some statements of others, 200 Afghan trained locals were at large in India. V.N. Gadgil, a member of the Congress party, wrote an article on the subject in *Hindustan Times* on 25 October, 1998 finally giving a call: 'Awake, Our Freedom Is In Peril' and said categorically that security of India 'can not be sacrificed at the altar of secularism.'

V.N. Gadgil further added that it was shocking that Osama bin Laden came to India, visited Mumbai, Delhi and Hyderabad. This remained unknown to Indian agencies.[33] Bangladeshis trained in Pakistan were sent to J&K. To create communal divide several churches were blasted in South India. Hindu organizations were initially blamed. The plan almost succeeded but for the chance capture of the ring leader along with explosives in the outskirts of Bangalore. Their vehicle turned turtle and caused grievous injuries to occupants who gave out the truth. This dangerous operation of creating communal divide failed. The organisation which was engaged in this task was Deendar Anjuman, whose chief has settled down in Pakistan. Evidence would show that some Anjuman, activists were trained in Pakistan. For example it was claimed that Syed Jilani, a radio mechanic, was trained in Mardan town of Pakistan.[34] On June 7, 2000 a meeting was held in Vijayawada where the activists were told about creation of a jihad army of Jamaat-e-Islami, Hizb-ul-Mujahideen to carry out more attacks.

The number of locals trained in Pakistan and Afghanistan need to be counted. Such details are available with state and central agencies. Such an all India exercise is necessary for the internal security of India. They are not spies but militants in disguise.

The ISI never gives up dividing India on communal lines. On January 4, 2000 Ankur Sharma a Hindu suspected to be an ISI agent banged into holy shrine of Badrinath in the wee hours. He

33 *Hindustan Times*, Sunday, October 25, 1998.

34 *The Hindu*, 28 July, 2000.

was nabbed from inside the temple. Some documents recovered from Sharma showed that he was working for the ISI which was confirmed by the police.[35]

On the basis of disclosure statement of Muhammad Dilshad, an ISI agent was apprehended in Siliguri on 4 January, 2002. One Ashique Ali alias Shahail Tahir, 22, a Pakistan national of Hyderabad district of Sindh province, was arrested from Nizamabad district of Andhra Pradesh leading to seizure of e-mail print-outs, pocket dairy containing telephone numbers and addresses of his handlers in Pakistan, sketch maps and photographs of defence areas. He was trained by the ISI to act as a sleeper. Dilshad transferred money to Tahir by draft from a bank in Siliguri and dispatched by a courier. Tahir was sent to India in June 2001. He destroyed his travel documents to conceal his Pakistani identity.

Pakistan links were found in various encounters with the police with Jihadis. There was a face to encounter on 12 March 2003 in Noida district of Uttar Pradesh with militants. The grenades recovered from them were of the mark of 'Arges'. These grenades are used by the Pakistan Army. In the Indian Parliament attack by Jaish-e-Mohammed (JeM) on 13 December 2001, grenades of this marking were found to have been used. The same type of grenades were used in 26/11 blasts in Mumbai.

Mohamed Aslam, a Pakistani hailing from Sindh of Pakistan province had a mobile with incoming calls from Pakistani handlers and also from local contacts. He was also carrying a document which shows 45 telephone contacts of Pakistan. On the basis of interrogation documents three more persons were picked up.

Fake Indian Currency- ISI's strategy to destabilise Indian economy and funding ISI's covert operations

Money is required for large scale covert operations. Nothing moves without money. Money is like oxygen. Money is required to train recruits, to maintain training camps, to move cadres from place to place. The so called jihadi army irregulars have to be supported by regular inflow of cash. Foreign donations are not enough. When the

35 *The Hindu,* January 6, 2000.

insurgency in Kashmir was in the peak from 1989 to 1995 ISI went to the extent of printing fake US dollars of $ 100 bills. When Benazir Bhutto got a call from Washington she was surprised. She was embarrassed too. A Pakistani military attaché Brig. Khalid Maqbool was caught red handed for running a fake US currency racket. The said officer was let off because of diplomatic immunity. He was sent back to Pakistan. He was the station head of the ISI in Washington. He refused to divulge facts relating to this racket. Benazir Bhutto could do nothing. Even a Prime Minister of Pakistan was not entitled to know who had authorized him to do so. As usual a cover story was prepared that fake notes were obtained from Afghanistan after the withdrawal of US contingent from there. The fake US notes were of high quality almost looking like genuine dollars. The US Treasury had to change the design of the notes.[36]

The same ISI has been able to repeat the same game of pumping fake Indian currency into India on a massive scale. It seems that this route has been adopted to finance terrorism in India and also subvert the Indian economy. The primary route is Nepal where such circulations were detected even in 1994. Like in the USA here also a Pakistani ISI Officer, diplomat in name, Arshad Cheema posted in Pakistan embassy in Kathmandu was caught red handed with huge fake Indian currency. He was masterminding Indian fake currency circulation and distributing RDX to ISI aided terrorist outfits. It was alleged that he provided logistic support to hijackers of IC 814.[37]

A Pakistani Embassy staff posted in Delhi similarly was found to have deposited fake Indian currency in a public school in Delhi for payment of school charges for his child.

In August 2003 another Pakistani embassy official in Kathmandu was caught red-handed with fake Indian currency of huge quantity. He was expelled from Kathmandu.

VK Shashikumar, senior editor with CNN-IBN, visited Nepal to investigate the depth and dimension of Indian fake currency

---

36 Adrian Levy and Catherine Scott-Clark, Deception, Pakistan, The United States and The Global Nuclear Conspiracy, Atlantic Books, 2007, p254 .

37 *The Hindu*, dated 7.12. 2001.

racket that operates from Nepal. He found law enforcement officials in Nepal and India admit that the long border is porous and security infrastructure weak and inadequate. Taking advantage of political uncertainty in Kathmandu Pakistan's Inter- Services Intelligence has set up a large and resourceful network of agents from Kathmandu to Birganj and all along the border to push hundreds of crores of counterfeit currency to India. One courier in confidence told him that 'hundreds of couriers bring bundles of fake currency—into India every day'. One dealer said that the ISI is pushing 100 crores of fake Indian currency every month into India from Nepal. It is estimated that if unchecked, by 2010 nearly 10,000 crores of fake currency will be in circulation in India.

Khalid Mehmood, a senior ISI officer posted in Kathmandu Embassy in a cover post ran the network, with the help of another ISI officer called Jamil Alam. These are assumed names to conceal their real identity. For country network the 'D'company network is used. D company has substantial presence in Nepal. This is widely known. Nepal has the photographs of some of the ISI operatives in this racket. The fake currency largely comes from Bangladesh and Thailand on international flights. Mufti Abdul Hannan, Chief of Harkat-ul-Jihadi Islam (HUJI) based in Bangladesh is reportedly the man behind this racket.

It is believed that ISI has managed to secure the support from some elements of the political system of Nepal. This is considered crucial for running the terror network in India. This appears true as money is required to run the terror network. As aptly said by Brig. Mohammed Yousaf of Afghan jihad fame that nothing moves without money. India will soon be facing subversion of her economy if this area of deep concern is not addressed. The Reserve Bank of India's role in controlling money supply will be at stake.[38]

There is a strong view that because of huge quantity of circulation of fake Indian currency, the money supply in Indian economy has increased manifold. As a result there is sharp increase in inflation in India. This is hardly discussed publicly for reasons

---

38 Nepal; export of fake currency, VK Shashikumar, *Indian Defence Review*, Oct/Dec-2008.

best known to economists.

There is no limit to the ISI's ingenuity to develop multiple methods of disruptive operations in India. The same trick of fake currency circulation can be played on Pakistan. Pakistan being small in size may not be able to withstand such disruptive activities for too long. Its economy will just collapse. But India has not played such a disruptive game, though this option is always available.

Northeast India

The ISI has special attraction for Northeast India. It is a long story of hijacking local discontent elements for promotion of its bases in that part of India. In early 1990, through ISI network of terrorists in India, Paresh Barua and many other of ULFA leadership were invited to visit Pakistan which they did via Bangladesh route. They even reportedly visited Hekmatyar's training camps. Gen. A.A.K. Niazi wrote in his book that Pakistan had raised a Brigade of Mizo and Naga troops in East Pakistan. After Mujib's assassination Bangladesh became the ISI's center of activity. On 8 August 1999 the Assam police busted a network of the ISI. 31 activists were nabbed, including two ISI officers, two agents and 27 militants belonging to different Islamic militant outfits. The most important was the Muslim United Liberation Tigers of Assam (MULTA). Grabbing of the Northeast is high on the agenda of the ISI as it was during the 'Muslim India' movement; Jinnah wanted Assam to be included in Pakistan. This is another unfinished agenda of partition for Pakistani establishment and Jihadis. Documents and interrogations confirmed this diabolical plot. The United Liberation Front of Assam (ULFA) operated from Bangladesh soil openly in tandem with the ISI and Bangladesh Field Intelligence Unit.

In 2000, Masood Azar's cassettes flooded Assam. These were highly inflammatory in content and tone and were released in minority areas with a sinister purpose. This was what the Chief Minister of Assam told the Assembly on 6 April 2000. He also tabled a detailed statement on ISI'S activities in Assam. It was an earth shaking account of the nefarious activities fomenting violence and terrorism in Assam by providing support to local militant outfits created by the ISI.

The main agenda of ISI for Northeast India are:

- To raise a large number of local Muslim fighters from Assam and launch Jihad to liberate Assam and neighbouring states and make it an Islamic state.

- To use ULFA and other local militant groups to create large-scale disturbances in the Northeast India.

- To collect money from local terrorist groups and pump in fake and counterfeit Indian currency notes.

- To foment communal troubles by inciting local Muslims.[39]

Denial strategy

Pakistani establishment has developed a denial strategy for all major attacks on Indian soil. Indian agencies are always blamed to defame Pakistan. Killing of Sikhs in Kashmir, hijacking of Indian Airlines flight IC 814, Kashmir Assembly attack and attack of Indian Parliament were attributed to Indian intelligence agencies. Maj. Gen. Rashid Qureshi was expert in the art of denial. The credibility of the denial strategy was finally dented in case of Daniel Pearl's kidnapping in Pakistan. Initially even the Pakistan Foreign Minister Abdul Sattar announced Indian hand from Berlin.[40] Maj.Gen. Rashid Qureshi announced that government would come out with such more details of India's involvement 'at the appropriate time'. Ultimately under international pressure the case ended in conviction of Omar Sheikh. He was awarded death sentence.

When the Christians were killed in Pakistan, the same game was played. Even some Christians were made to appear on Pakistan TV to allege Indian hand. This was humiliating to Christian community of Pakistan. Lt Col (retd) Zaman Malik found Indian conspiracy in IC 814 hijacking. In that case the three released from jail namely Maulana Azhar, Omar Sheikh and Zargar were part of the conspiracy. Pakistan denied presence of Omar Sheikh in Pakistan, when he was

---

39 *Sunday Observer*, January 9-15, 2000, Sujit Chakervarthy.

40 *The Hindu*, January 2, 2002.

running a business in Lahore and got married. Daniel Pearl's murder in 2002 opened a Pandora box.

On January 27, 2000 the Clinton Administration issued a public warning to Pakistan that it could be branded a state sponsor of terrorism, if the Pakistan Army continued to support terrorists blamed for the hijacking of an Indian Airlines flight in December 1999. The State Department spokesman, James Rabin, said that a possible connection between Pakistan's military and the group tied to hijacking, *i.e* Harkat-ul-Mujahideen was a matter of grave concern to US. He further said that this was an organization that US had declared as a foreign terrorist organization.

The ISI's links with Al Qaeda was well known. The ISI has managed to escape the critical attention of the US-led coalition as it is extending some cosmetic support to the USA in capturing some of the Al Qaeda operatives. Not a single catch was without the US intelligence. The ISI is marking its own time and waiting for another opportunity to enter Afghanistan by a series of covert operations. That has already started.

ISI – Internal

Benazir Bhutto made a genuine effort in her first term as Prime Minister of Pakistan to reform the ISI which is said to be 40,000 strong.[41] She constituted a Committee under a retired defence service officer. The Committee's Report was never made public. It was believed that the Committee had recommended that the ISI should not operate within Pakistan. It should restrict itself to external intelligence collection. Gen. Aslam Beg, then COAS of Pakistan army, killed the report in one stroke, saying that the character of the ISI would not be disturbed. Benazir Bhutto could do nothing. Instead, the ISI struck back by engineering her ouster. The internal political dynamics of Pakistan will not be allowed by the ISI to play its role and it has succeeded. This stark reality should receive international attention.

The internal role of the ISI was noticed from the days of Gen Ayub. He used the ISI for manipulating votes of the basic democrats

---

41 *The Hindu*, 4/1/1997.

for his Presidential election in 1964. 80,000 basic democrats were to be manipulated in favour of Ayub by fair or foul means. After all Miss Fatima Jinnah was contesting as the sole opposition candidate. She was the sister of the founder of Pakistan Mohammad Ali Jinnah, a Gujrati by birth and a Pakistani by accident of history. Brig Riaz was then heading the ISI. In 1965 war with India, the ISI could not locate the ground position of an armored division in India. He was given a dressing down by Gen Ayub. When Brig Riaz could not bear any more, he said that the ISI remained busy in the presidential election. Gen Ayub's temper soon changed. This was perhaps the first evidence of the ISI's involvement in politics of Pakistan. Thereafter the ISI never looked back.

The ISI could not give proper assessment of the Bangladesh situation. It framed up a case against Mujibur Rehman in Agartala conspiracy case. During the period of the alleged conspiracy Mujib was in jail and thus he could not be a part of the conspiracy.

Zulfikar Ali Bhutto on becoming the President of Pakistan in 1971 after the Bangladesh debacle, gave teeth to ISI. Then ISI chief Lt. Gen Jilani was more close to Rawalpindi GHQ than Bhutto. Apparently Bhutto trusted Gen Jilani and shared many secrets with him. Strangely, when Gen Zia staged the coup, Jilani was the only one who was not arrested by Gen Zia. Even Gen Tikka Khan, the previous army chief and a close confidante of Bhutto was arrested as also IB chief Rao Rashid and many others. Bhutto realised this when he was in jail and expressed wonder why Jilani escaped imprisonment. In fact, he remained ISI chief even during Zia's time for some time and on retirement he was rewarded with Governor's post in Punjab. The ISI always remained loyal to Army.

It was Gen Zia who made ISI as a strong instrument of state policy. He selected Gen Akhtar Abdur Rehman, a Pathan, as Director General of ISI. Gen Akthar remained in that post for more than a decade. He became a legendary figure during the Afghan war. He shaped the strategy of the proxy war in Afghanistan. He selected best of army officers for Afghan war. Brig. Yousaf was one of them, who headed the ISI's Afghan Bureau. Gen. Akhtar maintained close watch on Army Officers who were likely to cause trouble to Gen

Zia. Gen F A Chisti, who earned the reputation of Gen Zia'a storm trooper during the coup, had to suffer utter humiliation from ISI after his retirement. His phones were tapped and movements watched. No officer of the army could meet Gen Chisti, as anyone doing that would be exposed to severe questioning by ISI.

Gen Akhtar's success in Afghan war was largely because of US and its allies back-up as also of China's joining the jihad. As a result Gen Akhtar built up an image larger than his life size. He created a seven Afghan party alliance for fighting the war and backed up a wrong person Gulabuddin Hekmatyar who really had no popular base in Afghanistan. Before the formal end of the Afghan war, Gen Akhtar was shifted by Gen Zia from ISI to deprive him of the credit of success in the proxy war in Afghanistan.

Gen Akhtar's successor was Gen Hamid Gul, a passionate Islamist. He made a mess of Afghan policy. Gen Gul could not capture Kabul or consolidate the gains by keeping the Afghan parties united. The bitter infighting started between the Mujahideen parties and field commanders. His only reputation was that he managed to give practical shape of Mujahideen war in Kashmir. A modified plan for Kashmir operation on the lines of Afghanistan was said to have been formulated before Gen Zia's death in August 1988. India calls it "Operation Topac", but in Pakistani write-ups the code name of the operation is still a secret. On the basis of inputs and war-game analysis of Indian experts, "Topac" operation was conceived and has earned legitimacy as things have been happening the way it had been described. The Kargil intrusion was also drawn up in 1990 again on the basis of another war game called "Operation X file". It is now found from Pakistani sources that such a plan did exist, but Benazir Bhutto, as Prime Minister, did not approve of the scheme. She has given such news to the press from abroad. Musharraf was even contemplating to take action against her for violation of oath of office.

In September 2000 Benazir Bhutto accused Musharraf for inducting persons 'having direct or indirect connections with ISI'. She named Atiya Inayatullah, Gazi, Gen. Javed Ashraf Qazi, Col. Tressler for having ISI connections. Atiya had worked under with

Zia and Gazi also had links with former army dictator. Gen.(retd) Javed Ashraf Qazi was head of the ISI. She had described them as 'monster'. The ISI created a network of officers at district and Tehsil levels tasked to watch on the politicians, which was not its function.[42]

ISI during democratic rule

The army and the ISI, after Zia's sudden aircraft crash death, did allow reluctantly election and restoration of democracy. The Chief of the Army Gen Mirza Aslam Beg and Gen Hamid Gul wanted to defeat Benazir Bhutto's Pakistan People's Party. For this they built up a Zia portegee Nawaz Sharif. Money was provided to Sharif's party by inducing Habib Younus of the Habib Bank and Mehran Bank to part with Rs.14 Crore. Out of this Gul's share was 6 crore for Kashmir cell and rest was utilised by Gen Aslam Beg for political cell of the army. Such an open scandal, largely exposed by Air Marshal (retd) Asghar Khan, did not provoke the judiciary to react on the petition filed by him. The court almost exonerated these officers by saying it would not deal with the past corrupt activities of the ISI. It would confine itself to providing some guidelines for ISI. Nothing has come out this exercise so far.

Benazir Bhutto's first term was secured after she reportedly met the army chief and agreed to toe the army and ISI's line on Kashmir and Afghanistan. The waiting period was worrying her. She did not become Prime Minister immediately after the poll, a disturbing feature of the nascent democracy. The army under Gen. Aslam Beg and the ISI under Gen Hamid Gul never felt comfortable with her. There were attempts to topple her federal government. Within a week after taking over charge as Prime Minister in December 1988, Brig. Imtiaz of the ISI started contacting political parties to over throw Benazir's government. When evidence was produced, the army under Gen Aslam Beg merely removed him from ISI and not from the army. It was a gross defiance of orders of a civilian government. The next opportunity came in 1989 when a no-confidence motion was moved in the National Assembly by Nawaz Sharif's party. The members of the ruling party were under pressure

42 *The Indian Express*, 4 September 2000.

to vote for the motion for which heavy payments were promised to defectors. Major Amir of the ISI was the chief actor. One PPP member under instruction of Benazir Bhutto, decided to expose the ISI. The secret meeting place was bugged and conversation recorded. At an appropriate time the tapes were released and the whole exercise came to a grinding halt. The ISI was exposed in this dirty affair. The no-confidence motion was defeated. No action was taken against the ISI, the main operative was declared deranged by the military intelligence. They were merely transferred. The ISI chief Gen Hamid Gul was shifted from the ISI and elevated as Corps Commander of Multan. From Multan he continued to interfere in the affairs of intelligence agencies.

Benazir Bhutto recalled how on March 23, 1989 she was mobbed by the jawans and that panicked Gen Aslam Beg. Thereafter all the intelligence agencies mounted a slander campaign against her by spreading poisonous stories and circulating them to Corps Commanders and jawans. She was called an Indian agent, a Jewish agent and an American agent. The conspiracy to oust her was started. President Ishaq Khan was told that under Benazir a move was on to impeach him and he would to be replaced by Yahya Bakhitar, who was Zulfikar Ali Bhutto's defence lawyer during the murder trial against him. Even Benazir's husband was approached to take over as Prime Minister as the army officers 'could not salute a woman'.[43]

The most revealing disclosure was in respect of two meetings organised by a Corps Commander in which Nawaz Sharif and Osama bin Laden also participated. Bin Laden was told to provide money to overthrow a lady Prime Minister so as to bring Islam to Pakistan. She was on record to have said that $ 10 million was paid by Bin Laden to finance the conspiracy. The conspiracy failed as the MNAs refused to switch sides.

In 1990 the ISI, in spite of its previous failures, launched a similar exercise called 'Operation jackal'. The ISI was eventually trapped by a group of Benazir's supporters for inducing her MNAs to defect. The operation was videotaped. In the tape Brig Imtiaz who was not technically in the ISI said: the army does not want her, the

---

43 *The Herald Annual*, January 2001-Page 41-61.

President does not want her, and America doesn't want her'. The tape was handed over to Gen Beg, COAS, who merely retired Brig Imtiaz 'with a fault' and not proceeded against him for high treason. Even after this Gen Beg told some of the MNAs from NWFP that army 'wants to get rid of her......could you please move a no-confidence vote against her?[44]

In a similar fashion the PPP led opposition was on the verge of toppling Nawaz Sharif's government in Punjab by obtaining support of some members of the Nawaz Sharif's party. A day before the motion was to be put to vote, Gen Aslam Beg gave a press interview to the Editor of the Jung newspaper. Next day the news paper carried the headline. "Punjab Government will not fall-says Beg". That unnerved the dissidents and the entire scheme fizzled out. The unusual statement of the Army Chief was considered as another instance of political interference by the army.

Gen Javed Nasir became the new ISI chief after Gen Hamid Gul. He was an active member of the Tabligi Jamaat which is a world wide organization and works without much of fanfare. The Tabligi Jamaat believes in approaching individual Muslims calling them to shun practices which have Hindu or alien touch. They believe in purifying Islam in its original pristine Arab glory. This organization was found recruiting volunteers for Afghan jihad from all over the world. Gen Javed Nasir would regularly visit Raiwind to meet Tabligi leaders when he was in service. With Gen Nasir's taking over there was intensification of Jihad in Kashmir. He is a die-hard fundamentalist and was very close to Nawaz Sharif. When Nawaz Sharif came to power, he became his security advisor. Gen Javed's transformation as a fundamentalist came late. Lt Gen Satish Nambiar of the Indian Army had met him as a junior officer in a course in Australia and found Javed without any religious bug. Nawaz Sharif made him the President of the Pakistan Sikh Gurudwara Prabandhak Committee which was an unusual step. Imagine Praveen Togodia becoming chief of the Delhi Jama Masjid. Sikhs in Pakistan protested without any result. The idea was to reorganise terrorism in Punjab is largely financed any engineered by some misguided Sikh expatriates mostly

---

44 *The Herald Annual*, January 2001.

living in USA or Canada. They often visit Pakistan to exchange notes with authorities. The deals are not secret. On 14 August 2000 Independence Day celebration they were honoured by Pakistani establishment by seating them in the front row. The Pakistan TV gave good coverage to them. It was like India calling Altaf Hussain, Ataullah Mengal and some Pakistan leaders on 15 August celebration publicly congratulating them for the cause they uphold. Such cheap tactics is beyond imagination. It is a question of time when India too may extend invitation to all Pakistani dissidents to have their annual jamboree in India and foment trouble in Pakistan. So far India has not played this ball game.

Benazir Bhutto wanted to reform the ISI. She appointed a committee to look into this aspect. The committee's report was never made public. However, the knowledgeable people believed that she wanted ISI to concentrate on foreign intelligence operations and the IB entrusted with counter-intelligence operations. The Committee favoured ending of ISI operation in India. All these proved an useless exercise when Gen Aslam Beg announced that the character of the ISI would not be disturbed. That ended the reformation and reorganization of ISI.

ISI was used twice to create and split MQM. Karachi is the base of mujahirs who are migrants from India during partition of India. In 1984 Gen. Zia created 'fissures' in Karachi by sponsoring the birth of Muhajir Qaumi Movement (MQM). Soon it became a strong political force. In 1992 to counter Benazir Bhutto, ISI again was used to break the MQM by organizing a split and creating MQM(H). H means haqqiqi *i.e.* real as rival to MQM renamed as Muttahida Quami Movement.

All politicians of Pakistan feel insecure because of ISI's internal operations. Many feel reluctant to speak openly as like Najam Sethi they would have to face the wrath of the ISI. ISI has a network of detachment officers in each district of Pakistan with two senior officers of the rank of Colonel drawn from the army in position. Not only districts, but even Tehsils have ISI's presence. Their job is to spy on politicians, bug their telephones and mount surveillance, too obvious to be ignored by deviant politicians. Even Gen Chisti was under ISI's observance after retirement. He was harassed by ISI to an extent unbelievable in any other country. Gen Arif, a protégé of Zia, confirmed how ISI would take picture of visitors meeting Zia and produce them before Zia blaming IB for mounting surveillance on Zia[45] At that time Mohammed Khan Junejo was the Prime Minister of Pakistan. ISI wanted ouster of Junejo as he was insisting on Gen Akhtar's accountability for Ojhiri blast of April 10, 1988. To defame IB, ISI even bugged Zia's telephone and recorded the conversation of his daughter with someone. The tapes were played back to Zia. ISI blamed IB. The ISI claimed that such tapes could be secured by managing a Watergate on IB.

Mohd Edi, mother Theresa of Pakistan, was not spared either. Out of disgust he approached Prime Minister Benazir Bhutto, who advised him to leave the country as she was unable to deal with ISI. When Benazir was ousted in August 1990 by President Ishaq Khan, she blamed the army. The army never trusted her on sensational national issues. She even complained ISI's interference in domestic political affairs to Aslam Beg. Such is the humiliating position of a Prime Minister in Pakistan.

The ISI's structure and its character will always remain in a thick fog of secrecy and mystery. Old fossils of ISI (retired) are often re-appointed for collection of intelligence. However, Lt Gen Riaz Khan who succeeded Gen Jilani dispensed with this. Riaz Khan was, not sure if Islam permitted unethical intelligence operations. There is a religious section in GHQ which deals with such matters. Yes, according to GHQ, intelligence collection is backed by Holy Quran and Sunnah. This saved the conscience of Gen Riaz who was considered an upright officer in the Pak army. Brig Tirmazi also argued that in Islamic history deceptions and espionage were practiced by Prophet Mohammed as directed by Allah.[46]

Theoretically, the field detachment commanders, as they are called, remain under the charge of Deputy Directors of ISI, but the DG often would receive reports direct from detachment commanders bypassing Director, JCIB on need to know basis. This

---

45 Arif, page 395/396.

46 Tirmazi, Brig Syed A L, Profiles of Intelligence, Combined Printers, Lahore, pp 22-23.

was the practice widely prevalent when Gen Jilani was heading the organizations.

Gen Zia tasked Gen Hamid Gul to raise survey sections within ISI reporting on political pulse. Zia and Akhtar were also blamed[47] that they promoted mediocre and brilliant officers were shunted out.

In 1996 in her second term, Benazir came to know that DG Military Intelligence, Gen Mahmud had told an official that she would go in the month of March and he would sort it out. Gen Mahmud got stories published defaming Benazir. Gen Karamat when informed did not interfere.[48] President Leghari was under pressure from DGMI to get rid of Benazir and if he did not then the army would get rid of the President and the Prime Minister'. She was ousted on November 4, 1996 and she came to know about her ouster when Colonel Asif arrived at her residence to ensure takeover by the President. The army had taken over the airports of the country. Before that her telephones were being tapped in October and November 1996 by the intelligence agencies. The intelligence managed to spin out stories of her involvement in the murder of Murtaza Bhutto. She recalled that President Leghari was informed that Asif Zardari had made a videotape of Leghari's child's relationship with some one based in Lahore. This infuriated President Leghari. The same trick was played on Zia by the ISI when some taped conversations of her daughter was played back and the blame was given to IB which was under the charge of Prime Minister Junejo. Junejo was dismissed by Zia.

The ISI former chiefs do not repent for their acts of gross violation of democratic practices. Gen (retd) Hamid Gul in an interview to a news magazine proudly admitted having influenced the 1988 elections (Herald Annual 2001). The former DG ISI Gen (retd) Assad Durrani admitted influencing the 1990 elections. Gen Hamid Gul has perverted notion of the will of the people. He said 'the will of the people was reflected on October 12, 1999' (coup) and justifies that Nawaz Sharif was a hoax by the intelligence agencies as was Bhutto created by Ayub. He blatantly admitted to have created

---

47   Muslim, Nov 6, 1993.

48   Herald Annual, 2001.

IDI (Sharif party) and 'one must not be puritanical about this' and Nawaz Sharif fell into the American trap and was removed.

The country is thus under full grip of army controlled ISI. They work independent of government. Under the so called civilian rule ISI remained nominally under the Prime Minister who did not have the power or capacity to deal with it. Its presence is over-bearing. It decides posting of civilians including postings of GHQs. Even the names of the chief ministers need prior clearance of ISI. ISI has the capacity to hire people from all walks of life and can direct any organ of the government to take extra legal action in the name of nationalism and attempts to feed stories to a number of journalists on leash.

Henri Levis while he was in Pakistan studying political situation in Pakistan soon found out that his local guide was being shadowed. Mysterious calls received by him without caller's ID. He soon found out from his sources that in Pakistan one can safely assume that such calls originate from the ISI or the military. President Zardari reported to have received a threatening call from Indian Foreign Minister after the Mumbai terrorist strike. One can not rule out ISI's game in this in future also.

ISI's greatest allies are the Islam pasand parties and their fighting jihadi outfits. Gen (retd). Hamid Gul was frank enough to admit that the right parties and jihadi groups are the natural allies of the army and the ISI. Gen Gul, after retirement, is the guide and philosopher of many of the jihadi outfits. He is anti-American and has intense hatred for India. He smokes pipe with Laskher-e-Toiba chief Hafiz Mohammed Saeed too often. Army's real ally said Gen (retd) Hamid Gul, are the religious parties and the Mujahideen and not the secular elements.[49]

JCIB

The Joint Counter Intelligence Bureau is not be confused with IB. It is the most important counter intelligence unit of the ISI presided over by an officer of the rank of a Brigadier. Brig. Syed A.I. Tirmazi was picked up by Gen Jilani for ISI. He remained in ISI during the

---

49 *The Friday Times*, Pakistan, July 21-27, 2000.

turbulent period of Bhutto's trial and after for a good length of time. Previously as a Captain he had stint in Intelligence Bureau and claimed to have picked up an Intelligence on September 2, 1965 of Indian attack on Lahore on September 6 and bombardment of Rawalpindi from a source in the Indian High Commission office in Islamabad. This does appear to be true as Altaf Gauhar claimed that such an information was received from a source in Delhi. Tirmazi worked under Gen Riaz who succeeded Gen Jilani. Gen Riaz was a God fearing honest person. While in service he died of heart attack without leaving behind a plot of land or a house. Gen Riaz was succeeded by Gen Akhtar Abdur Rehman who was a die-hard Zia loyalist. Brig Tirmazi like many others in Pakistan Army was always critical of the US intentions. He blamed US for hanging of Bhutto.

'Counter intelligence is like searching a needle in a haystack'. The head of JCIB reports to DDG internal as also DG ISI. From his accounts of counter intelligence operations the following claims have been revealed by him. What type of needles did he find in a haystack? His disclosures are amusing and ridiculous.

Pakistanis who meet Indian High Commission Officials are 'followed and questioned'. The Indian ladies who were wives of embassy officials have been described as 'aphrodisiac nagmanis with naked bellies' and 'a few older Pakistanis lose their head on a 'bhabhi'. In most cases one can judge 'from the wife, the position and appointments of the husband'. The staff not connected with intelligence 'escort their oversized wives' to market to 'end up with purchasing a solitary cauliflower or a quarter kilogram of potatoes'. 'The ISI is dreaded organization in India' writes Tirmazi. 'Even some mothers scare their children to sleep lest the ISI men lurking in their streets would come into the house".[50]

ND Khan, Pakistan's Ambassador to UAE was reportedly hooked by sister-in-law of the Indian Ambassador and Khan decided to marry her. 'He became a victim of her' lascivious charm'. He was proceeded against and removed from service.[51] A first Secretary of Pakistan High Commission called Gaffar in Delhi 'smuggled' an

---

50 Tirmazi, p 93.

51 Ibid, p 97.

Indian girl to Pakistan and got married. He was court martialled and dismissed.[52]

A case of an Indian girl Veena (not real name) managed to trap one Parvez of the Pakistan Atomic Energy Commission in a hotel. The ISI 'waiter' fixed a small transmitter in the trolley to overhear their conversation. She subsequently became a double agent. She even prepared to cross over, embrace Islam and marry a Pakistani. Brig Tirmazi lamented that the ISI 'could not arrange for a husband for her'. She went back to India when recalled.

All Embassy phones are regularly taped by the ISI.[53] In one operation a Pakistani Major spoke to one Brig. Singh and he was booked and dismissed. He was a recipient of Sitar-e-Jurrat. Pakistan's Air Attaché Younus in Afghanistan was enticed by the wife of an Indian Defence Attaché. Once he was allegedly spending his holidays at the residence of the Indian Attaché. He was recalled and punished.

The most important catch of Brig Tirmazi was trapping Mohan, a domestic servant of one Dodi of the Indian High Commission. All these names are fictitious. Mohan was a drug addict which brought him close to an ISI's pathan operative for regular supply of charas. The pathan got easy access to Dodi's residence to plant bugs. This was made easier by Bittu, the daughter of Dodi, as she started smoking charas. Dodi was flirting with the wife of another official. 'She was a real gajagamani'. Tirmazi's knowledge of 'gajagamani' is startling. His knowledge is better than our MF Hussain. As her sex was insatiable, she too was trapped by putting a Pakistani 'handsome' man on her. Her love making with the handsome Pakistani was videotaped. She agreed to play the role of a double agent and benefited the ISI by providing 'endless' flow of information. She left Pakistan when her husband was posted out.

These big achievements real or imaginary, do not give a good image of JCIB. He blamed RAW for various anti-national activities and failed to provide any information on such operations. His failure

---

52 Ibid.

53 Tirmazi, p 101.

to book any Indian agent of RAW proves that either JCIB failed to catch the agents or the agents were not many to be caught. Indian counter intelligence cases at least end up in court trials in India and accused like Mohd. Sharif received sentence from Court of Law. No such court cases could be cited by the Director JCIB, Brig. Tirmazi.[54] Such make believe petty cases are flaunted as great achievements of the JCIB.

Strength of ISI

No one knows for sure the strength of ISI. Some feel that it may be around 25,000, much more than RAW and IB (India) combined together. Its budget is secret. During the Afghan war it operated private bank accounts for crediting CIA and Arab contributions for jihad. It is widely believed that the main source of fund is derived from drug trafficking. The drug lord's profit is shared by ISI. The foreign press reporters had reported how the army convoy escorted by the ISI after dropping arms at Quetta and Peshawar used to return with drugs loaded into those trucks.

ISI's worldwide jihad by proxy is not sustainable by Pakistan government's budgetary contribution. How can Pakistan finance Kashmir jihad operation and operations in India and elsewhere, when its own finances are in a mess. India spends heavy amount in counter-insurgency operations in Kashmir. In what way Pakistan can match with India in the area of spending. Jihad has been largely privatized by ISI by adopting unconventional methods of fund raising.

The internal political dynamics of Pakistan will always be derailed by the ISI. The ISI removed Benazir Bhutto from the post of Prime Minister twice as she was projected pro-India, an agent of Israel and the USA. Its dirty trick department churned out defamatory stories against her. Nawaz Sarif did try to put the army back to barracks. The army coup was planned much before 12 October, 1999. In September 1999 the US strongly advised the Pakistan army not to dethrone Nawaz Sharif. This was ignored. Sharif's utterances

---

54 Profiles of Intelligence by Brig. Syed Al Tirmazi, printed at Combined Printers, Guardi Trust Building, Lahore, 1995.

against the army for Kargil misadventure was not liked by the army. They decided to get rid of Sharif. Only a truckload of army men in uniform from 10 corps in Rawalpindi was enough to change a civilian regime in Pakistan. The judiciary is incapable to deal with the army and the ISI. The judges who refuse to toe the line of the ISI and the army is literally shunted out. Their images are tarnished by painting them black through the obliging press and leaks.

The ISI is known for breaking and building political parties in Pakistan. When democracy was restored after Gen Zia's death in 1988 the ISI and the army promoted anti-Benazir alliance under Nawaz Sharif. Sharif was chosen to lead the government of Punjab during Zia's time. He was selected because the Sharif's family businesses like steel manufacturing units were nationalized by Zulfikar Ali Bhutto. Sharif is otherwise a lovable person with love for Indian filmi music and good food. Every district has ISI presence. It collects money from dubious sources. Gen. (Retd.) Aslam Beg made a bold statement before the court that it was a practice with the ISI to fund candidates in the general elections. He said the ISI distributed Rs. 60 million to the candidates of the Islamic Alliance which included Nawaz Sharif.[55]

The ISI kidnapped PML (N) leader Ahsan Iqbal on January 13, 2001 when he was on his way to meet a friend in Islamabad. Two white Corollas blocked his way and six jumped out and dragged him out of the car. They took him to a house and locked him in a dark room. At 10:30 pm his face was covered with a black cloth used for prisoners to be hanged and dropped him after 20 minutes in front of his car. Five other colleagues were also picked up in the similar way and detained at various places in Islamabad. Their only fault was that they were raising voice for restoration of democracy after Musharraf's coup. He lamented in spite of wide publicity as the chief of the police took no notice of this incident. Pakistan's Supreme Court also took no notice on press reports of illegal detention. The idea was to break the PML and isolate Nawaz Sharif which they succeeded by creating PML (Qaid). This is not the only

---

55 *Asian Age* 20/02/1997.

case to illustrate the illegal action of the intelligence agencies.[56]

Benazir Bhutto was on record to have stated that Osama bin Laden provided money in 1988 to a Corps Commander at Rawalpindi for dislodging her government. Her accusation was not challenged. The ISI's drug trafficking links were established by foreign journalists during the first Afghan Jihad. Corruption in the ISI has never been exposed. All ex-ISI generals live in style barring one Gen Muhammad Riaz Khan who never received admiration and died in service. The ISI's budget is outside the purview of accountability. According to a US Congressional Report, 35 percent of the refugee aid of $1.2 billion was misappropriated by the ISI.[57] The blue-eyed boys of the ISI are given residential plots at throw away price. [58]

Pakistan's democratic future is under constant threat from its army and the ISI. The ISI's dubious role in exporting terrorism is widely known. Can Pakistan army survive without the ISI? No. Therefore, the Pakistan army needs the ISI. Without intense international pressure the ISI will never change. For democratic Pakistan the role of the army and ISI need to be curtailed. Under the present dispensation this is not likely to happen. Pakistan's Lahore High Court justified illegal long detention of Najam Sethi, a respected journalist, on the ground that the ISI was an extension of the army and, therefore, court has no jurisdiction to look into the role of the ISI under Article 193 (3) of the Constitution. By providing this legal legitimacy for the first time the ISI has become a more dangerous institution. Pakistani intellectuals, academicians and politicians live under the fear and threat of the ISI. It is a threat to regional and world peace as it promoted terrorism abroad.

If the role of the ISI is not curtailed the proxy war in Kashmir will continue. This has to be understood as the Jihadi outfits are maintained and sustained by the ISI. The ISI's hardcore elements are strongly indoctrinated with the concept of Jihad. After all the army in Pakistan are being trained on the basis of 'Quranic Concept

---

56 The Herald, February 2001, Mukashir Zaidi who interviewed Ahsan Iqbal.

57 *The Hindu*, 4/1/1997.

58 Tirmazi, p18.

of War'. The book written by Brig. S.K. Malik on Quranic Concept of War was endorsed by Gen. Zia as a standard literature for Pakistan army. The book explains how terror has to be practiced on enemy to win long and short wars. The Pak army and the ISI are out of tune with the present day world which vehemently rejects terror as a state policy. Will the world wake-up and face this stark reality? This can perhaps happen if the belly of the eagle (USA) is again hit by some Islamic outfit. After 9/11 there was slight change of the ISI strategy. The financial times of May 2002 provided the truth by quoting a jihadi leader "Pakistan has told us to suspend our activities". Some jihad leaders realise that they were being used as cheap and dispensable commodity. If a soldier dies, pension and other financial aids have to be provided to the family. In case of jihadis who embrace martyrdom nothing is to be paid except some amount from the ISI's secret service fund. Even a part of that is eaten up by the jihadi organizations to keep the organizations going.

How to deal with the ISI

Has Pakistan been able to build up its fifth column in India? The fifth column derives its name from Spanish civil war from 1936-1939. A fascist revolutionary general Gen Zalo Quiepode Llano Sirro moved to Madrid with his four Army columns. The general referred to his armed supporters within Madrid as his 'fifth column' who were tasked to undermine the loyalist government from within.

Thus, the security of a nation can be threatened by large scale infiltration of sympathisers at the nodal points by planting its adherents at the decision level or at the level of national defence services. Our porous borders have been used by Pakistan for sending its people, men and women, in large numbers without documents. They just melt into the crowd. One bright Brigadier D S Dhillon could bust such infiltration in the armed forces in the Northeast in 1998 when he referred to police the doubtful applications for verification. The applications contained bogus addresses. GOC Eastern Command Lt Gen J.S. Verma said that Pakistan's ISI was working on a long term plan of getting ISI operatives recruited in three wings of the armed forces. Such ISI infiltrators after obtaining fake ration cards are trying to get enlisted in the armed forces in the ranks of jawans. He said that the ISI has bases in Bangladesh as well as in the Terai region of Nepal where changing demographic pattern had helped in its functioning.[59]

What has to be understood very precisely and clearly that the ISI and its jihadi outfits are making outright 'incremental invasion' of India in violation of international law and UN conventions on terrorism. This has escaped the attention of many in India for reasons best known to them. India has legitimate right to respond to counter this 'creeping invasion' of the fifth columnists. Obviously, the beat system of the police should be tasked to identify such anti-nationals and deal with them as enemy agents under a separate law. Only harshest penalty may stop this creeping invasion or else the nation will perish. They are not spies, but jihadis out to destroy the secular fabric of India.

The Punjab Police had seized two cyanide consignments from ISI agents in 1998. Immediately after this one Kg cyanide was seized from a Bombay gang. These consignments are being stored in safe houses for use at a critical juncture. So is the case of stockpiling of RDX and sophisticated weapons by ISI within India. The critical situation scenario will be built up gradually by aiding and abetting local militants like ULFA, Bodo Militants and many others. In 2008 the name of Indian Mujahideen has surfaced. They were trained in Pakistan and ideologically motivated Pakistan based Jihadi outfit like Lasher – Toiba. The ISI has operational control on many of them. Why ISI paying host to Paramjit Singh Panjwar in Lahore? It is believed that Koyalapattinam village in Tamil Nadu was the meeting ground between LTTE and ISI.[60]

White Paper on ISI

The government of India's indecision to publish a 'White Paper' on ISI has created a negative impression. There is a doubt if ISI is really involved in India the way it has been projected in media or otherwise. It is perhaps believed by government that if such reports are revealed in the White Paper it would compromise our future

---

59 *Times of India*, August 30, 2003.

60 Ghosh, Rinku, The seize within, *Pioneer* dated January 23, 2000.

counter-intelligence operations. But nothing remains secret after arrests or liquidation of ISI network. Press comes out with full details. There is no secrecy either when the ISI operatives are convicted in courts of law. Such news of court convictions are hardly reported in the press. There are plenty of open documents openly available to build up a White paper on ISI for internal awareness of threats and external consumption of people who need to know how to deal with the situation globally. In the interest of transparency, facts need to be told and absorbed by people at large.

The Singapore Government, in its wisdom, released a White Paper on Jemaah Islamiya (JI) and its links with Al-Qaeda after busting of JI and Al-Qaeda network in Singapore in 2001-2. These outfits were planning large-scale bombing attacks in Singapore. All the links of these organizations in Southeast Asia and Pakistan have been brought out in significant manner, how the terrorist activities were being organised in the region. These disclosures prompted Southeast Asian countries to take note of the reality and initiate action. Bali bombers have been hanged in 2008. Because of these strong steps the South East Asian region is now more peaceful than before. There is an agreement now in place to cooperate with each other.

India's experience is no different. There was a conspiracy to bomb Madras Stock Exchange in the early nineties much before the Bombay serial blasts in 1993. There was a dry-run of the Madras Stock Exchange building carried out by Mohd. Sharif, along with some locals. Sharif, an ISI trained sleuth, was visiting frequently Delhi, Bombay, Tamilnadu, Hyderabad, Nepal, Western UP and Kolkata for setting-up cells and recruitment of locals for spreading the ISI network for jihad and anti-national activities. His memory is phenomenal. He needed no camera to capture the area details. He visited Avantipur airbase in Kashmir. When arrested he pleaded that his forefathers were Hindus. He used to communicate with his handlers in Pakistan using STD facilities. His trial ended in conviction. His case deserves to be told to the public for awareness campaign and included in the White Paper if ever published as part of historical record.

A time has come now when the intelligence gathering system has to be revamped the way Mossad and Sherbet work. Every useful information is passed on to these agencies by Israelis. Each Israeli abroad work for Mossad free of payments. Mossad's strength lies not in its numerical strength, which is much less than what we have in our country, but it has fine networking of mass based intelligence collection system. Mossad and Sherbet have good network of intelligence gathering capability. To combat terrorism in India a similar system has to be built up.

Revamping of intelligence collection & system

A proper motivation is required now for generation of mass based intelligence gathering. It is no use blaming one agency or other for not spotting anti-national elements. For example Sivarasan, who masterminded the actual execution of the conspiracy to kill Rajiv Gandhi, was roaming around in Tamil Nadu, but he could not be targeted in the absence of mass based intelligence gathering system prior to Rajiv Gandhi's killing. No intelligence system can be effective without mass support. Patriotic citizens have a role to play to secure their children's future.

Beat system

At any point of time thousands of anti national conspirators are in this game. The basic structure of the police administration is supposed to cover every part of the country by a beat constable. He is supposed to take care of criminals who appear and disappear from his beat jurisdiction. The beat constables, if smart in their work, can also pick-up bazaar information on suspicious characters, suspicious meetings of strangers who appear and 'melt into the crowd'. Where the beat system works, the policing are effective and crime is generally controlled.

Beat system is effective only when their supervisory officers brief and debrief them. This is the critical area of supervision where the system either works or fails. The first task of revamping of the police system is to revive the beat system, which is conceptually correct and operationally effective as one method of dealing with crime and criminals and anti-national elements in a vast country like

India.

The district police system, under the charge of Superintendent of Police, takes care of the criminal side of the administration. On political side, collection of intelligence largely rests with State and Central Intelligence Agencies. Their net-work is loose and do not cover the every landmass of the country. As a result, their intelligence gathering capacity is very limited. The ISI functioning within Pakistan is unique. The ISI has covered the entire state of Pakistan by posting detachment commanders of the rank of Colonel/ Brigadiers in all the districts. Where necessary its net-work goes to Tehsil level also. This system has pitfalls as it tends to suppress political activities of political parties and tends to play the role of a mediator in politics. This system of army controlled agency is not at all suited for India where democracy needs to be strengthened and not curtailed as has happened in Pakistan. It does not take much time to build up a parallel Indian version of the ISI to deal with Pakistani ISI. Wisely we have not taken this disastrous route, although we have enough supporters for creation of such a Frankenstein organisation in India also. Let the police beat system be focussed on anti-national elements.

Central Criminal Intelligence Organization – a need of the hour

Instead, India can build up a system of collection of mass based intelligence on a different pattern. Information on transnational organised crime needs to be centralised and no such central criminal intelligence collection agency exists to take care of growing threats from international organised crime groups. These organised crime groups are often used by the ISI for subversive activities. Money generated by transnational organised crime groups are obviously shared by the ISI. It is natural. Why else Pakistan would keep Dawood Ibrahim to operate his syndicate from Karachi? Each threat or kidnapping fetches substantial amount of money. Such ransom/ or extortion money would be sent abroad through Hawala net-work or otherwise.

"Intelligence" is a central subject under our constitution. That is how IB functions in States. IB's earlier avatar was called the

Central Criminal Intelligence Bureau. It grew out of Col. Sleeman's operations against Thugges in the eighteenth century. The manner of documentation of Thugges by Col. Sleeman was enough to launch successful operations against Thuggies all over India. It was a very systematic effort to deal with organised crime syndicates. Gradually the word 'criminal' was dropped to make it Central Intelligence Bureau, largely dealing with political intelligence. No institution was built up to take care of collection of criminal intelligence at all India level. This lacuna needs to be plugged. For this a separate agency is required or pending creation of a separate agency this task can be entrusted to any agency. As 'intelligence' is on the central list, perhaps no amendment of the constitution is required to create such a set up.

To deal with organised crime syndicate an Act is necessary to provide tools for collection of criminal intelligence and prosecution of cases in courts. A law now exists in Maharashtra, where Organised Crime Control Act is in position and the first conviction from court has already been received. The Maharashtra Act has been extended to Delhi. Results are noticeable.

Security Audit

How does one spot out likely targets from a vast mass of people? Theoretically it is as easy as fishing by a trawler. How can a fishing trawler be introduced in the system?

All decent and shady characters have to come in contact with one establishment or other. The establishments are now largely computerised. What is the game like then? The answer is to hold small sample checking. A top Pakistani spy, after entering India with genuine passport, stayed in various five star hotels giving fake names and addresses. He visited Calcutta without reporting to local police, visited Nepal posing as Indian citizen with fake documentation, talked to Pakistani handlers from STD booths, visited South India and stayed in hotels with false names and addresses. He contacted many people for building up local bases. If he had been subject to a sample checking, the falsity of his address and name could have been unearthed and his movements was like suicide jihadis of 9/11 as they too entered the US with valid visa. Some had past records of jihadi connection. Such linkages could not be found out as the US immigration authorities lacked such information in their computer as none of the agencies gave these vital inputs to other agencies.

Such a system is not in place. Such a simple sample checking may not only lead to spotting of anti-national targets, but may lead to detection of persons involved in conventional and economic crimes. They too appear and disappear without leaving any paper trail. To explain the point another real life example may be explained.

In a study conducted by an agency in the eighties, it was found that bank-drafts of substantial amounts originating from a particular locality in Delhi either contained fake names and addresses of the payers or the payees of such bank drafts. Nearly forty percent of these bank drafts contained substantial element of concealment. This is an example of black money operation which escaped tax-net conveniently in the absence of sample checking system.

The efficiency and transparency of our existing method of functioning needs to be checked by sample checking to know to the extent of variation. In areas of Tax Deducted at Source, it would reveal how tax deducted at source by companies is not deposited with the Tax authorities. Even big establishments are not out of this game of tax avoidance.

This system security auditing by a process of Retrieval And Analysis of Public Records can be a part security audit. For such sample checking man-power requirement would be minimal. What we need is to have some computer experts who can cull-out records from the system on the basis of some basic leads and subject them to field checking in discreet manner by competent existing agencies. A pilot scheme may be introduced to check the efficacy of the system.

The adoption of this system does not mean discarding the well established methods of collection of intelligence and counter-intelligence operations. This will be in addition to the existing system and will just enable faster generation of hard intelligence. The complexity of the present world would require innovations to strengthen the homeland security. When Col Sleeman could build up vast intelligence data manually, why not now when the systems have been largely computerised and available for easy retrieval and analysis?

In our computerised system of working there are vast reservoirs of intelligence waiting just to be tapped. In a way it can be called Security Audit. Other agencies will have the benefit of target spotting without their extra effort. The Security Audit concept will tone up the system itself.

Diplomacy of engagement with neighbouring states

The ISI network in the neighbouring states would require focussed attention. It has implications on domestic security. 'That is the Cold Calculus of US Diplomacy Today.'[61] We too should engage the neighbouring states. Saying no is the beginning of further negotiations. After long negotiation and with international pressure results are obtained. Line of credit should be extended to such states willing to take notice of the Indian security concerns. India too can manage neighbouring states with substantial aids and grants. For internal security of India such states would include Nepal, Bhutan, Myanmar, Bangladesh, Thailand and many more. 12 UN conventions on terrorism do provide a framework of effective cooperation in the areas of third party's land use for terrorists, funding, extradition and judicial assistance.

Need to enact an Enemy Agent Act

India needs to enact a separate sunset law on enemy agents. Enemy agents do not always involve themselves in the terrorist acts. They are merely booked under Foreign Act or Passport violation or under the Official Secrets Act if some documents recovered from such a foreign agent. If any one is found to be an enemy agent, he needs to be punished and not acquitted for want of evidence. Indian system provides scope for enemy agents to escape punishment by way of legal loopholes. India needs to deal with 'sleepers' planted by a hostile state with effective deterrent and long punishment.

---

61 Homeland Security begins abroad; *The Statesman* dated 13 August, 2003, by N.D. Batra, Professor of Communications, Norwich University, Vermount.

The ISI has played havoc with the security of the world. It has derailed democracy in Pakistan. The US establishment is not keen to put pressure on Pakistan to revamp the ISI. Therefore, there is need to inform people that the ISI is a threat not only to India but also to other countries of the world. 9/11 connection with the ISI will never be made public by the US for want of their clarity on the issue. The civil society of Pakistan perhaps in future may raise this question. How long Pakistanis suffer in the hands of the ISI. Only Benazir Bhutto had raised these fundamental questions. Others are maintaining silence for fear of arrest, intimidation and perhaps liquidation. It is no wonder that Benazir Bhutto's murder case will never be solved. Therefore, her husband had called for UN investigation as he had no faith in Pakistan's police investigation.

Conclusion

Indians needs to counter 'incremental invasion' of India by the ISI and jihadi outfits. Ideological invasion is more dangerous. This has to be understood by critical analysis of events and happenings. As apply said by late V.N. Gadgil this deeper understanding should not be sacrificed at the altar of secularism or else India will perish by a slow poisoning process. A study of partition of India shows how a vague concept formulated in 1930 by the Muslim League by Allama Iqbal and formulated by adopting a resolution by the Muslim League in 1940 become a reality within a period of 7 years. Balkanization of India is high on ISI's agenda. A White Paper on ISI is the call of the hour.

The international opinion is not fully aware the dangerous role played by the ISI controlled footloose jihadi warriors radiating outwards to India and all countries to install Islamic rule of the Wahabi and Salafi version of Islam. The jihadi factories are in India's backyard. India has no option but to deal with this dangerous situation jointly with international community. The day is not far off when the jihadi generals will be in control of Pakistan's nuclear arsenal.[62] Pakistani retired generals often speak of a nuclear flashpoint in South Asia before 9/11. USA, G-8 and the rest must act, and act quickly, before it is too late, if they have to save the vast population of people

---

62 *Indian Defence Review*-Jan-March 2000.

of South Asia and the rest of the world from a nuclear holocaust.[63] After 9/11 the serving generals and diplomats of Pakistan used the nuclear threat to prevent India from attacking Pakistan even after the daring Parliament attack. The nuclear blackmailing has gone too far. It is being used to provide space to jihadis for proxy war. This has to be understood in the wider context of international terrorism.

In the future of Al Qaeda chapter the possible real threat to the world has been discussed. The danger of a real 'confrontation' and catastrophic disaster is not imaginary but appears to be real. The blueprint has already been drafted and circulated. It is time that the world takes notice of this dangerous emerging situation. The best book on this subject is 'Deception', which every analyst and strategist should study for understanding and policy formulation. The moderate Muslim with traits of Sufism need to be taken on board who express love for humanity and not hatred as witnessed today because of Whabbi and Salafi interpretation of Islam.

The dangerous jihadi character of the ISI emerged out of Afghan Jihad from 1979-1998. This jihad was sponsored and led by a secret alliance of countries under the US leadership for their own reasons to fight against Soviet troops in Afghanistan. The US called it officially Jihad. Therefore, it is relevant to find out how the ISI was empowered to lodge jihadi activities elsewhere in the world. The next chapter on Afghan jihad deals with that.

---

63 Possibility of a Nuclear War, *The News*, September 7, 2000.

2

Afghan Jihad
(1979-89)

'Religious extremism did not arrive in Pakistan from nowhere. It was approved by Washington, funded by Saudi Petrodollars and carefully nourished by Zia'

- Tariq Ali

The terror network of Al-Qaeda was conceived in Peshawar in Pakistan, during the decade long Afghan jihad. This jihad was sponsored and sustained by the United States to avenge its earlier humiliating defeat in Vietnam. In Vietnam War, the US had suffered 58,000 casualties and utter humiliation. The US defeat was attributed to the Soviet Union which had rendered logistic and material help to Vietnamese. A keen observer of events Bob Woodward said that it was Brezezinsky (US National Security Adviser) who was the hardest believer that the Soviets had ever extended themselves beyond their area of jurisdiction in the cold war era. Afghanistan was their Vietnam and Brezezinsky wanted it badly and ruthlessly exploited. "Bleed them", he had said.[1] So was the case of William Cassey, CIA chief, whose 'impact could be felt most strongly when he argued about the extent and persistence of Soviet expansionism. It was a matter on which the key players in the Administration concurred'.[2]

---

1   Bob Woodward, The Veil, The Secret Wars of CIA, p71.

2   Ibid. p455.

A dying Soviet Union committed a 'terminal error' by inducting its troops in Afghanistan on 25 December, 1979, a sin that could have been avoided in the name of protecting the pro-leftist regime in Afghanistan. As found by some researchers now the Soviet Union was more interested at that point of time, to protect its 'underbelly' rather than to open out to blue waters of the Arabian sea as perceived by the US-led secret alliance. President Nixon made the US position clear in May 1980 in West Germany that Afghanistan was just a phase in World War III.[3] Globe London published an article in May 1988. It was argued that Moscow, five months before the actual Soviet troop induction, conveyed its intention to the United States. The US kept quiet about it and surprisingly the US did not confirm or deny the substance of Globe article. If this silence was deliberate then it can be argued that the US had a game-plan to trap the bear and breakup of the Soviet Union by way of revenge of its humiliating defeat in the Vietnam War. Washington's silence was presumably taken by Moscow as a tacit green signal for its military intervention in Afghanistan.[4]

Now we have the same version from Dr. Zhigniew's interview published in the French Weekly *Le Nouvel Observateur* in January 1998, a decade after the end of the Afghan Jihad. He admitted that the CIA was aiding the mujahideen in Afghanistan six months before the actual induction of Soviet Troops in Afghanistan. The fact was that the US President had signed a directive on 3 July 1979, much before Soviet induction of troops, for secret aid to the opponents of the pro-Soviet regime to induce a Soviet military intervention. On the day of the actual Soviet military intervention he wrote to President Carter that US got an opportunity for giving the USSR its own Vietnam.[5] His priority was to end the cold war era and it was beyond his imagination that the same US sponsored and aided fundamentalists would attack the US on 9/11 in a manner never seen

---

3   Georgy Arbator, Cold War or Détente, the Soviet View Point, Zed Books Ltd, London 1983.

4   Gen. K. M. Arif, 'Working With Zia, Pakistan's Power Politics 1977-1988, Oxford University Press, p317.

5   The Clash of Fundamentalisms, Crusade, Jihads and Modernity, Tariq Ali, Verso, London, p207.

before.

This explains the US and its allies suddenly discovered hitherto unknown sterling qualities of President Zia. President Carter telephoned Zia affirming US support in case of Soviet aggression on Pakistan.[6] There was flurry of high level visitors to Pakistan. These included British Foreign Secretary Lord Carrington on January 18, 1980, the UN Secretary General on 23 January and OIC General Secretary Habib Chatti on 25 January 1980. Other dignitaries visited China and Arab countries to build up a coalition against USSR. Andrei Gromyko had to warn Pakistan on 12 February 1980 not to convert Pakistan into a 'springboard' for further escalation and hurting Soviet interests.[7]

The US found a God-given opportunity to wage a terrific decade long bloody proxy war in the name of jihad in Afghanistan. Gen Zia-ul-Haq, then President of Pakistan, was an international pariah after hanging Zulfikar Ali Bhutto in a sham trial in April 1979. He was seeking an opportunity to come out of his international isolation. The soviet troop induction in Afghanistan came really as a 'Christmas gift to Zia'.[8]

While building up a secret US-led coalition against the Soviet troops in Afghanistan, the US under President Ronald Reagan and the CIA under William Cassey did not calculate all the possible 'blow-back' effects of the Afghan jihad. The US and the CIA thought that by siding with hardcore Islamists they would win over the hearts and minds of the Muslims all over the world. As aptly said by a former General of Pakistan that Pakistan 'was used as a condom to reach out to Afghanistan.'[9] Pakistan was the funnel to the Afghan resistance.[10] This is the perception of the all Pakistanis now. Seizing the vast opportunity Zia had used the US-led alliance for Pakistan's

---

6   Gen. K. M. Arif, 'Working With Zia, Pakistan's Power Politics 1977-1988', Oxford University Press, p314.

7   Gen. K. M. Arif, 'Working With Zia, Pakistan's Power Politics 1977-1988', Oxford University Press, p415.

8   Shah, Mehatab Ali , The Foreign Policy Of Pakistan, IB Tauris, London, 1997, p13.

9   Tariq Ali, on the Abyss.

10 Bob Woodward, The Veil, The Secret Wars of CIA, p104.

financial and military benefits. In a way Gen Zia could legitimize his dictatorial role in Pakistan as the world lapped him up as darling of the 'free world.' 'The CIA and the Reagan administration wanted Zia to stay in power.[11]

The US-led secret alliance included US partners of the cold war, China, Saudi Arabia, Egypt and even Israel. Each of them was driven by its own consideration. China was having border problems with USSR and China's keenness to lead the communist ideology in the Asian sphere. Saudi Arabia was motivated by a desire to be seen as a true Wahhabi version Islamic country severely dented by the capture of Mecca's holy place by a Wahhabi sect in 1979. The rebels had declared rulers of Saudi Arabia were apostates, which tarnished the image of the regime vastly. Added to this was the success of the Iranian revolution where the Islam was seen more effective in driving out the king of Iran. These two basic reasons prompted Saudi Arabia to join the secret alliance to prove its Islamic credentials. Egypt was facing attacks from fundamentalists and wanted them to shift their venue of attacks elsewhere. It did happen that way as all major leaders of Al Qaeda were from Egypt and played a big role in shaping the Al Qaeda movement all over the world. They could never return to Egypt. Israel has been always been a part of US partner for its own regime protection. It joined the alliance out of its own compulsion and not by any desire to promote jihad in Afghanistan.

One of the first acts of Ronald Reagan after being elected as President was to induct William J Cassey, as head of the CIA. He was Reagan's campaign chairman. During World War, Cassey had worked in the Office of Strategic Services (OSS). OSS was CIA's 'organizational ancestor'. Cassey was in charge of dropping spies behind German Lines during the last six months of World War II. Admiral Turner his predecessor misread Khomeini as 'a benign senile clergy'. The Iranian revolution was a surprise to CIA. Much of this was because the CIA operatives were deficient in Persian Language.[12] Brig. Yousaf of ISI's Afghan Bureau described Cassey

---

11 Bob Woodward, The Veil, The Secret Wars of CIA, p31.

12 Bob Woodward, The Veil, The Secret Wars of CIA, p30-31.

'with a quick brain, and a bold and a ruthless approach to the war against the Soviets. He hated communism. In fact, like many CIA officers, he regarded Afghanistan as the place where America could be avenged for its defeat in Vietnam. The Soviets must pay a high price in blood for their acts in the North Vietnam. This was his off repeated view. 'Those bastards must pay' was his war cry.[13] The authors of Deception have described him as 'affluent, rigorous and unconventional', a risk taker with little regard for process who wanted to transform the agency into a mace with which to batter Moscow. He acquired a cabinet seat, a first for a CIA chief.[14]

The emergence of Al-Qaeda will never be understood unless the US-led jihad in Afghanistan is studied in depth. Countries and volunteers from abroad that took part in this 'unholy war' eventually faced a serious jihad within their own countries. This is a lesson of this religious war which climaxed into unprecedented attacks on US soil on 11 September 2001. Thus, the International Front of Islamic Jihad is the product of 1979-89 unholy war. This chapter attempts to unfold the events of this period from 1979-1989.

Unleashing a CIA-ISI proxy war in Afghanistan

President of Pakistan Mohammed Zia-ul-Haq was responsible for empowerment of ISI for mounting proxy war in Afghanistan against Soviet troops and intensification of Jihad in Kashmir. After executing Zulfikar Ali Bhutto in a show trial, Zia's international standing was largely isolated; Yasser Arafat never visited Pakistan during Zia's time by way of protest against hanging of Bhutto. Zia became an international pariah and not to be courted by major powers.

All that changed with induction of Soviet troops in Afghanistan in December 1979 to defend the left regime in Afghanistan. Zia seized the opportunity to turn the events into his favour. He could easily convince USA, the need to check the Soviet influence in Afghanistan. Seven Afghan Mujahideen political parties were available in exile. Out of seven, four were fundamentalist, while

---

13 Yousaf and Mark Adkin, The Bear Trap, Jung Publications, 1992, p79.

14 Adrian Levy and Catherine Scott-Clark, Deception, Pakistan, The United States and The Global Nuclear Conspiracy, Atlantic Books, 2007, p78.

three were moderate Islamic groups.

Zia's plan was to harass the Soviet through the mujahideen groups by guerrilla tactics keeping sufficient margin of deniability. The proxy was to be such as not to provoke Russia to mount counter attacks against Pakistan. The western border of Pakistan is always vulnerable. He had also to ensure that peace was maintained on the eastern front which is India. So Zia cultivated Indian personalities with his 'denatured smile and triple embrace' and mango diplomacy. He even visited India on the pretext of watching a cricket match between India and Pakistan at Jaipur. However, he remained anti-Indian throughout and managed to arm the Punjab militants when they took shelter in Pakistan after the ill-conceived "Blue Star" operation at the sacred Sikh Golden Temple of Amritsar.

The Afghan war strategy was conceived and executed by Zia's closet ISI Chief Lt. Gen Akhtar Abdur Rehman. Rehman was the most important key figure as Chief of the ISI. If death had not intervened, he would have taken over as Chief of the Army Staff, as Zia never vacated his post of the Chief of the Army Staff. An army dictator in Pakistan always keeps tight control over the army to sustain the regime. Even under pressure of the right parties General Musharraf had refused to vacate the post of COAS till the much delayed election. If he had vacated the COAS post, he would have been toppled earlier by another army general or by a political upsurge.

Brig Yousaf, who was inducted in ISI by Gen Akhtar Abdul Rehman, played a dominant role in Afghan proxy war on behalf of USA from 1983 to 1987. After retirement he took the risk to write a book called "THE BEAR TRAP". He has described in vivid details about the CIA-ISI proxy war in Afghanistan, delivery of arms and finances to ISI without any audit trail. Certain bare facts of the ISI's Afghan Bureau need recapitulation to understand the working of the ISI-CIA combine. After all 'the CIA's station in Islamabad was biggest in the world.[15]

The ISI HQs is located in Islamabad and the Afghan Bureau

---

15 Bob Woodward, The Veil, The Secret Wars of CIA, p311.

was located in Rawalpindi. The Afghan Bureau of ISI was given a staff of sixty commissioned army officers and 400 senior non-commissioned officers from the Pakistan army. The ISI's total strength, however, consisted of hundreds of officers and thousands of staff under Lt. Gen. Akhtar Abdul Rehman, the most trusted general of Zia-ul-Haq. For the first time in the history of Pakistan the ISI started handling covert and military operational matters for which it lacked expertise and resources. The task of an intelligence agency is to collect intelligence. In case of ISI, it was both external and internal. In matters of military operations, the task was performed by the defence services, particularly the army. "For reasons of secrecy these were combined in the ISI Directorate to support the mujahideen struggle."[16] A decade long Afghan Jihad sponsored and sustained by the ISI made it a powerful organization. The ISI acquired 60 skills of covert operations from the CIA and the jihadis were trained in such activities. Thus, the ISI acquired a new extraordinary capability which was subsequently extended in Jammu and Kashmir and elsewhere in the world for promotion of jihad world over. All ISI chiefs, after Gen. Akhtar Abdur Rehman, like Gen. Hamid Gul and Javed Nasir became hardcore extremists. Both of them targeted India in a big way.

Brig. Yousaf, as head of ISI's Afghan Bureau, claimed to have trained 80,000 Mujahideen. This force level was almost equal to Russian troops in Afghanistan. The Pakistan army officials, dressed as Mujahideen, regularly entered Afghanistan along with the regular Mujahideen, who were called 'soldiers of God'.

Arab Jihadis

Brig Yousaf did not speak much the Arab jihadis. He did not disclose how many of them were trained by his Bureau. This part of the information has come from people who were interviewed by the author Jason Burke who were involved in the process. The Arab volunteers were attached to various mujahideen factions and no separate Arab Brigade was created, may be for operational reasons. The CIA estimate was that at any given point of time there were

---

16 Gen. K. M. Arif, 'Working With Zia, Pakistan's Power Politics 1977-1988, Oxford University Press, p319.

25000 Arab jihadis and half of them were spending their time in providing support activities much away from frontline fighting.[17]

There was a bit of side story. Many of the Arabs married locals and settled down in Pakistan or Afghanistan. The Arabs were generally disliked as there was a gulf between Wahhabi and Salafi Islam practiced by Arabs and South Asia Muslim traditions and practices. The Afghans are Sufi oriented visiting shrines and dargas. The Afghans did not like temporary marriages performed by Arab mujahideen with local girls. This was not a part of Afghan culture. Afghans are mostly Sunnis. This practice is prevalent among the Shias of Iran. Such marriages are called 'mutta marriages'. Islam practiced in Afghanistan 'was, and is, a tolerant, flexible religion, similar to that practiced throughout much of the south and southwest Asia, east and north Africa – full of mysticism, shrines, saints and tokens. It shares little with 'hard' Salafi and Wahhabi Islam or the political ideologies of Islam'.[18]

The war in Afghanistan was carried out in the name of Islam and not for the establishment of a democratic state in Afghanistan. Gen Zia had a vision of Islamic Umma, a nation of Islam, with no political boundaries. In other word, the Afghan issue was viewed for obtaining 'strategic depth' for Pakistan which it lacks. During Zia's time the strategy was to wage a guerilla war and make the Soviet bleed by inflicting 'thousand cuts'. Zia wisely formulated the view that the water in Afghanistan should remain warm, but not to be brought to boiling temperature. The proxy war was to be kept under control so as to prevent Russia - India team up in a possible joint operation against Pakistan. Any such joint operation, covert or overt, would have led to a breakup of Pakistan, as it happened in 1971. For Zia, Indira Gandhi was a real threat to Pakistan army. Many Pakistani believe that Zulfikar Ali Bhutto would have escaped hanging if Indira Gandhi remained as prime minister of India.[19] When Indira's assassination was communicated to Gen. Zia, he could not conceal his real happiness and said that 'God would take

---

17   Jason Burke.The True Story of Racidal Islam, Penguin Books, 2004, p58.

18   Jason Burke, The True Story of Racidal Islam, Penguin Books, 2004, p60.

19   Shah Mehatab Ali , The Foreign Policy of Pakistan, IB Tauris, London, 1997, p180.

care of those who harm Pakistan'. Having said such harsh words Zia was possibly the first head of the state to reach Delhi to attend her funeral.[20]

The Afghan Bureau of ISI was located 12 km away from Islamabad. ISI HQ is, however, located in Islamabad. Actually the Afghan Bureau was located in the infamous Ojhri camp. It has a prison too, where severe torture is inflicted specially to suspected Indian spies. Tehmina Durrani author of *"My Feudal Lord"* fame has described that one day's stay in Ojhri prison camp is equal to one year's stay in any other ordinary Pakistani prison. Even now it is believed that Indian soldiers captured in 1971 war are still being kept in this camp and other prisons of Pakistan. Bhutto used to hear cries of such Indian detainees from his Rawalpindi cell awaiting his hanging. This was purposely done to make the life of Bhutto miserable.

The ISI's Ojhri camp had all the facilities for training including the facility to test the American newly developed Stinger missiles. Each staff had a cover name to hide his real identity. The ISI had two forward detachments at Quetta (Baluchistan) and at Peshawar (NWFP), so as to be close to the Afghan border. From these two detachments stores, arms and ammunition were supplied to Afghan political parties for eventual distribution to mujahideen commanders. Thus, seven political parties were the political fronts for mujahideen groups fighting in Afghanistan.[21] This system was devised to keep the field commanders under control of parties and parties in turn remained under the control of the ISI. This strategy is being replicated in Jammu and Kashmir with no apparent success. Basically, the parties received allocation of money and on the basis of their combat effectiveness by way incentive.[22]

For 29 provinces of Afghanistan, operational plans used to be drawn up and executed by ISI. The Afghan Bureau had three branches *viz.* Operation Branch, Logistic Branch and Psy-war Branch, each under the charge of a Colonel of the Pakistan army. Brig. Yousaf,

20 *Op.Cit*, pp18, 21, Shah Mehatab Ali.

21 Yousaf and Mark Adkin, The Bear Trap, Jung Publications, Lahore, 1992, p79, 90.

22 Ibid, p90.

as head of the Afghan Bureau, was reporting directly to Lt. Gen. Akhtar Abdul Rehman. The seven Afghan party alliances were forged by the ISI. The leaders of the seven parties were Gulbadin Hekmatyar, a strong favourite of the ISI, Khalis, Rabbani and Prof. Sayyaf. All of them were hard-line Islamists. There were moderates too but were largely sidelined by the ISI. They were Nafi, Gailani and Mujadadi. The rank and file of Mujahideen was drawn from six million Afghan refugees who took shelter in Pakistan and Iran. They were used by Tanzims (Political Parties) as foot soldiers. For obtaining the loyalty of the refugees, the political parties provided food and shelter largely obtained from the relief organization set up by the ISI. Some refugees took shelter in towns like Karachi. Their presence in Pakistan led to local conflicts, ethnic imbalances and a tremendous pressure on utilities.

For supply of rations to mujahideen, a separate organization was created under the charge of another Brigadier. Obviously, rations were purchased out of US funds. For supply of ration to civilians in Afghanistan, another set up existed. The idea was to collect intelligence in lieu of free ration and keep them under the control of Afghan parties. This may be called collection of intelligence through welfare. The total population of Afghanistan in 1979 was 15 million only. Afghanistan is basically a Sunni state with ten per cent of Shias and other ethnic minorities.

Motivation

A popular notion exists that unless a Muslim fights Jihad, he can not be a mujahideen *i.e.* a soldier of God. To quote Yousaf 'once Jihad is declared by their religious leaders it was the duty of all men to fight to save faith and families....'.[23] Again he says that' the mujahideen's willingness to die in a battle stems from the promise of Allah that Shaheeds go immediately to paradise. No matter how many sins they have committed in this life, to die as a soldier of God ensures complete forgiveness. A special place in Paradise is assured.[24] Thus there is no greater glory for a Muslim warrior than to fight for jihad.

---

23   Yousaf and Mark Adkin, The Bear Trap, Jung Publications, 1992, p33.

24   Ibid.

When jihadis are captured in India they speak in the same language. This explains why thousands of jihadis came from other countries to fight in Afghanistan.

Those who do not die in Jihad become a 'Gazi' again with a promise for "rewards in paradise". Even a Mujahideen who performs one day's static guard duty, according to Prophet, has performed a thousand nights of prayer. This type motivation in Islam for Jihad has a strong appeal to Muslims. Indians do not fight for Hinduism, but fight for mother India only. The level of motivation for Jihad is strong to attract recruits from all walks of life. Those who are unable to fight one are required to provide money for the cause of Jihad. Thus, there is always a free flow of fund for Jihadi cause. Jihad is thus a total war on infidels. Reward and punishment has a strong bearing on Jihadis.

An Afghan Mujahideen by temperament hated digging bunkers and trenches. He believed in action to be observed by all. He did not like pipeline busting by explosives. He did not like to crawl either. It is in the nature of an Afghan to fight with each other face to face. The ISI had to set up an alliance of seven parties to give a semblance of unity. The four hard-line parties had enough private donations from Arabs more than three moderate parties which were always starved of funds and arms and almost remained marginalized.

By being more fundamentalist than others, Gulbuddin Hekmatyar emerged as a strong Afghan Mujahideen leader with the total support of the ISI. He was born in 1946 and had education in Kabul military school and, thereafter became an engineer by profession. He was said to be ruthless, arrogant and inflexible. While visiting US to address the UN, he rejected even an invitation to meet the American Officials including the President Reagan in 1985. He was determined to give the message that he was not a lackey of the Americans and not promoting the US cause in Afghanistan.[25]

The US game plan was to teach a lesson to Russians as their perception was that the Russians aid to Vietnam enabled a high rate of casualty to US soldiers. Some 58,000 US soldiers died in

---

25 Yousaf and Mark Adkin, The Bear Trap, Jung Publications, 1992, p41.

Vietnam War. The CIA Director William Cassey, Congressman Charles Wilson, a strong supporter of US aid to Mujahideen were depressed with the US Vietnam experience. Said Charles Wilson: "I thought the Soviet ought to get a doze of it."[26] Wilson visited Afghanistan more than once, dressed as a Mujahideen and obtained sadistic pleasure that Russians were being killed in the proxy war. Thus, the Americans were aiding the proxy war not only to contain the Soviets, but to take revenge of the Vietnam War. Wilson, Democratic leader of the Congress, made 14 trips to South Asia to promote the Afghan Jihad.

Strategy

The Soviet and Afghan government troops were guarding the towns and cities. The Mujahideen were operating from rural areas where the writ of Kabul did not exist. Often Gen. Akhtar Abdur Rehman, himself a Pathan, used to advice inflicting 'thousands cuts to bring down the bear.' The Mujahideen in the given situation could freely move into the rural areas for mounting attacks on installations. The ISI strategy was to ambush and carry out standoff attacks with rapid frequency and ferocity to weaken enemy's morale and ability to continue the war.[27] The Soviet strategy was "Search and Destroy policy" which was to search for enemy and destroy their hide outs.

The total induction of Soviet troops were around 85,000 and this force level was never increased, which was a wise policy, as they never intended to stay in Afghanistan for a long period. In Vietnam the US did the opposite. In 1964 the US troops were 16,000 men and officers. As war progressed within five years the US force level went up to 5,00,000. The force level of mujahideen was 85,000 at any given point of time.[28] Thus, the situation was no win situation for ISI-Mujahideen and Soviet-Afghan in Afghanistan. This proved by the fact that even after Soviet withdrawal of troops in 1989, the ISI-mujahideen could not even capture Jalalabad which is just near Pakistan border.

---

26 *Daily Telegraph*, 14 Jan 1985, Bear Trap, p62.

27 Yousaf and Mark Adkin, The Bear Trap, Jung Publications, 1992, pp 65, 68.

28 Ibid, p48.

Largely, the Soviet army in Afghanistan was conscripts who were not keen at all to fight in an alien country. In both the countries, USA and Russia the army generals just promoted their career prospects and received medals of honour for fighting bogus wars without any commitment.

Funding

In a guerilla war, the requirements are to have loyalty, shelter and food for Mujahideen with a firm belief for the cause *i.e.* Jihad. The terrain was favourable as the majority landmass of Afghanistan is covered with mountains. A neighbouring country should provide sanctuary which Pakistan provided as it has long boarder with Afghanistan. Mujahideen were in need of plenty of funds which came from USA, Saudi Arabia, and rich Arab nationals. The funds received by the ISI were credited into a bank. The utilization of such funds was never checked by any authority, not even by the CIA which was the major donor. The money also came from the black account of the USA. Brig. Yousaf's comments on this score are worth quoting. He wrote "nothing moves, in a war, without money". The Mujahideen could achieve nothing without financial support. No matter how brilliant he might be, the implementation depended on the availability of a vast reservoir of cash required to arm, train and move the forces. Almost half of this money originated from the US taxpayers, with the remainder coming from Saudi Arabian government or rich Arab individuals.[29]

This admission of a former ISI officer would also apply to ISI's India wide operations immediately after termination of Afghan Jihad in 1989. Till now some 85,000 AK 47 rifles have been recovered by India in anti insurgency operations. Who can provide such investments and payments for training and giving monetary support to Jihadis. Brig. Yousaf has explained the quantum of finance required for such sustained operations and the same is applicable to jihadi war in India.

Without provoking a regular war with the Soviet Union, the ISI supported the strategy of 'thousand cuts' to bleed the enemy and

29 Ibid, p77.

demoralise the Soviet and Afghan government troops. The Soviet troops were guarding the static points, while the Afghan Mujahideen were moving in the inhospitable areas for regular strikes against the government positions. The strategy was to ambush, stand off attacks with rapid frequency and ferocity to weaken enemy's ability to continue the war.

The Soviet strategy was to hold grounds and organise blasts in Pakistan to weaken Zia politically and neutralise the zeal to fight for Jihad in Afghanistan. Afghanistan even helped Al-Zulfikar to operate from its soil against Pakistan. The Soviet and the Afghan government did try to raise the cost of Jihad unbearable for Pakistan. It did not succeed as Pakistan was waging a war free of cost.[30]

This war by stealth was master-minded by CIA director William Cassey. He visited Pakistan incognito to hold talks with the ISI Director General Lt. Gen Akhtar. Cassey hated communism. He was earlier directing CIA operation in Nicaragua, Angola as also in Afghanistan. Intelligence Chief of Saudi Arabia Prince Turkie was ensuring logistics and flow of Saudi funds for Afghan Jihad. For each American dollar it was ensured that Saudi would also contribute another dollar for Afghan Jihad. After all Saudi dynasty is secured by American support or else it would have collapsed long ago.

The cost of CIA's clandestine operation in Angola, Nicaragua and Afghanistan was to the tune of $30 billion, which was more or less the foreign exchange reserve of India during the late 1990's. With such colossal investment every thing moved, men and material. Saudi's yearly income out of sale of petroleum is estimated for $2000 billion a year. Rich Saudis have been investing in USA for real estate, income generating securities, which are not revealed as per a secret agreement with the USA.[31] Saudi Arabia always plays a major part in promoting Islamic fundamentalism in lieu of peace obtained from fundamentalist groups. "Rabiat" which is a charitable institution of Saudi, donates funds for madrassas to Muslim and non-Muslim countries. Pakistan is always a major beneficiary of Saudi money. Indian Muslim institutions also reportedly received money from "Rabiat".

---

30   Yousaf and Mark Adkin, The Bear Trap, Jung Publications, 1992, p49.

31   Jan Goodwin, The Price of Honour, Little Brown and Company, UK, 1994, p 22.

As said earlier, for Afghan War, Saudi and CIA contributed money in equal proportion. In addition rich Arabs also funded Jihad by way of contributions to fundamentalist parties supported by ISI. Prince Turkie was the chief of the intelligence of Saudi Arabia who maintained regular contacts with the ISI and the CIA. The CIA, the Saudi intelligence and the ISI developed a close relationship over the years. Most of the ISI high ranking officers like Hamid Gul, Brig Yousaf had visited CIA's HQ's for training, briefing and consultation.

CIA and Saudi funds received by ISI were credited into special bank accounts under the control of ISI HQ's at Islamabad. This money, it may be mentioned, is separate from money used up for purchase of arms and ammunition by CIA. Money received from CIA and Saudi Arabia was actually controlled by ISI Director General Lt. Gen Akhtar Abdur Rehman and his administration which was functioning under a Director.

Supply of arms to ISI

Brig Yousaf said that during 1983, 10,000 tons of arms/ammunition was received from CIA which went up to 65,000 tons in 1987. The major contributors were China, Egypt and many other countries. It is interesting to note that one hundred thousand Indian 303 rifles were also purchased by CIA at rock bottom price. When questioned on this, the CIA officer told Yousaf. "The Indians are mean bastards, not trustworthy at all. For money they would even sell their mothers."[32] The Indian side of the story remains to be explained. Did the Indian authorities take precaution to prevent resell of such arms to parties hostile to India? If sold as scrap, they should have been broken up so as to make them non-functional. If true, this smacks of corruption which calls for an enquiry by Indian authority.

Admittedly, in the whole Afghan proxy war ISI could achieve result only because of financial and arms support from CIA, Saudi Arabia and Arab individuals and other Muslim donors. Brig Yousaf asserts that without the backing of the US and Saudi Arabia, the Soviets would still be entrenched in the country.

---

32 Yousaf and Mark Adkin, The Bear Trap, Jung Publications, 1992, p85.

Procurement of arms and training of Mujahideen

Without massive cash inflow nothing would move. The USA took the responsibility for procurement of arms/ammunition of all descriptions. Billions of dollars out of US tax payers' money went towards purchase of arm etc. from a very close circuit of US friends and allies. China had already become a trusted friend of Pakistan. China's friendship with Pakistan was dictated by a policy of containment of India. The perception of the Chinese policy makers was that, if unchecked, India would emerge as a power in south Asia, which was detrimental to Chinese interest.

The Chinese have no fixed border. Territories are claimed as and when it suits them. The Chinese has border problems with Vietnam and other South Asian countries. Even Sikkim, Arunachal Pradesh and a vast track of Uttar Pradesh of India are often claimed by China. After getting admitted to UN, for which India played a vocal part and its admission in 1954 for Bandung conference at Nehru's initiative, China raised the border issue after Dalai Lama's retreat to India in 1959. China tested India's capacity when it just took over Tibet in 1950, where India had a garrison to defend the country. India agreed China's claim on Tibet. When Aksai Chin in Jammu and Kashmir was stealthily taken over, Nehru justified the occupation on the ground that not a 'blade of grass' grows in that vast track of land. China taught the Pakistanis how to fight a long drawn war against India. All evidence indicates that Pakistan had received nuclear technology and missiles N-18 from China. In 1994, Nawaz Sharif in a public meeting in POK admitted of having nuclear weapons. The weapons were said to have been tested at Lopnor in Xinjiang province of China.

It is but natural that the Chinese arms were purchased by CIA for ISI in large quantity. It did not matter to USA to ensure that such arms were not diverted to other areas. In Punjab, during raid of a shrine, a lot of Chinese made AK 47 rifles were recovered. Even Interpol enquiry to China did not yield any reply. They all bore China's manufacturing details.

Egypt did help CIA's war in Afghanistan by providing old

weapons procured from the USSR. So did UK, Lebanon and Turkey. Jack Anderson wrote in Washington Post in May 1987 that "CIA's secret arms pipeline to Mujahideen was riddled with opportunities for corruption" It was highly suspected that many agencies made windfall profit in procurement of arms for Afghan Jihad. All the deals were possibly laced with corruption. Not a single American could decide who would get the weapons. Brig Yousaf admitted that corruption was a way of life in Pakistan[33] and said 'that the CIA's secret arms pipeline to the Mujahideen is riddled with opportunities for corruption'.[34]

From all available evidence arms were procured by CIA by spending directly. It was CIA's job to unload the cargo at Karachi or at Chaklala airport and nothing beyond. ISI thereafter would transport such consignments to its Ojhri camp near Rawalpindi from where they would be sent to Quetta or Peshawar detachments for eventual handing them over to parties, who would distribute them to their Mujahideen commanders. This type of distribution system enabled the ISI to keep the commanders under the strict control and also provided the cover of denial to conceal covert operations via Mujahideen route.

Thus, four layers of transactions were involved *i.e.* CIA, ISI, Parties and Field Commanders. Parties were allotted arms on the basis of their 'combat effectiveness.' As parties had to arrange dispatch of arms into interiors, a lot of expenditure was incurred on transport by trucks, mules, horses. Chinese mules and Argentine horses were procured by CIA as they were sturdy and useful for the Afghan terrain. The four fundamentalist parties also received direct funding from rich Arabs and were in a better position to bear the cost of transport. The three moderate Muslim parties lacked financial backing of rich Arabs and had to be content with smaller supply of arms from the ISI. The fundamentalist parties like Hekmatyar were favoured as they were vocal and ardent supporters of Jihad and were pro-Pakistan. The whole game plan was to promote Hekmatyar and eventually install him as the supreme leader in Kabul. Hekmatyar's

---

33 Yousaf and Mark Adkin, The Bear Trap, Jung Publications, 1992, p90.

34 Yousaf and Mark Adkin, The Bear Trap, Jung Publications, 1992, p97.

obsession ruined the peace prospects after the withdrawal of Soviet troops in February 1989 from Afghanistan.

Training

Training was vital for guerilla war. ISI arranged seven secret training centres around Quetta and Peshawar. For this the ISI had developed a huge infrastructure capability to train Mujahideen on a large scale and this capability is now being used to train terrorist outfits against other countries. It was estimated at one time that 2,50,000 trained terrorists were floating in Pakistan with deadly arms, causing internal and external attacks and all Sunni Jihadi groups were organically linked to Al Qaeda.

To lead the parties of Mujahideen in Afghanistan, Pakistani soldiers mostly non-commissioned officers were sent for target attacks, blasting of installations etc. When caught Pakistan just denied their existence. Such Pakistan army men were dressed as Afghans with long beards mostly speaking Pasthu. The Pakistani men and Mujahideen even launched attacks of installation deep into Soviet Union. That ended when the Soviet Union issued a strong diplomatic warning to Pakistan. This happened during the time of Lt. Gen Hamid Gul. It created a panic in Pakistan of a possible Soviet retaliation, a possibility which Zia always thought to be a danger to be avoided.

Stinger Missiles

A Stinger Missile Training Centre was established at Ojhri camp with simulators. Americans supplied these newly developed Stingers to Pakistan. A part of it was diverted to Kargil in 1999 by Pakistan. Even after the Afghan war the US did not force the ISI to handover the left over Stinger missiles to CIA. In fact, the Pakistan did misappropriate a large quality of arms for Jihad in Kashmir. No protest was made by USA to Pakistan in the face of strong evidence of recovery of such American weapons in proxy war in Jammu & Kashmir. The former officers of ISI claim that no Chinese experts were used for training. That was not required as Pakistani instructors had apparently received training for handling the Chinese weapons. They in turn trained the Uighur Mujahideen who were sent for Afghan jihad.

There is an interesting story of induction of Stinger missiles by US in the Afghan war. Stinger was relatively a new weapon system with a heat seeking system device to attack war planes and helicopters. The efficacies of the Stinger missiles gifted by the USA were tested when the UK used them to shoot down the Argentine fighter bombers in Falkland war. This act of generosity enabled the USA to secure the British support for Afghan Jihad. Congress pressure was mounted by Charles Wilson (D-Texas), David Driev (R-California), Bill McCollum (R-Florida) and Gordan Humpprey (R-Senator) to release Stinger missiles for Afghan jihad. The first American Stingers were in the hands of Mujahideen by the summer of 1986. In all 800 stinger missiles were delivered to ISI out of which some 600 were given to Mujahideen groups. Hekmatyar group got the maximum. 'The Stingers were not fitted with night vision and could not be used in the dark'.[35] Moreover automatic decoy flame dispensers by ejecting at two second intervals was enough to confuse the heat seeking stingers as they burned much hotter than engine fuel and the stingers were not in a position to distinguish one from the other. Many of these were stockpiled or sold.[36] The first Stinger hit was a Soviet helicopter in September 1986.[37] Stingers were thus distributed like 'lollipops'. After the Afghan war the Stinger missiles reached other theatres of war during the Iran-Iraq war. These were reportedly pumped in by Gulbadin Hekmatyar. It was said that 16 Stinger were sold to Iran for about $ one million which was denied by Iran. Elsewhere, the left over Stinger missiles were in Georgia. Pakistan kept some stock of Stingers and many were lost in Ojhri Camp fire in 1988. Brig Yousaf claimed that if ISI had supplied Stingers earlier the Afghan war was winnable much earlier.[38] But the fact was that much earlier to induction of Stingers, the Soviet leadership had decided to exit from Afghanistan as found out by Sarah Mendelson in her research. Even with Stingers the

---

35 Sarah E. Mendelson, Changing Course Ideas, Politics and Soviet Withdrawal from Afghanistan, p98.

36 Oliver Roy, The lessons of the Soviet Afghan War, International Institute for Strategic Studies, Summer 1991, p36.

37 *See* John K Coolly, Unholy War, p172 & 173.

38 Yousaf and Mark Adkin, The Bear Trap, Jung Publications, 1992, p156.

Soviet troops withdrew in 1989, after three years of induction of Stingers.

The CIA Director William Cassey visited the ISI controlled training centres in 1986. He was highly impressed by ISI's performance. Zia-ul-Haq used to entertain Cassey for dinners. Zia was so thrilled by account given by Cassey that he too visited training centres subsequently without fuss and publicity.

To speed up training, ISI sent Mobile Training Teams to Afghanistan. All these efforts, backed by CIA, enabled ISI to build up a formidable force and ultimately the Soviets decided to withdraw. They were not willing to sustain such a war on a foreign soil for such a long period.

Gifting of secured communication to ISI by USA

To avoid communication interception by the Russians, CIA in 1985 provided ISI 'secured radio sets'. The long range system is known as "burst communication set" having range of 1000 kilometers. The short range set is called a 'frequency hopper' with a range of 50 kilometers. The technology was to ensure transmission of messages sent out in few seconds with no possibility of decoding. Frequency hoppers were meant to be used by field commanders. To operate this system 20 week special programmes had to be arranged for ISI officials. Many of these sets were noticed to have been used in J&K by ISI officials, thanks to US aid to Afghan jihad.

Explosives were widely used by Mujahideen. For this extensive training courses were arranged. As said by Brig Yousaf: "the covert use of explosives is a honoured tactic of a guerilla" He did not mention extensive use of RDX by ISI, but one has to conclude that the best kind of explosive must have been used on a large scale in Afghanistan. This expertise received from USA has been used extensively by ISI in J&K and elsewhere in India after the ISI sponsored Afghan jihad.

The greatest difficulty faced by diverse guerilla outfits was "feuding and fighting", lack of cohesiveness and a central command and control structure acceptable to all the Afghan groups.

Ideologically all the Mujahideen groups were different. In addition, ethnic factors did emerge, as Pasthuns were dominating the scene, leaving behind the Shias, Tajiks, Uzbeks and other ethnic groups. Therefore, the Mujahideen could not consolidate even after the Soviet withdrawal from Afghanistan in February 1989. By design or by default the ISI under Gen Hamid Gul failed to consolidate the gains of the US proxy war. He could not even snatch a bit of land from the Afghan government forces. To conceal his failure he became anti-American as it was made out that he was shifted from the ISI in 1991 on US pressure. All the seven fundamentalist parties just vanished.

Mosquito Operation

During the Afghan jihad the CIA drew up a covert operational plan called Mosquito Operation. "The Mosquito operation" was the brain-child of the French Intelligence Chief who gave the idea to the President Ronald Reagan who just lapped it. He literally jumped from his seat in total ecstasy. The elements of the operation were: -

(a) To print Koran in local languages for free distribution in Muslim republics of the Soviet Union to arouse their passion for Jihad;

(b) To distribute free drugs to Soviet soldiers to cripple their fighting ability; and

(c) To print duplicate Russian newspapers for Soviet troops with plenty of disinformation.[39]

All the three elements worked to the benefit of Jihadi forces. Now evidence has surfaced that many textbooks extolling Jihad against non-Muslims were prepared by the University of Nebraska and funded by the USA. The text books were distributed to madrassas in Afghanistan and Pakistan to motivate the Islamic Mujahideen to fight Soviet troops in Afghanistan. The US domestic law, however, does not permit funding of religious texts at taxpayer's expense.

---

39 Cooly, John K., Unholy War, (and partly corroborated by Brig Yousaf) that CIA had printed and distributed 10000 copies of Holy Koran in Central Asia, *see* Bear Trap, p193.

The CIA and ISI combine fought the Afghan proxy war. Their mutual relationship became close and intimate at personal level. The ISI's skill to fight proxy war was upgraded considerably. That gave them confidence to carry out similar proxy war in Jammu and Kashmir. For a decade the CIA and the US administration remained silent. There is now some shift in US policy largely because the US has become an 'enemy of Islam'. The ISI, if not controlled by the internal dynamics of Pakistan, is soon likely to emerge as the greatest challenge to US and Western interest. An ex-ISI Chief has since published an account of his expertise being used for transporting anti-tank missiles to Bosnian Muslims which turned the tide in favour of Bosnian Muslims. This happened when there was UN sanction for supply of arms to warring groups.[40]

Pak strategy for induction of foreign Jihadis

The ISI managed the Afghan war with so called seven party alliances. The same strategy has been adopted by the ISI for its Kashmir operation by creating a United Jihad Council nominally under Salahudin. The real operator is the ISI.

The Afghan jihad also gave a unique experience to Pakistan. The call of jihad has universal appeal. Visa restrictions were slackened by Pakistan to allow the inflow of foreign jihadis of all shades and character to Pakistan. The USA allowed top Jihadi leaders like 'Abdullah Azzam' to visit America for large scale recruitment of Arabs and American Muslims for Afghan Jihad. Some of them even declared Jihad against US from US soil even before the end of the Afghan Jihad. These early signals were just ignored. This has been discussed elsewhere in great details.

The Soviet leadership crisis

The Soviet policy was largely influenced by the internal political dynamics of change in political thinking. The induction of the Soviet troops was decided by a four member group. Andropov was more concerned with political corruption; Molotov was non-committal while Brezhnev was seriously sick. "Admiral Stransfield

---

40 *Statesman*, 28 December 2002.

Turner, CIA chief had top secret report on the health of Brezhnev.[41] He was incapable to sustain intelligent conversation for more than 20/30 minutes (Mendelson). The issue of induction of troops in Afghanistan was largely forced by the defence minister Ustinov. By mid eighties the political turmoil in USSR was observed even by casual Soviet watchers. By 1985 the Soviet Union decided to withdraw from Afghanistan. This was obviously known to the CIA and American leaders. Thus, there was no genuine need to induct Stinger missiles in Afghanistan. On December 7, 1988 Mikhail Gorbachev announced at the UN that the Soviet Union would make unilateral military cuts of 5,00,000 troops and 10,000 tanks and did not seek a reciprocal cut by the US.[42] Such a decision could not have been taken in a day or two. This matter must have been deliberated for some years. Therefore, the Soviet Union was not at all keen to stay in Afghanistan. To ally the US fear, in a luncheon meeting Gorbachev told the then President-elect George Bush that he was not playing a trick and impressed on Bush that the Soviet Union was undergoing a genuine reform process since 1986. His statement had 'ring of truth'.[43] Bush took office in early 1989. Sarah E. Mendelson made a deep study of Soviet withdrawal from Afghanistan and came to conclusion that 'US Policy in Afghanistan did not cause the withdrawal of Soviet troops' as the Soviet Union had decided to withdraw before induction of Stinger missiles during the period from 1985 to 1989.

The Soviet strategy was largely defensive. Like Zia, the Soviet leaders did not favour escalation of the war into Pakistan. The Afghan regime was capable to hit back Pakistan with sufficient logistic support from the Soviet Union. That was not the policy to be followed by the Soviet Union. Mendelson found that the Soviet Union inducted only 2.1 percent of the Soviet forces in Afghanistan as against the US deployment of 21 percent at the height of Vietnam War.[44]

---

41 Bob Woodward, The Veil, The Secret Wars of CIA, p31.

42 Bob Woodward, The Commander, Simon and Schuster, New York, 1991, p52.

43 Bob Woodward, The Commander, Simon and Schuster, New York, 1991, p52-54.

44 Ibid p27.

Therefore, the Soviet and the Afghan government strategy was to engage Mujahideen in selected counter intelligence operations to cripple the resistance and disrupt the weapon supply routes. By 1983 the Soviet divided Afghanistan into seven military districts or zones, each headed by a Soviet General with troops and MI 24 helicopter gunship. Because of mosquito operation the Soviet troops had to be rotated on a six monthly cycle. At any given point of time the total Soviet troops were around 1,20,000 as per Khan's book. It was much less as admitted by Brig Yousaf.[45] Gradually it was thought prudent to use more airpower, fire power and wider use of helicopter gunship. The strategy was to hold the key areas which included towns and cities and left out the vast country side unprotected. This enabled the Mujahideen and Pakistan army regulars to enter freely the countryside without much resistance.

The Soviet Union in principle accepted the involvement of US-led secret coalition in Afghanistan being implemented by Pakistan by proxy war. If the Afghan government troops with backing of the Soviet Union had wanted a similar proxy war in Pakistan, the situation would have been totally different. The force ratio was in favour of the Afghan-Soviet combined force. The Soviet did not increase its troops, nor did it follow a hot pursuit policy.

The fear of the possible Soviet inspired proxy war haunted Gen Zia and, therefore, he did not wish to give India a cause for an Indian attack. He was keen to secure the eastern border by managing side shows of public relationship with a variety of Indian opinion makers and politicians. In the event of war with India, Pakistan would have disintegrated into several parts. He was literally afraid of return of Indira Gandhi to power. His mango and cricket diplomacy had to be seen in that light. The 1987 possible war was averted as he himself took the initiative to visit Jaipur in February to see a cricket match.

The long peace negotiation process ended by signing a Geneva Agreement on Soviet withdrawal of troops on 14 April 1988. The Soviet completed withdrawal of troops by February 1989.During the decade long war the political scene in Soviet Russia changed. New leadership emerged after successive deaths of stalwarts like Leonid

---

45 Riaz M Khan, p85.

Brezhnev in November 1982 followed by death of Yuri Andropov in March 1985. Gorbachev announced eventual withdrawal of troops from Afghanistan in 1985.[46]

In May 1986, Dr Najibullah replaced Barbak Kamal in Afghanistan and proved quite effective. He could not be ousted by the ISI-CIA-Mujahideen combine. The so-called seven party alliances of Mujahideen parties too collapsed. Now the force ratio was in favour of the ISI/Pak army and Mujahideen combine. The ISI staged in March/April 1989 launched an offensive to capture Jalalabad which just ended in a fiasco followed by a few more ineffective offensives. The end result was total chaos and confusion. It was seen as a failure on the part of Gen Hamid Gul who was the ISI chief. It was his plan that failed. He covered up this failure by mounting jihadi attacks in Jammu and Kashmir by inducting foreign jihadis.

Fallout of the Afghan War

The most damaging fallout of the Afghan war was huge empowerment of the ISI as a political force, independent of civil authority and accountability. The ISI influenced the political alignments in Afghanistan through the prism of Pakistan's strategic view. There was convergence of Gen Zia's Islamization of Pakistan and extension of that policy in Afghanistan. It was called international Jihad against the Soviet infidels. Strange as it may sound, infidels from the USA, West and China joined the Jihad. Each nation had its own agenda against the Soviet Union. This has been rightly called 'An Unholy War' by John K. Cooly who made a deep study of this war where there was no convergent of interests. Each player had divergent interest in this Unholy War.

The legitimization of jihad as an effective international instrument of another kind of war was the greatest folly of all participants. President Ronald Reagan and the CIA chief William Casey literally accepted the nodal role of Pakistan as a 'frontline state' against the Soviet Union. The ignited minds of the

---

46 Gen. K. M. Arif, 'Working With Zia, Pakistan's Power Politics 1977-1988, Oxford University Press, p320.

concerned Americans gave Pakistan fantastic Islamic ideological inputs and the latest technology to Pakistan to fight a Jihadi war on their behalf. A vastly improved and technologically sound and effective infrastructure for promotion of international terrorism was permanently created in Pakistan to wage similar proxy wars in Jammu and Kashmir and other hotspots like Chechnya, the Philippines, Myanmar, Sudan and other parts of the world. The Islamic terrorism has become a hard reality.

The Mujahideen drawn from various parts of the world to Afghanistan were injected with a new vision of Islamic Ummah. Soon the 'blow-back' effects of the Mujahideen in their respective countries were observed. There was emergence of Islamic revivalist forces in Egypt, Algeria, Sudan, Myanmar, the Philippines, Indonesia, Algeria, Egypt, Tunisia, and China. India too was sucked into this process. The returnees of the Afghan Jihad became heroes for the cause of Islam.

The blow-back effect of Afghan war was tolerated and not dealt with severely by nation states till 9/11. The UN failed to define terrorism as some of the Islamic countries propounded the theory of 'one man's terrorist is another man's freedom fighter'. Afghan Jihad is squarely responsible for rapid growth of international Jihadi terrorism with organization, structure and a much secured base in Afghanistan and Pakistan for promotion of jihad worldwide. For spread of Jihad internationally a base was required and that was readily available in Pakistan and Afghanistan, both being ruled by jihadi leadership.

The greatest fallout was the promotion of international Jihad, soon after the departure of the CIA contingent from Pakistan. The CIA built-up an impressive proxy war infrastructure with capability to carry out covert operations all over the world. The CIA's training manuals were converted into Jihadi manuals. The ISI under Zia picked up the cause of Kashmir from 1988 in a virulent manner and this did not die down even when Benazir Bhutto became the civilian Prime Minister. She could secure her post of Prime Minister on the understanding that the ISI and the army under General Mirza Aslam Beg would decide on Pakistan's policy in Kashmir and Afghanistan.

'The Intelligence agency to be allowed to make or break political parties or alliances and dictate the policy of the elected government against their better judgment.'[47] There was unprecedented growth of poppy cultivation and narcotic trade in Afghanistan largely controlled by narcotic mafia groups. Drug mafia proliferated due to support extended by the military establishment of Pakistan for sharing profit. A part of the income was reportedly to be given to the ISI for Jihad. The CIA and the American Drug Enforcement Agency stationed in Pakistan were aware of these arrangements but preferred to ignore them in the interest of Jihad, a task much holier than drug trafficking.

Drug trafficking, Kalashnikov (AK 47) and an army of criminals engaged in these operations prospered at the expense of the civil society. The civil society in Pakistan had been squeezed out vacating space for criminal and anti-social elements. Terror had gripped the ordinary citizens of Pakistan. There was extra–ordinary marriage of alliance of evil forces.[48] In such a situation people lived on 'a razor's edge' of extreme anxiety and a sense of outrage at the break-down of utility services, law and order triggering clashes on small and big issues. These evil forces still operate in Pakistan.

The Shia Sunni clashes in Pakistan came out of the Afghan Jihad. The Sunnis dominated the proxy war and the Sunni extremists of Deoband and Arab Wahhabi version found expression in Afghan Jihad. Die-hard Sunnis got shelter in Afghanistan. People like Riaz Basra, a Sunni extremist, escaped to Afghanistan and operated from there. Riaz Basra was subsequently killed after the collapse of Taliban.

The icons of the Afghan Jihad were largely controlled by the ISI. The group unity was lacking. The preferred leadership of Hekmatyar, as propped up by the ISI, did not last long. Many of them proved to be token heroes.[49] This is what is precisely happening in

---

47 Mazhar Ali Khan, Pakistan: The Barren years, Oxford University Press, New York, 1998.

48 *See* Akmal Hussain, Communal Riots and survivors in South Asia, ed by Veena Das, Oxford University Press, 1990, Delhi.

49 Khaled Ahmed, *The Friday Times*, August 14-21, 1997.

ISI promoted Jihad in Kashmir. The leadership lived in style while the ordinary folks laid down their lives. The Geneva Agreement on Afghanistan was never implemented largely because Pakistan continued to play a divisive role in the politics of Afghanistan. There was growth of local warlords who ruled there respective areas with imposition of multiple taxes by creating road blocks.

The central lesson of Afghan Jihad is yet to be fully understood by the US policy makers. As John K Cooly has aptly said: 'when you decide to go to war against your own enemy, take a good long look at the people behind you when you choose as your friends, allies or mercenary fighter. Look well to see whether these allies have already unsheathed their knives – and one pointing them at your back.'[50]

The period between 1989 and 1994 was one of worst civil war in Afghanistan. Even after capture of Kabul in 1992 by Taziks, there was no end to civil strike. The UN failed to bring in stability in Afghanistan. Dr. Najibullah virtually abdicated when his trusted ally General Dostum changed sides. Najibullah had already dispatched his family to Delhi. He could not make it himself as he was detained allegedly at the tarmac.

Jan Goodwin remained in Pakistan during the period of Afghan Jihad. She recorded closely the happenings of that period. As a woman she remained in touch with female resistance leaders like Fatima, daughter of Pir Sayed Ahmed Gailani, Laili, and all western educated who lived in US three years before the Soviet entry. Laiti's family was close to king Zahir Shah. These people were opposed to communist taking over the country. As Jihad progressed they were disillusioned, as women were subjugated under the influence of Arab Wahabism. Arab Jihadis had virtually taken over as the Liberal Afghans were targeted and killed. Laili married Roger Helms, blue-eyed nephew of former CIA director Richard Helms after getting converted to Islam. Mujahideen groups issued death threats to them as 'the CIA was hated by Afghans despite the fact they supplied them with arms' and enraged to see an Afghan cohabiliting with an American' as that would 'rub the people the wrong way. Western aid

---

50 Cooly, John K., Unholy War, p241.

agencies were attacked in1989 and 1990. Many of them were killed. Fatwas were issued by clerics banning women from indulging in luxuries of freedom of movement. The schools were closed to keep the women under 'chader and chardiwari'. The stage was set for Taliban take-over of the country. 'Women are one part of the society that can be controlled, so the Islamists manipulate them as symbols. Women have become the powers of men in this Islamization process',[51] and others were deeply influenced by Wahabism, and Afghan trained Jihadis separately took initiative in the first WTC attack in 1993. Libya too promoted Gulbuddin Hekmatyar, who has been described by Jan Goodwin as the 'most brutal and repressive Afghan Resistance leader'. He attempted a coup in 1990 against the Kabul regime of President Najibullah, which fortunately failed. The most Afghans 'abhor and fear' him. Hekmatyar's followers were known for acid attacks on women in Kabul, for dressing up in western attire. He even offered sanctuary to Sheikh Omar Rehman, a blind cleric, when he was in Afghanistan. He was subsequently arrested for 1993 WTC attack. Planning more such attacks was unearthed by FBI mole.

The Revolutionary government of Iran too supported and funded the Shia groups. The 'Great Game' again started surfacing as the petro-dollar domination of Afghanistan through a number of proxies. The oil reserve of the central Asian countries acted as magnets. The country drifted towards anarchy as Afghan fault lines were many. There was no charismatic leader to unite Afghanistan, nor did the US and the western world take a firm political stand on the future of Afghanistan. Fundamentalism feeds itself with more fundamentalisms. In Muslim world in a crisis situation the answer is on 'more Islam'. The stage was set for Talibazation of Afghanistan.

Interim Government

When Kabul fell in April 1992, the Afghan resistance spearheaded by the CIA-ISI combine was expected to triumph, but the wave of liberation soon became a fight for the different varieties of Islam. These factions fought for their dominant positions. The moderate Muslim Afghanistan was soon turned in a theocratic state, more rigid

---

51 Jan Goodwin, *The Price of Hours*, Little Brown and Company, UK; 1994, p79.

than Iran and Saudi Arabia. The first act of the interim government in May 1992 was to issue a decree (fatwa) that women must adopt the Islamic dress code and tent like burqas appeared in bazaar and sold out quickly. The same edicts are periodically issued in Jammu and Kashmir by an unknown outfit called Lashker-e-Jabbar. Islamic revolution starts with enforcement of dress code and ends in killing of innocents who just cross the line. The king Zahir Shah's constitution of 1964 guaranteed both men and women equal rights and obligations and women were empowered to exercise voting right in 1965. The interim government took away the female voting right. 'Kabul was emptied of women'.

There were deep ideological divisions among the Afghan Jihadis. The US committed the greatest blunder by allowing Zia to use the funds through his ISI. Zia on his turn ensured diversion of funds to fundamentalist parties over the moderates as part of his Islamization programme. In addition, the Saudi Arabia funded the Arab Wahabis to indoctrinate the Afghans to practice pure Islam.

The Afghan jihad had impacted on ISI which became all powerful and obstructed the growth of democracy after tragic death of General Zia on August 17, 1988. Zia trained officers, pampered and indoctrinated, played havoc by manipulating the political destiny of Pakistan. The ISI under Gen Hamid Gul and COAS General Mirza Aslam Beg cobbled together nine political parties under ISI command, a political front to confront the PPP of Benazir Bhutto. Lt Gen Hamid Gul takes pride in such maneuvering of political forces. It played, as Brig Tirmazi of the ISI fame said, the role of a political broker, a complete departure from the British Army Tradition of political neutrality. The Army and the bureaucracy stood polarized and politicized. As an offshoot of the Afghan Jihad the ISI even did not bother about the principle of deniability. The joke is that the ISI secret reports are available at the Pakora shops of Aadpara, a market situated near the ISI headquarters. Brig Tirmazi regrets that the ISI' had been gang raped'. He hints at embezzlement of funds donated by the Americans towards the Afghan Jihad.[52]

---

52 Brig Tirmazi Syed, Profiles of Intelligence, Combined Printers, Lahore, p358 and the Herald Annual , January 2001 featuring an interview of Lt. Gen Hamid Gul. Gul who took pride that Zia, Bhutto and Nawaz Sharif 'were the creation of the military.

This happened as there was no accountability about the use of money and arms supplied by CIA to ISI. It was an accepted principle 'that no American ever involved in the actual distribution of funds and arms once the money had arrived' and 'cash was fungible'. Covert wars demanded it.[53] Brig. Yousaf admitted that US cash was being stolen between the point of delivery of handing over cash to ISI, and its distribution to the forward lines controlled by Yousaf, money just evaporated and a part of the siphoned off money was directed to KRL *i.e.* A Q Khan laboratory for Islamic bomb.[54]

The Russian withdrawal of troops in February 1989 was a great occasion for big celebration at CIA headquarters at Langely. The Vietnam War was avenged. The celebration was short-lived as Pakistan messed up the fruits of Jihad by pursuing a systematic policy of gaining strategic depth' in Afghanistan, a concept introduced to Pakistan by China[55] for waging a relentless proxy war against India. Pakistan's ISI mostly dominated by Pasthuns, were promoting a purely Pakhtun regime under Hekmatyar, who was not liked by other minority ethnic groups like Tajiks, Shias, Uzbeks and Hazaras. There was an interregnum of fratricidal war in Afghanistan from 1989 to 1994. The US policy was that Afghanistan should remain under the control of Pakistan for America's strategic oil interest of Central Asian Countries. The situation was ripe for Taliban to emerge to restore some sort of order by imposing more Islam.

---

53 Adrian Levy and Catherine Scott-Clark, Deception, Pakistan, The United States and The Global Nuclear Conspiracy, Atlantic Books, 2007, p130.

54 Adrian Levy and Catherine Scott-Clark, Deception, Pakistan, The United States and The Global Nuclear Conspiracy, Atlantic Books, 2007, p130-131.

55 Altaf Gauhar.

3

The Taliban

The Taliban, when finally captured Kabul in September 1996, became known to all over the world. It was a stark reality that Taliban controlled almost 90 per cent of Afghanistan. From nowhere it appeared in 1994. Its onward journey to Kabul was unstoppable. It came much after Soviet withdrawal of troops from Afghanistan on 14 February 1989. The Soviet Union collapsed in 1991. The Pakistanis and jihadis claimed victory for the collapse of the Soviet Union which was doubtful as Mikhail Gorbachev had already initiated a reform process in the mid eighties. The CIA celebrated the withdrawal by opening champagne at Langely, USA as Afghanistan was viewed as Soviet's Vietnam.

The period 1989 to 1994, after the Soviet withdrawal of troops, was one of chaos and extreme disorder. When the reality of freedom came, the seven-party alliance forged by the ISI to fight jihad in Afghanistan collapsed like a house of cards. Each party with their fighting outfits started moving towards Kabul. Dostum and Ahmad Shah Masood were first to reach Kabul. Governments that came after Dr. Najibullah in 1992 could not last long, due to lack of sense of unity. Intense ethnicity and feuding dominated the scene.

The chaos was largely due to 'low-IQ handlers' of the ISI namely; Lt Gen Hamid Gul and Lt Gen Javed Nasir. They were determined to crown Hekmatyar as the supreme leader of Afghanistan and not king Zahir Shah. Out of seven Jihadi parties, five favoured return of king Zahir Shah to Afghanistan. Zahir Shah had a track record of anti-Pakistan stance over the Durrand Line issue. An

Afghan intellectual favouring return of the king was murdered in Peshawar. Benazir Bhutto in her first term as Prime Minister of Pakistan favoured a policy of non-interference. The ISI obstructed that policy. The ISI acquired the authority 'to dictate the policies of the elected government against their better judgments'.[1]

Again in February 1992 Nawaz Sharif wanted to endorse the UN sponsored Peace Plan. Nawaz Sharif's two ministers Ejaz ul-Haq and Abdus Sattar Niazi threatened the government with street agitations if the sane UN Peace Plan was carried out. They made it abundantly clear that the war in Afghanistan would continue till their favourite leader Hekmatyar was installed on the throne of Kabul. The duo even wanted an aggressive policy on Kashmir with crossing the Line of Control even at the risk of war with India.[2]

Traditionally, Afghans never had a strong central government. The tribal chiefs had their areas of influence. The Loya Jirga was mostly composed of such chiefs. Afghanistan always had Pushtun head of the state. Even in the scheme of operation designed by ISI, Pashtun Hekmatyar was propped up as a leading force. Dostum and Ahmad Shah Masood were just marginalized as they were non-Pasthuns. But Hekmatyar had no popular support and was unable to deliver as discussed below. The 'Game' shifted to Peshawar region of Pakistan where the bigwigs of the ISI played their own game. An interim government was announced on 23 February 1989 with Sibghat Allah Mujadidi as acting President and Abdul Rasul Sayyaf as acting Prime Minister. This was done as the last convoy of the Soviet troops headed by Gen Boris Gromov crossed Amu Dariya River on 14 February 1989.

In March 1989, Jalalabad was attempted to be captured with a nod from the ISI and Americans. It was not a replay of what happened in Saigon in 1974, when the North Vietnamese troops entered Saigon with a great show of victory. The attack was repulsed by the troops under the control of Najibullah. It was a defeat for the ISI Chief Lt.Gen Hamid Gul. The Interim government just collapsed

---

1 Pakistan: The Barren Years 1975 – 1992, Oxford University Press, New York, 1998, p57.

2 Ibid, p503.

as Hekmatyer withdrew his support.

What really led to fall of Najibullah's government was due to series of defections from his camp. In March 1990, the most powerful General and minister of defence of Najib's forces General Shahnawaz Tanai defected to Hekmatyer's Hizbe-Islami, while others defected to Rabbani.

Only in March 1991 the Pakistan based mujahideen captured the district of Khost bordering on Pakistan. To add to misfortune of Najibullah, General Rashid Dostum and Sayeed Mansur Madri, Uzbek and Ismaili, combined with Ahmed Shah Masood managed to occupy Kabul on 25 April 1992. Najibullah took shelter in the UN compound in Kabul.

On 28 April, 1992 Mujaddidi arrived from Peshawar to Kabul. Under Peshawar Accord, Mujaddidi would rule for 2 months followed by Burhanuddin Rabbani for 18 months as a transitional government to be replaced by an elected government after holding general elections. On 28 June 1992, Prof Rabbani took charge as President. But there was no end to fighting between the ISI sponsored Hekmatyer and General Dostum and Masood's forces. In the process Kabul was virtually destroyed. Only Ismail Khan in Herat and Dostum in Mazer-e-Sharif could maintain a semblance of order in their respective jurisdictions. The country was ripe for emergence of religiously motivated Pasthun consolidation under the banner of the Taliban with the patronage of the Pakistan regime which 'was actively trying to establish a safe and direct route of communication with the newly established Central Asian Republics'.[3]

The role of Pakistan in Afghanistan was motivated by 'strategic depth' and capturing of oil market in the Central Asian republics. The ISI's lower ranks in Pakistan were mostly Pasthuns. They were pursuing an aggressive Pasthun agenda and neglected other ethnic groups.

Each Mujahideen commander and their sub-commanders started to rule their areas of physical control. After departure of the Soviet troops, the local commanders had to raise money by imposing

---

3   The Afghan, Willen Vogelsang, Blackwell Publishing UK, 2002, p321-330.

heavy tax on vehicles. Eventually, more unethical practices were adopted. The local chiefs started enjoying life. Rape became too common. Inter-party fights became the order of the day. Nawaz Sharif did intervene resulting in two agreements. These agreements did not work as the parties did not follow the rules of the game. The situation was akin to pre-1747 when Afghanistan was an amalgam of different Tribes and Khanates ruled by Tribal Chiefs and Khans. It was Nadir Shah's 23 year old General Ahmed Shah Abdali who reached Kandahar from Persia with a force of 4000 Afghans and succeeded and founded his kingdom of Afghanistan with capital at Kandahar. Kandahar and Herat had remained with Iran for centuries. Till today these areas have flavour of Iran. The Abdalis are considered half-Persians.

Taliban in Arabic means desire. In Urdu it means seeking. A person in search of knowledge is called in Urdu Talib-e-ilm. Thus Talib is a student. Plural of Talib is Taliban. The students who study in *deeni madaris* are called Taliban.

Thus, Taliban phenomenon represents the power and urge of *deeni madaris* students for a political objective of bringing in a state of Islamic Afghanistan. The madaris students who had received military training during Afghan jihad had battle experience as the fighting outfits depended on them for recruitment. However, Taliban as a separate force emerged in 1994, out of a shocking incident often narrated by some scholars.

A Herati family on its way to Kandahar from Herat was intercepted by a local mujahideen who behaved like highway bandit. Apart from looting, the boys were molested and the young girls were gang-raped by the mujahideen bandits. Thereafter, they all were killed on 20 September 1994 and bodies were half burnt. On hearing this Mulla Omar reached the spot, washed the bodies and gave them decent burial as per Islamic practice. He then addressed some Talibs and pledged them to start a campaign to get rid of criminal-minded jihadis. He went from mosque to mosque to collect students and initially only 50 joined the movement. It is said one of these fifty had a dream of angels descending from heaven. This was taken as Allah's blessing for the cause. This story is often cited for creation of Taliban.

The first Mujahid commander to give them arms was Haji Basher. The movement then was called Tehreek-I-Islami-Taliban Afghanistan. They were tasked to liberate areas out of criminal jihadis and hold the liberated areas to enforce the Islamic laws. Soon a big faction of Hizb-e-Islami and Ittehad-e-Islami of Abdul Rasul Sayyaf joined Taliban. Initial success of Taliban brought more within its growing fold. The most important was Gen Shahnawaz Tanai, a communist General of Najibullah who joined the Taliban. He soon became a devout Muslim and started growing beard. 30,000 students from various madaris also joined the Taliban movement subsequently.

The ISI led Taliban intrusion into southern route to Herat to Central Asia was not to the liking of Rabbani. Rabbani insisted on clearance from Kabul for such road opening journeys sponsored by Pakistan leadership unilaterally. The US too was trying to explore opportunities under the Taliban regime. After capture of Kandahar by Taliban, John Manjo, American Ambassador to Pakistan, visited Kandahar.[4]

Taliban, as widely reported, also used large sums of money to win hearts and pockets of their opponents. This trick of bribing was introduced by the CIA during the Afghan jihad. This brings us to the question whether such money was provided by the ISI or by the CIA. It was impossible for the Taliban to raise that kind of money from their own resources. Hekmatyar, eventually became the common enemy of the Taliban and Rabbani. They cooperated 'in pushing Hekmatyar out of the way'. The Taliban pressed for capture of Kabul. On 27 September 1996, Masood seeing the ground reality ordered withdrawal from Kabul and the Taliban entered the capital. The first act of the Taliban was to commit gruesome murder of Dr. Najibullah. He was taken out from the UN custody, 'castrating and jeep-dragging him before hanging him from a traffic post.[5] Najibullah's family had already been shifted to Delhi. He too was supposed to leave for Delhi. He failed to make it as the secret plan was leaked out to mujahideen. This part of the story needs deeper probe.

---

4   Ibid, p 327.

5   *The Atlantic Monthly*, September 2000.

Hamid Karzai remained deputy foreign Minister from 1992-1994 when Afghanistan was governed by the mujahideen. Initially he too had good opinion of the Taliban movement. Karzai soon found strangers appearing in the Taliban meetings. 'That was the riddle of Pakistan intelligence'.[6] In July 1999, Hamid Karzai's father was assassinated in Quetta. The murder was attributed to the Taliban and the case remained unsolved largely due to indifference of the Pakistan police. The Pakistani police and agencies had built up a poor reputation of not solving any of its political murder cases from Liaqat Ali Khan to Benazir Bhutto. This is largely because of interference in the investigation of cases by various forces in Pakistan.

Deeni Madaris

Islamic schools are called *deeni madaris*. Madaris were functioning in Afghanistan from before and many came up in Pakistan especially during Gen Zia's Islamic drive period. In Punjab alone there were 2512 *deeni madaris* in 1997[7] with a student strength of 2,18,939. Many of these institutions provide not only free education but also free boarding and lodging. It was beyond the capacity of the government of Pakistan to run so many free schools with free boarding and lodging.

The common basic syllabi of these *deeni madaris* included the following:

1. Learning of holy Koran by heart.

2. Tajweed, correct pronunciation of the Koranic verses in Arabic.

3. Tafseer *i.e.* interpretation of the holy scriptures.

4. Fiqh *i.e.* Islamic jurisprudence.

5. Shariah *i.e.* Islamic Laws.

6. Hadis *i.e.* life and decisions of the holy prophet on various

---

6   The Atlantic Monthly, September 2000, Robert D Kaplan.

7   News, 26 May 1997.

issues brought to him.

7. Mautiq *i.e.* philosophy.

8. Riazi *i.e.* mathematics.

9. Falakiat *i.e.* astronomy and

10. Tabligh *i.e.* spreading the word of God.

Talib can become a mullah if he completes his studies and has gone through further studies in different madaris under different religious scholars. To become a mullah he has to have a proper '*daster bandi*'. A mullah is one who has been trained in religious schools for at least 12 years.

A mullah can become an *imam* or *khatib* of a mosque or often become teachers of religious schools. Some may become *kazis* or *muftis* with authority to act as local judges or conduct religious rituals. By application of this rigid standard, "many of those who call themselves mullah amongst the Taliban did not really qualify for this title as they were only half educated and were not fully conversant with the injunctions of Islam and the correct interpretations of the Holy Koran and the Sunna".[8]

The Taliban were divided into two categories on the basis of their aptitude. One was trained to fight for jihad to subdue their rivals and the other confine themselves to studies. They often interchanged their roles depending upon the situation. During the period of Afghan jihad and after, the Hanafi and Wahabi Islam of Saudi Arabia got mixed up on the soil of Afghanistan and in the neighbouring frontier areas of Pakistan. Thus, a new breed of jihadis emerged out of this mix, promoted and supported by the ISI. Till 1997, the US did not object to the rise of Islamic fundamentalism in the form of the Taliban movement. The US was more concerned to obtain transit rights for flow of oil and gas from Turkmenistan to Pakistan via Afghanistan.

---

8 Matinuddin Kamal, The Taliban phenomenon, Lancer Publications and Distributors, New Delhi, 2000, p 16.

Directives of Taliban

Imposition of Islamic Shariah was the primary task of the Taliban. Shariah would include not only holy Koran or Sunna but also fatwa (religious edicts) given out from time to time by Islamic scholars. These wider applications of Shariah, according to some, have largely injected and influenced extremism in the minds of the Taliban.

Some of the directives of the Taliban were as follows:

- It was compulsory for Afghan women to cover themselves fully from head to toe when they venture out of their homes. The Prophet did not impose such restrictions, but the movement leaders believe that 'women's eyes and hands can be cause of immoral deeds'. This, many feel, had brought a wrong image of Islam but no Muslim cleric has clarified the issue in terms of Koran, Sunna or Hadith.

- Girls were denied education and women their jobs.

- Even veiled women needed to be accompanied by a male relative when they venture out of their home. Women caught violating these rules were imprisoned. So were the shopkeepers and rickshaw pullers who picked up unveiled women for shopping.

- Doctors were forced to cut off the hands and feet of thieves on the basis of decisions of Kazis. If a crime was committed by an outsider against an Afghan, the court of Kazi has the authority to award punishment. Thus, a Pakistani was hanged in Afghanistan on the allegation that he had killed two Pasthuns in a district in Pakistan. This was a case of extra territorial jurisdiction of the Taliban laws.

- Cinemas were closed and turned into mosques.

- Taking photographs or displaying them was banned to prevent idolatry. On the basis of this, Taliban at one time even vowed to destroy the world famous sixty-meter high statues of Lord Buddha, carved out of a rock of a hill in Bamiyan province dating back to the 5th century BC. When protests were lodged by the Buddhists world over, Taliban denied to have adopted any such programme. But subsequently these Buddhist statues were demolished as such statues were un-Islamic. A Taliban delegation refused to sit in a room in Chitral (Pakistan) on the occasion of signing of a transit trade agreement with Pakistan just because a photograph of the Quaide-I-Azam Jinnah was hanging there.[9]

- Video shops ware destroyed not in Afghanistan but also in neighboring Frontier Province of Pakistan like Miranshah. Television was a taboo too, often used for practice firing. Playing football was considered un-Islamic. Chess was looked upon as an idle occupation. Kite-flying was forbidden and keeping pigeons was banned and the caged birds were killed. People indulging in such pleasures were often jailed.

- On one occasion Taliban leaders attending a Pakistan Day Parade remained seated even at the time of playing of the national anthem of Pakistan in keeping with their religious understanding.

- Celebrations like New Year's Day and Iranian Nauroz were not allowed.

- The Radio Kabul was re-named as the 'Radio Shariat'. Songs or music were banned on radio as people need to be prevented from bad and evil influence.

- Mixed parties, even of foreigners, were not allowed as these were evils and have corrupting influence.

- 12 murderers were hanged in public between November 1994 and April 1997. Relatives of victims were ordered to fire the shots to kill the accused. These were termed as 'revenge killings'.

- Some of alleged informers of rival militia gangs were killed and bodies hung in the streets of Kabul in October 1997.

---

9 Matinduddin Kamal, The Taliban phenomenon, Lancer Publications and Distributors, New Delhi; 2000, p 35.

- Men with trimmed beards were beaten. All men have to grow long beards.

- Namaz was made compulsory and those violating faced arrests and imprisonments.

The Taliban concept of Islamic purity was based on a deep commitment. Because of local conditions prevailing in lawless areas, there was a need to reorganise the social structure on religious moral grounds. Eradication of crime and criminals was uppermost in their mind. This type of spartan life style did show that there was commitment and dedication. These directives were enforced by the Taliban Religious Police Force.

Hate Schools

Some describe madrassas as 'hate schools'. They produce a class of militants totally dedicated to jihad not only in Afghanistan but elsewhere also. The prominent seminaries which preach and teach jihad are mostly located in Pakistan. One of the famous madrassa is located at Akora Khattack in NWFP. It was called Jaamiah Darul Uloom Haqqania founded in 1947. On an average, at any given time, some 2000 Talibs receive education free of cost including free food and lodging. The Talibs were drawn mostly from Pakistan, Central Asian States and about 30 to 40 per cent would be Afghans. Annual budget was estimated to be Rs. 60 lakh. Funds are received from Islamic countries as also from rich individuals. Their educational programmes were in conformity with the Taliban directives. These madrassas were under the control of the faction of JUI headed by Samiul Haq. His chain of religious schools has been responsible for training of many of the Afghan Taliban leaders. He was said to be close to Osama bin Laden. Of late, after US retaliation, he founded the Afghan Defence Council to protect the Taliban regime and Osama bin Laden. He took to street agitations with the Talibs from his religious schools. Samiul Haq of JUI(s) believed that the Taliban movement has given a new life to the Islamic movements throughout the world.[10]

---

10 News, 9 Aug 1998.

The Binori Mosque – the cradle of Taliban

Another famous seminary is located in Binori Town on the outskirts of Karachi. It is known as Jamaitual Uloomil Islamiyyah, founded by Maulvi Mohammad Yusaf Binori. The bulk of Taliban were trained by these two seminaries.

Binori or Binori Mosque in Karachi derives its name from Maulana Muhammad Yusuf Binori. The Jamait-ul-Uloom-il-Islamiyyah of Maulana Binori was set up to teach students for propagation of Islam. Tajweed is to pronounce correctly the holy book the Quaran in Arabic. The range of activities includes all facets of Islamic teaching.

The Taliban leadership as also foot soldiers of Islam basically was drawn from two Pakistan based schools; the Dar-ul-Uloom Haqqnia and the Bonori chain of madrasas controlled by the Binori mosque.

It was said that at least three members of Mullah Omar's six member's council had studied at Binori Town Madrasa. Mulla Omar and Osama bin Laden reportedly met with each other for the first time at the Binori mosque. Any teacher from Binori chain of madrasas, when they visited Afghanistan, were treated with great honour and entertained as state quests. Such was the reputation of the Binori mosque in Afghanistan. Some top military commanders of Taliban had previous training in madrasas controlled by the Binori mosque.

At any given point of time the Karachi Binori mosque would have 8000 students, drawn from different nationalities. They go through a course of intense Islamic studies covering a wide range of subjects. They follow a strict Hanafi code of Shariat within the Sunni sect of Islam. In Islamic terms the school of thought here was Sunni Deobandi. The Deobandi School was launched more than a century ago as part of the Islamic revival movement in India to 'cleanse' Islam from later accretions like worshipping of graves of saints. The philosophy of mother institution cannot be different now. During the Kargil War a fatwa was allegedly issued by the learned Islamic scholar Ali Mian calling the followers to maintain its separate religious identity and not to pray for India's success in

Kargil war. This was reported by *The Hindu*, a prestigious daily newspaper of India. There was a controversy and denial, but no affirmative statement was issued in favour of Indian soldiers fighting on Kargil heights.

The way the Deobandis behave with other Sunni and Muslim sects lead to occasional feuds and bad blood. There was no desire to compromise. This rigid attitude becomes a part of Taliban culture. Because of this rigid attitude to other sects, sectarian clashes take place in plenty in Pakistan. Pakistan regime calls these clashes as acts of terrorism.

The training schedule of a Talib was rigid. The training started with morning prayer at 6 am and ended at 8 pm, with breaks for five prayers and food. Hundreds of foreign students were groomed here that would also include Afghans. Many of the Afghan students were said to be illegal immigrants registered as Pakistanis to avoid visa and passport formalities. They were safe once they entered the mosque complex.

After completion of studies the Afghan talibs used to cross the border mainly from Tokhan and Chaman. Taliban administration recruited such Talibs for various types of work. Talibanised Afghanis considered Afghan Taliban regime as 'a true Islamic state'. Many Pakistani students imbibed with Islamic glory did desire to settle down in Afghanistan so as to live in a truly Islamic state. Many Taliban educated students wear black turban as sign of action on Afghan front.

On a Sunday in the month of November 1997 an activist of the Islamic Students Federation got injured in a scuffle in Karachi. Two hours later, two very prominent Sunni scholars were burnt alive in a car while their driver was shot dead when he tried to escape. Interestingly, both Shia and other organizations, besides Americans and unknown Indian agents were named in the FIR. Taliban took to the streets in a most violent manner indicating that in future they can utilise their Afghan training in any violent clash in the name of sectarianism on the soil of Pakistan.

There was infighting between Sunni Tehreeq and the Sipah-

Sahaba, following the Multan incident in which at least four Deobandis were killed by Barelvis. The religious fanatics of Afghan war veteran enforced complete strike on Friday. Even the Hasan Square which had never seen a bandh before was under the control of the fanatics. Wine shops and schools were attacked by young activists of the Taliban.

Maulana Masood Azhar, after release from Indian prison, was left at Khandahar in exchange of captive 159 Indian and foreign passengers of IC 814. The first thing he did was to reach the Binori mosque to announce jihad against India.[11] Salman Hussain reports how religious fanatics brought most liberal metropolis like Karachi into a standstill. Karachi soon became one of the hot favourite places for promotion of international terrorism. The Singapore case had shown how the jihadis used Karachi for meeting of Al-Qaeda operatives to hold conspiratorial meetings for multiple target attacks in South East Asia.[12] This document brings out the links between Jihadi outfits in South East Asia and Al Qaeda. Pakistan was used for holding meetings with operatives from both sides mostly in Karachi and as transit route to Afghanistan for operational meetings with Mohd Atef, operational head of Al Qaeda whose sanction was necessary for target attacks in South East Asia or elsewhere.

Taliban's Worldview

The Taliban movement was not confined to Afghanistan but was liberally exported to neighboring countries. The Taliban prominently displayed maps in 1998 in all the main squares in Kanduz city after capturing it. The map showed how with the passage of time Taliban Islamic movement would be pushed into Iran, and the Central Asian Republics. Delhi had been shown as the future target of the Islamic militia. Other target areas were Bukhara, Tashkent, Dushanbe, Isfahan.[13]

Taliban massacred thousands of Hazaras in locations between

---

11 *The Friday Times*, Nov/Dec 4-20, 1999.

12 White Paper, The Jemaah Islamiyah, Arrests and the Threat of Terrorism, 7 January 2003 Singapore.

13 Muslim, 26-08-1998.

Mazar-e-Sharif and Hariatan. 10 Iranian diplomats and one Iranian journalist were mercilessly killed when the Taliban guards entered the Iranian consulate in Mazer-e-Sharif.[14] Iran has not forgotten this incident even today.

Not only Shias, the Taliban targeted Ismailis on 3 September 1998 living in Kiyan valley of Baghlan province of Afghanistan. Their eagle shaped 'Assembly Hall' was blasted on the ground of prohibition of carving and worship of statues in Islam. This justification was provided in the Taliban sponsored weekly 'Zarbe Momin'.[15] The reality of the Taliban situation was the rejection of anti-Shite Deoband or Wahabi and Naqsbandi of Uzbelelan spiritual coalition. The Taliban was recognized by Pakistan, Saudi Arabia and UAE immediately after capture of Kabul. All these schools of Islam are totally opposed to fidda (innovation) in Islamic rituals, separation of local accretions from the pure Islamic faith. Jahangir was forced by the Naqasbandi order to prosecute Sikhs and the Muslim mystical orders which had developed a spiritual consensus with the Hindus. Sheikh Ahmed of Naqsbandi order decreed that the Shias were apostates.

Destruction of Bamiyan Buddhas

Taliban movement and governance of Afghanistan carried all the elements of Islamic fanaticism. The movement suffered from a sense of insecurity of Islam. For more than 2000 years standing giant Buddha statues remained in Bamiyan province of Afghanistan. Bamiyan is located 330 kms of northwest of Kabul. Other Buddhist relics are available in various parts of Afghanistan and in some Central Asian States, signifying inter-cultural contacts much before the advent of Islam.

Hussain Shaid Suhrawardy, while defending the Pakistan Resolution, had said that Pakistan idea was very much Indian. He said Pak signified purity while 'Isthan' was the place, which had Sanskrit origin. Therefore, all the regions which have 'Isthan' suffix form part of this regional ethos. This would include Afghanistan,

---

14 The Muslim, 04-09-1998.

15 News, 06-09-1998.

Baluchistan, Kazakistan and many such areas. The Buddha's message went far and wide.

For centuries the statues of Buddha survived in Bamiyan. The march of Islam did not touch these images of Buddha. Genghis Khan and Tamerline campaigns did not involve the destruction of Bamiyan Buddha statues. Why did then the Taliban undertake this wanton destruction? Did a Taliban Mulla not issue an edict in 1999 assuring preservation of all ancient relics 'as integral part of the heritage of Afghanistan'? The change in attitude needs to be explained. The official position of Taliban was that the decision was taken by 400 ulemas of Afghanistan and Mullah Omar was bound by the decision of the ulema council. It is believed that no such ulema's meeting was held. Mullah Omar declared the destruction as 'tribute to Islam' and 'Muslims should be proud of smashing idols'. "It has given praise to God that we have destroyed them. These idols have been the Gods of infidels who worship them even now. The real God is Allah and other false Gods should be removed".[16]

When Bamiyan was first captured by Taliban in 1998, the three Buddha's statues were bombarded with rockets, blowing away the legs of Buddha and blackening his faces. That was not considered enough. There are reports that these massive destructions of Buddhas in 2001 are somehow linked with Osama bin Laden, whom a Pakistani journalist called 'a Saudi born terrorist'. The hardliner Taliban commanders having close links with Osama bin Laden forced the issue. After all Taliban depended on Osama's Arab fighters as also on Pakistanis. They formed the critical mass of the Taliban war machine. The Taliban depended on them for their annual summer assaults against the Northern Alliance. Arabs in large number lived in Kabul, Kandahar and Jalalabad.

As rightly said by a Pakistani journalist that 'the blowing of the Bamiyan Buddhas has not only erased an era of Afghanistan's past, but it also heralds a gloomy future.[17] This happened inspite of 27th February 2001 warning by UN that 'destroying any relic, any monument, any statue which are part of common heritage, will only

16 *News line*, Karachi, April 2001-A Special Report.

17 *Newsline*, April 2001, Pakistan.

prolong the climate of conflict'. In March 2001, Francesc Vendrell discussed with Muttavakil, foreign minister of Taliban regime, not to carry out the destruction of the statues.

Funding

All Pakistani writers on Taliban and fundamentalism have categorically said of foreign funding of seminaries, mosques and madrassas. Apart from foreign funding; the rich expatriates of Pakistan have been financing seminaries by way of substantial contributions. Gen Zia-ul-Haq had also authorized the district Zakat Committees to give them money from their Zakat funds.[18] Zakat fund is raised by deducting an amount from bank deposits of individuals. Tax on heroin was another area of fund raising by Taliban, although it was un-Islamic to encourage poppy cultivation. Much of the Afghan jihad funding was out of drug trafficking. This has been fully corroborated by accounts given by various authorities and was even known to CIA. All principles were thus compromised even by Taliban when it suited them. Addressing the UN sponsored Drug Summit in New York, the President Burhanuddin Rabbani of recognized Government of Afghanistan functioning from North Afghanistan said on June 8, 1998 that 'one can not turn a blind eye to the symmetry that exists between the extraordinary increase in drug production and the raise of Taliban'.[19]

Talibanization of Afghanistan

Talibanization of Afghanistan did go a long way. The Taliban controlled before its collapse more than 90 percent of the landmass of Afghanistan. The linkages between the Taliban and Pakistan were quite deep. The Taliban commanders holding position of authority were the products of madaris of Pakistan. This bonding had a spill over effect on Pakistan. They secured almost free access to Pakistan and in some areas they had even held influence. The bordering areas of Pakistan have been largely Talibanized. In Miranshah in Pakistan Talibans smashed the video shops and TV sets. Arms were flaunted

---

18 Matinduddin Kamal, The Taliban phenomenon, Lancer Publications and Distributors, New Delhi, 2000, p14.

19 *Dawn*, 26-06-1998.

openly. It was estimated that 2,50,000 jihadis fully armed were floating in Pakistan. Such a huge strength of jihadis in Pakistan became a destabilizing factor. These jihadis were exported all over the world for terrorist activities. There has been no effort to de-weaponize them by force or control them by invoking law for illegal holding of arms. The strength of floating jihadis in Pakistan has not been officially registered, but it was believed to around 2,00,000, which also included Afghanis.

Iran with Shia majority felt that Taliban was a monster. It was often criticized in Iranian press. Shias were victims in Afghanistan. Newspaper Kayhan International published from Iran quoted Ahmed Shah Masood in 1997 that the ISI was the major backer of Taliban. In a battle with Taliban, Masood claimed to have captured 37 Pakistanis. A Persian Daily Akbar on 12 Dec 1997, termed Taliban as a 'malignant tumour' similar to Ale Hadee and the Wahabis. These two Sunni movements inflict blows to Islam and Shiaism. Gen (retd) Hamid Gul, ex-ISI chief is a diehard Sunni and often lambasted USA for conspiracy to divide Afghanistan and often urged China to recognize the Taliban regime.[20] As aptly remarked by Robert D Kaplan[21] 'the Taliban embody a lethal combination, a primitive tribal creed, a fierce religious ideology, and the sheer incompetence, naiveté, a cruelty that are begot by isolation from the outside world'. The Taliban was largely controlled by invisible ISI, described as the hidden hand of Pakistani intelligence,[22] a view widely shared by all those who had been watching developments in Afghanistan for a long period.

Pakistan may have helped the Taliban with military training, fuel and weapons including servicing the military aircraft they captured in Kandahar areas. Islamabad may also have helped the Taliban recruit pilots. Additionally, hundreds of Pakistanis were involved in fighting alongside the Taliban. There were many other sightings of Pakistani military personnel in various parts of Afghanistan.[23] A UN

---

20 Frontier Post, dated Feb. 26, 1999.

21 The Atlantic monthly 2000.

22 The Atlantic monthly 2000, p72.

23 Zalmay Khalilzad, Anarchy in Afghanistan, Journal of International Affairs, Summer

report on war-torn Afghanistan accused a neighboring country [read Pakistan] of arming and fuelling the hardline Islamic militia. This was however, denied by Taliban.[24]

The fact was that the Pakistan army controlled the Taliban militia. A Pakistan general called Eid Qaffor (may be a false name), was killed in fighting between the militia and the opposition forces in Faryab province in 1998.[25] Ahmed Shah Masood in his last interview before his assassination on 9 September named a Pakistan general Zaman leading the Taliban militia in northern assault. There was no dearth of oral or documentary evidence to prove how the ISI and Pakistan army had manipulated the Taliban regime to the strategic interest of Pakistan.

Taliban's acquisition of arms

Taliban seized considerable quantity of Soviet arms, tanks, rocket launchers and a variety of arms and ammunitions. These were cannibalized by the Pakistani engineers. Pakistani pilots used to fly the Taliban aircrafts seized from the Najibullah government. Taliban reportedly seized 110 Russian made Scud missiles along with four launchers on August 14, 1998 near Mazar-e-Sharif. They included Scud A and Scud B with 80 and 270 km range respectively. Scud missiles were inducted by the Russians in 1985.[26]

Taliban had a good quantity of Stinger missiles donated by US to Afghan Mujahideen during 1979-1989 Afghan jihad against the Soviet troops in Afghanistan. Taliban had also seized heavy stockpile of Scud, Luna, Oragan missiles after capturing Baghlan province dominated by Ismailis in September 1998.[27]

The Taliban representative in UN even told the BBC: 'I would not be surprised if some of the most deadly weapons, which have never been used in that area, would be used, which would certainly

---

1997, page 48-49.

24 *Dawn*, 2-7-1998.

25 *Tehran times*, 28-7-1998.

26 *Frontier Post*, 15-8-1998.

27 *The News*, 6-9-1998.

involve the interests of the Western world'.[28] It was a threat to the USA for retaliation in response to US missile attacks at Khost on 20 August 1998 in response to 7 August 1998 attack of US embassies in East Africa by Al Qaeda.

The Taliban strategy was bound to boomerang and did pose a threat to Pakistan itself. It did lead to further sectarian violence and domestic instability. This was the biggest legacy of US-Pakistan unholy alliance during the Afghan war.

India too was hit by insurgency in Jammu & Kashmir by Taliban and Al Qaeda trained militants. Pakistan strategy was to keep terrorism at a high level just below the India's "threshold of tolerance". To test the tolerance level of the Indians, Pakistani sponsored terrorism was gradually escalated ending with an attack on Indian Parliament in December 2001 and Mumbai attack on 26th November 2008.

China - US - Pakistan and the Taliban

For Pakistan the strategy was to consolidate power in Afghanistan by proxy so as to reach out to Central Asian republics for markets, to obtain Central Asian oil and in the process enrich Pakistan and secure 'strategic depth' against India. As Taliban had the official backing of Pakistan since 1994 and its military establishment, army officers belonging to earlier Kabul regime joined the Taliban force in large numbers. There was desertion from other fighting groups also. As a result it became a dominant force, serviced by Pakistan for its strategic and tactical needs. The credit for creation of Taliban was generally attributed to Gen (retd) Nasirullah Babar, who was then Interior Minister in the cabinet of Benazir Bhutto. She was often called as the mother of Taliban.

Osama bin Laden returned to Afghanistan in 1996 and he took up seriously the cause of jihad world over. This created an impact on neighboring Muslim countries in Central Asia, Russia, and India and to some extent in China's Muslim majority province of Xinjiang. Osama's contacts reached out to USA, Egypt, Turkey, and Algeria. While staying in Sudan from 1991 to 1996, he established

---

28 *Dawn*, 7-9-1998.

a network for resurgence of Muslims in Africa leading to clashes between Islam and Christians as witnessed in Ethiopia, Sudan and other trouble spots.

Abu Sayyaf group in the Philippines became active with a Muslim homeland slogan. Most of the troubled spots had mujahideen trained in Afghanistan. They had Afghan war training and on return to their respective countries they took up the cause of separate Muslim homeland. This is akin to 'two nation' theory of M.A. Jinnah and the Muslim League in undivided India.

Taliban thus became a worldwide movement for which credit goes to Osama. A fully Taliban controlled Afghanistan, by way of simple logic, became a threat to moderate Islamic regimes which did not conform to Taliban's view of Islamic Ummah and purity practiced in Afghanistan. Thus Egypt, Algeria, Tunisia, Saudi Arabia became targets of Islamic fundamentalism.

Taliban's expansion was limited by Ahmed Shah Masood in the Northern Areas of Afghanistan. Every year there was summer assaults on Northern Area by Taliban aided by Pakistan army volunteers drawn from ISI and army and joined by mujahidien from Arab countries. All their efforts failed to dislodge Ahmed Shah Masood or Dostum.

The US strategy was to keep the Taliban and Osama influence confined within the Indian subcontinent, or else Osama and Taliban will move westward to target US interest. The US also felt that Iran could be contained by Taliban. Even after the US twin Embassy bombings in Africa, the US President Bill Clinton retaliated by one time missile strike only. Robin Raphel of the State Department was breaking bread with Mulla Omar. The US was only negotiating for extradition of Osama bin Laden to face trial in the US for bombings of its embassies in East Africa.

The Chinese who faced a major Muslim unrest for a separate East Turkestan state was engaging its 'all weather friend' Pakistan in controlling flow of Afghan trained Uighur Mujahideen entering into Xinjiang. The Chinese had gone to Kandahar on several occasions to buy peace with the Taliban. For some time this strategy did work, but not for a long time as Taliban and Osama bin Laden would lose credibility by not supporting Muslim fighters of Xinjiang and for not achieving an Islamic state in China. One reason for the Chinese policy of nuclearisation of Pakistan is traceable to this factor of containment of Mujahideen onslaught on China in Xinjiang and help Pakistan to standup to India. The Chinese repressions of Uighur revolts were not criticized by the Pakistan's right parties, an indication of so-called Chinese success in its diplomacy. In Islam, there can be temporary peace pacts but final victory has to be achieved. The Chinese Ambassador to Pakistan Lu Shulin met with Mullah Omar for an hour in 2000 and got an assurance that Kabul would not create troubles in Xinjiang.[29]

The balance of power would have tilted in favour of Taliban in case Masood was eliminated from the Northern Area. In that event the world would have witnessed a spurt of more terrorist activities in several trouble spots. Thus, the strategic alliance that developed eventually between USA & India, India & Russia were manifestations of deep-rooted strategy to use India as a front-line state to deal with Taliban and Osama bin Laden. Between US and India, US, was more threatened than India. India has been absorbing shocks. In the US, casualties create a political turmoil. The US after the Vietnam War suffered from a 'body-bag syndrome'.

The Taliban factor did succeed in Tajikistan where there was a sort of a civil war. The next target was Kazakhstan and Kyrgyzstan. Uzbekistan was showing signs of nervousness and its president Karimov became ambient. Four states *i.e.* Uzbekistan, Kazakhstan, Kyrgyzstan and Turkmenistan signed an agreement in April 2000 to conduct 'joint operations to combat terrorism, political and religious extremism, multinational and organised crime, and other security threats'.[30]

Xinjiang threatened by Uighur Muslims seeking independent East Turkestan, reinforced by emergence of Central Asian Republics of independent states, is a product of US sponsored Afghan war.

---

29 News, 14-4-2000.

30 China, Pakistan and the Taliban syndrome- Asian Survey, Vol XL No. 4, July/August 2000, p659.

Uighur Muslims trained by China participated in Afghan jihad and acquired battle experience to face the Chinese repression, more acute than Tibet. Reports of Uighur revolt did come to the knowledge of China watchers. Xinjiang is one sixth of China with vast oil and mineral reserves. In no way China can afford to lose this region, nor can China allow a political settlement by holding plebiscite in Xinjiang, a formula being floated for Kashmir by Pakistan. This would have multiplier effect on Xinjiang. The Chinese stand on Kashmir, therefore, remained ambiguous with the show of solidarity with Pakistan. The Chinese managed a dangerous game and did achieve tactical results.

The Chinese hostility towards India is the product of a peculiar Chinese strategic thinking. India has to be kept on the boil by a policy of encirclement with hostile forces. China is not at all keen to settle the border issue with India. The peace and tranquility of the border is not to benefit India, but is the result of internal problems of China in Xinjiang, Tibet and Taiwan. Any misadventure now will invite India's reply and adverse world opinion. The internal turmoil will be heightened and the internal threats will be insurmountable if China adopts policy of confrontation. What India has really received out of efforts to build bridges with China? Nothing. In fact China holds a substantial Indian territory out of its 1962 aggression and still claims 93,000 Sq Km of Indian territory.

Nuclearisation of India has changed the balance of terror used one sidedly by China so far. Soon India will be able to reach out to China, the way the Chinese have already done against India. India's nuclear programme is the result of the Chinese nuclear test of 1964. A big country like India cannot remain under threat of a hostile power for a long time.

All these equations have changed after 9/11. China promptly changed its position by supporting the UN Security Council resolution 1373. The turmoil in Xinjiang is now under control. On China's insistence, the Uyghur separatists have been declared by the USA as Foreign Terrorist Organization (FTO) of foreign origin (FTO). Pakistan realizing certain massive hit back promptly took U-turn and joined US-led coalition against its own Taliban regime and Osama bin Laden more as a strategy than real change of heart.

Who's Who in Taliban

The Chief of the Taliban was secretive Mulla Omar. Like Sivarasan who organised and participated in killing of Rajiv Gandhi, Omar too is also one-eyed Mullah. Many of them lost their eyes in guerrilla battles. Omar lived in Kandahar and visited Kabul only once in 1996. He was rarely visible and was guarded by the militia. Every decision of the Taliban regime had to be approved by him. His worldview was said to be 'no better than an ordinary villager'. He passed an edict of death sentence of any Muslim who converts to Christianity. He disallowed functioning of political parties.[31] It was like Saudi Arabia where conversion to another religion invites death penalty under its laws and amounts to blasphemy of the prophet and liable to involve death penalty. These provisions violate article 18 of the Declaration of Human Rights. In these countries conversion is only one way traffic.

Mulla Omar was born in 1961 in Nodeh village of Punjwai district of Kandahar province. He hails from Gilgia Pushtun Hotak tribe. He was educated in a madrasa school up to the seventh grade and did not complete 12 years of religious education to call himself a Mulla. He is married with five children. It is said that he also married Osama bin Laden's daughter which stands unsubstantiated. He is tall and keeps flowing black beard and wears black turban He has battle experience as he fought the Russian troops and lost his right eye in combat of which he is proud of. He avoided meeting foreigners and does not speak much. In April 1996, in a gathering of 1500 mullahs in Kandahar, he was declared Amirul Momineen, the same status the Mullahs gave to Prof Rabbani earlier. After all loyalty of Mullahs depends on ground reality.

It is believed that Omar suffers from 'brain seizures' as a result of a shrapnel lodged in his brain in 1989. He was rarely seen outside his bomb-proof residence built by his alleged father-in-law Osama bin Laden.[32] His visit outside his Kandahar residence was always

---

31 *Frontier Post*, 6-7-1998.

32 *Indian Express*, Oct 8, 2001.

accompanied by dozens of body guards in a convoy of deluxe Japanese vehicles with darkened windows.

Mulla Mohammed Rabbani was second in command in the Taliban hierarchy. His year of birth was not known but was said to be about forty years. He is a Pasthun of Kakar tribe of Peshmul area of Punjwari district of Kandahar province. Much is not known about his educational qualification. He is considered intelligent and matured. He worked with a number of jihadi groups during 1979-89 Afghan Jihad. It was his decision that led to hanging of Dr. Najibullah after Taliban's capture of Kabul in 1996. It was an avenge killing of his brother by Dr. Najibullah. Due to differences, he had to leave Afghanistan, but later rehabilitated. He attended OIC meeting at Islamabad in March 1997 as an observer from the Taliban side.

Mullah Nooruddin Turabi, a middle-aged bearded former guerilla commander, was the minister of justice in the Taliban administration. He was considered as the closet ally of Mullah Omar and "the most extremist of the extremists". While signing the order or destruction of Buddha statues he said: "we have obeyed the order of Allah by destroying the idols"! After the fall of Taliban he promptly recognized the Karzai government and obtained clemency.

Mullah Muhammad Saleem Haqqani held the post of a deputy ministry in the dreaded ministry for Prevention of Vice and Preservation of Virtue. This outfit was the religious Islamic police charged with enforcement of Islamic laws. His job was to spot out people who did not grow beard of the prescribed size and women who did not veil themselves from head to toe. He is a Pakistani madrassa product. It became his additional duty to enforce a newly enforced ordinance to ban on the celebration of Nauroz, which is the Afghan New Year on the ground that tradition was the tradition of infidels.

Mullah Obaidullah was the powerful defence minister. He had to supervise the destruction of Buddha statues as the local Bamiyan Shias refused to cooperate with Taliban to carry out the destruction. That delayed the destruction for a longtime. Because of this procrastination Mulla Omar later ordered the slaughter of 100 cows to seek forgiveness of God. Mullah Obaidullah was said to be close to Osama bin Laden for operational needs. Mullah Fazil was the Deputy Defence Minister, while Chief of the military was Mulla Berader. Obaidullah was captured and released by the Karzai government. He was not charged for destruction of Buddha statues.

Mullah Abdul Wakil Muttawakil was the Foreign Minister of the Taliban regime. It was his task to give human face to Taliban. As foreign minister he had no prior information of the edict of Mullah Omar for destruction of Buddha statues. The tragedy was noticed when just before the issuance of the edict by Mulla Omar, he was assuring a delegation of the society for preservation of Afghanistan's heritage. He said the Taliban's intention was for preservation of the heritage. The foreign minister came to international limelight at the time of hijacking of Indian Airline flight IC 814 to Kandahar. He manipulated the show to the advantage of the hijackers and allowed hijackers to escape after unloading their luggage. He reportedly provided official vehicle to hijackers to travel to Chaman from where they proceeded to Pakistan. He was however considered, moderate as also his deputy Abdul Rehman Zahid. He was under the US custody for some time and released.

Health Minister Muhammed Abbas Istanakzai was considered a moderate. He is fluent in English.

Northern alliance

Ahmed Shah Masood, the leading leader of the Northern Alliance, was killed by a blast on 9 September 2001. He was most charismatic leader who gave good leadership to Northern Alliance. He was born in 1956 and came from a relatively well off family. His father was an army officer. He was a Tajik from Panjsher Valley. He studied in a French School in Kabul and also studied engineering in Kabul. He was against the regime of President Daud and as a result had to shift to Pakistan in 1973 and joined the resistance movement in 1975. He was trained in guerilla tactics in Pakistan in 1977 and went back to Panjsher in 1978 and thereafter rarely visited Pakistan. The ISI never favoured him and did not provide him enough arms to fight the Soviet troops. That made him anti-Pakistan and anti-ISI. He was liberal in outlook and that gave him international recognition.

General Abdul Rashid Dostum of Mazar-e-Sharif fame was born in the year 1955 in a farmer's family. He had education up to the age of 14. He joined a state owned gas company as an unskilled worker and soon became a union leader. He is tall, stocky and well built. He was in Uzbeck and had standing army Uzbeck militias to support. He was holding the post of deputy defence minister in the Karzai government. His present activities are not known.

Taliban-ruthless killer of opponents

On 27 March 2000 Gen Ismail Kahan and Abdul Zaheer, both war veterans of 1979-89 jihad were opposed to Taliban and escaped from Kandahar jail. In July 2000 Taliban arrested its own commander Bashir Baglani and hundreds of his fighters. Reason for this action was not provided, as the regime was highly secretive.[33]

Several killings were attributed to Taliban's hit squad based in Peshawar and Quetta. For example governor of Kunduz, Arif Khan was killed on 14 April 2000, possibly because of his indication to switch over to other factions.

Maulavi Mohammed Siddiquah was a retired Posthun Commander. He was killed on 24 April 2000 in Peshawar.

On Taliban's request Pakistan arrested Abdhul Qahir Shariati on 5 July 2000. In July the dissidents organised six bomb blasts in Kabul near Pakistan embassy.[34]

When the Taliban captured Mazar-e-Sharif in August 1998, Mulla Omar, had given permission to kill for two hours, but they killed for two days. The Taliban went on killing frenzy, driving their pick-ups up and down the narrow streets of Mazar shooting to the left and right and killing every thing that moved up like cart pullers, women and children, shoppers and even goats and donkeys. Contrary to all injunctions of Islam, which demands immediate burial, bodies

---

33   Nation, 27-28.12, 2000.

34   Ibid.

were left to rot on the streets; dogs were eating human flesh and going mad and the smell became intolerable.[35] 'People were shot three times on the spot, one bullet in the head, one in the chest and one in the testicles 'and their throats were slit in the halal way.[36]

If there was any sign of discontent, the Taliban would deal with the situation severely. 60 people were arrested in October 1988 in Jalalabad on the suspicion of a coup attempt by former military officers and men loyal to General Shah Nawaz Tanai, who deserted Najibullah's army in 1990 and joined Mujahideen. His Pasthun faction had been an ally of the Taliban army. In January 1999 right hand and left feet of six Taliban soldiers were amputed as they were allegedly involved in looting. The severed body parts were hung in the city center for public viewing until they rotted'.[37]

Taliban's anti-Shia torture and operation

Osama bin Laden was largely instrumental in bringing in Saudi version of Wahabbi Islam in Taliban ruled Afghanistan. The Taliban depended on Saudi for financial assistance. Prince Turki, intelligence chief of Saudi Arabia, visited Kandahar in mid-June 1998 and provided the Taliban with 400 pickups and huge financial aid. Pakistan provided 2 billion rupees through the ISI pipeline. The ISI officers frequently visited Kandahar to help the Taliban prepare the Northern Assault, the area held by Tajiks and Uzbeks.

There was a misconception that the Talibs were pure Islamists with no vices. Like any other conquering army they too raped women. The Taliban aimed to cleanse the north of the Shias. After capture of Mazar, the Taliban mullahs under Nazi who became governor of Mazar, offered three choices; convert to Sunni Islam, leave for Iran or just die. Shia mosques were ordered to be closed. The Hazars were to be killed as they practiced a different version of Islam.

The Taliban led by Mullah Dost Mohammed and Pakistani Sunni militants like Sipah-e-Shaba entered the Iranian Consulate

---

35 Ahmed Rashid-p73.

36 Ibid.

37 Ibid, p104.

in Mazar-e-Sharif. 11 Iranian diplomats and journalists were shot dead in the basement of the building. More then 45 Iranians were also taken as prisoners. Reportedly the ISI too took part in this heinous operation. The killings were reportedly carried out on the instructions of Mullah Imam.[38] The Iranians were so outraged that there was total mobilization of Iranian forces to launch a possible attack on Taliban, which however never happened.

Haq Nawaz and Salim were die-hard Pakistani Sipah-e-Sahaba militants. They took refuge in Afghanistan when Pakistan police were closing on them for Shia killings in Pakistan. They were under the protection of Harkat-ul-Ansar who had good presence in Afghanistan. After the fall of the Taliban regime, Haq Nawaz was eliminated by the Pakistani establishment.

The Bamiyan fell to the Taliban on 13 September 1998. In one village 50 old men, who were left behind after the younger generation escaped, were mercilessly killed by the Taliban.[39] There was nothing holy in holy war. No one was taken to task for such inhuman massacre of old people who did not know how to defend themselves.

How puritans were the Taliban

The hero of Mazar-e-Sharif attack Mulla Dost Mohammed ultimately landed up in jail, not because of his ruthless killing of Iranian diplomats but because 'he had brought back two Hazara concubines and his wife complained to Mullah Omar. It is said authoritatively that some 400 Hazara women were forcibly taken as concubines by the Taliban.[40] This is happening in Kashmir too. Recently it is said that Hizbul Mujahideen killed a Lashker-e-Tayaba commander for trying to do the same mischief with a girl in Doda as reported in the Statesman.

Taliban, bin Laden and India

The ISI of Pakistan used Taliban and Osama bin Laden for promoting

---

38 Ahmed Rashid, p 75.

39 ibid, P.76.

40 Ibid, p75.

jihad in Kashmir. On 20 August 1998, 70 cruise missiles hit six targets in Khost killing 20 people and wounding 30 more. Osama bin Laden escaped the attack 'Most of those killed were Pakistanis and Afghans who were training to fight in India-controlled Kashmir'.[41] All the jihadi groups of Pakistani origin like Harkat-ul-Mujahideen, Al Badr, Lashker-e-Toiba and Jaish-e-Mohammed were organically linked to Osama bin Laden, the Taliban and the ISI. All Pakistani watchers have noted this link. There was nothing covert about this relationship. India was thus greatly concerned with the Afghan situation.

Pakistan-Taliban - bin Laden nexus

After failure to capture Osama bin Laden, the US attention focused on the Taliban as the Taliban kept Osama bin Laden under its protection. On 8 December 1998, the UNSC passed a resolution threatening imposition of sanctions against the Taliban for not handing over Osama for trial in USA. Pakistan was the only country that did not support the resolution calling it biased. Pakistan stood isolated internationally. The civilian leadership in Pakistan in 1998 could not change the Afghan policy due to its military establishment and the ISI.

On 15 October 1999, the UNSC imposed limited sanctions against the Taliban regime. This happened after military takeover of Pakistan on 12 October by Gen Musharraf. The sanction did not deter him to plead for the Taliban. He continued with Pakistan's policy for recognition of the Taliban on the basis of Musharraf's 'ground reality' theory. The reality was that Pakistan, the ISI and 2,50,000 armed jihadis were holding the whole Afghan population hostage to a new kind of Wahhabi version of Islamic Sunni regime which 'brought Afghanistan even closer to the edge of ethnic fragmentation'. Pakistan covertly violated the sanctions imposed by the UNSC and escaped being punished for violating sanctions imposed by UNSC. China and Malaysia abstained when UNSC resolution was put to vote.

Pakistan's Afghan policy was largely shaped by the ISI's

---

41 Ibid.

Pasthun cadre backed up by Zia ul Haq. It was to ensure 'a disunited movement with no cohesive organizational set up so as to keep the Mujahideen leaders obligated to Pakistan'. As a result the Soviet withdrawal of troops in 1989 did not make any difference. The disunity amongst the Peshawar based Mujahideen leaders was beyond repair. Therefore, a consensus government with adequate representation of ethnic minorities could not be evolved. Hamid Gul, Chief of the ISI, tried to capture the territories from the Afghan government troops. He conceived a frontal attack, which did not yield any result. He became a severe critic of the US as he felt that he was not made COAS after Gen. Beg's retirement due to alleged American pressure. Ultimately, he was removed from the ISI, but continued to meddle in Afghanistan politics. His one point programme was to promote the leadership of Hekmatyar. His successor Lt Gen Javed Nasir, a product of Tablighi Jamaat, was more interested in promoting jihad in India. He was largely blamed for Bombay bomb blast in 1993. The Bombay bomb blast took place a month after the first attack on World Trade Centre in 1993. These two cases have similarities. In both these cases cars and truck loaded with explosives were used. Ramzi Yousef, a Pakistani, was found to be involved in the first WTC attack in 1993, while Dawood Ibrahim, based in Karachi, was used for blasts in Bombay a month after. Yousef is now rotting in an American jail, while Dawood is enjoying good life in Pakistan under the protection of the ISI.

Pakistan till early 1990s continued to back Hekmatyar. As Pakistan army had more than 20 percent Pasthuns, the army remained determined to ensure a total Pasthun victory in Afghanistan. As Hekmatyar failed to deliver, the Taliban were propped up by Lt. Gen (retd) Nasurullah Babar, then interior minister of Benazir Bhutto 1994. He too was a Pasthun.

On 29 October 1994, the ISI's logistical branch pulled up a convoy of 80 vehicles with Pakistani ex-army drivers. On board was Colonel Irani of the ISI with two Mullahs in toe. The convoy was detained 12 miles outside Kandahar. The Taliban was used to free the convoy on 3 November 1994. The local mujahideen commander was chased and shot dead with ten others. His body 'was hung from a tank barrel for all to see'.[42] To win Kandahar, local mujahideen were bribed by the ISI. The capture of Kandahar enabled the Taliban to capture huge quantity of arms, 6 MIG fighter planes and six transport helicopters all of Soviet origin. 'The fall of Kandahar was celebrated by the Pakistan government.[43] By December 1994, 20,000 Afghan and Pakistan students joined the Taliban in Kandahar.[44]

Pakistan and the ISI attempted a political alliance of Hekmatyar, Dostum and others with the Taliban in February[45] for capture of Kabul. This offer was turned down by the Taliban as it considered non Taliban warlords as communist infields. This was the turning point when the regional powers took keen interest in Afghanistan either enhancing the capability of the Taliban or the opposition groups hostile to Taliban. The emergence Taliban was seen as a threat to regional balance of power in Central Asia, Russia, Iran and India. The training centers in Afghanistan were handed over to Pakistan outfit for promoting jihad in India. The Taliban after initial success dreamed of an outward movement of its ideology. Said a Taliban leader: "we can love our enemies but only after they have been defeated".

Gender war

Kabul was earlier a modern city with visibility of educated women in skirts. Teachers in schools were mostly women as also professors in colleges and universities. King Zahir Shah had introduced a series of reforms. The first task of the Taliban was to enforce a strict version of Sharia. The department of the Promotion of Virtue and Prevention of Vice or cultural police as they were called was run by Maulavi Qalamuddin who has been described by Ahmed Rashid as 'a huge Pasthun tribesman with enormous feet and hands, a long thick nose, black eyes and a bushy black beard that touches his desk while he talks'. He was soft spoken in contrast with his size.

Young zealots of the department vice and virtue walked around

---

42 Ibid, p 28.

43 Ibid, p 29.

44 Ibid, p 31.

45 Ibid, p 7-13.

with whips, long sticks and Kalashnikovs. The department became notorious for issuing edicts from time to time forcing women to wear tent like burqa covering the body from head to toe. Iranian chadar was not acceptable for ladies. Women were told to walk without hitting on the ground to make noises. Women were not allowed to work or sit next to the driver.

Beating of men and women were too frequent for enforcement of Sharia. The Religion police were drawn from madrassas from Pakistan. It acted as an intelligence unit for the Taliban. The edicts were broadcast on Radio Shariat a new name for Radio Kabul. In public gatherings there would not be clapping but chanting of Allah-o-Akbar. Five times prayer a day was strictly enforced, Kite flying was banned. No one was allowed to question the edicts as that amount to questioning the tenets of Islam. There was total collapse of education system. Many of the educated women in Afghanistan just fled. This educated women group in the USA campaigned against the harsh rule of the Taliban and influence the US policy makers who were willing to compromise with the Taliban regime in interest of oil/gas pipeline project of the UNOCOL. The Taliban were very clear on the subject of freedom to women. They believed that obscene freedom of women would lead to adultery and herald the destruction of Islam.

Collapse of the Taliban

The situation changed after September 11, 2001. The attack on US soil was too blatant to be ignored by the USA. This time the US did not go in for negotiation with the Taliban. It decided to attack states sponsoring terrorism. The Taliban decided to fight against the US troops not realizing the US would engage the Taliban in striking the Taliban and Al-Qaeda's positions by precision bombing. The first US-led attack was mounted on 7 October and the Taliban regime just collapsed. The fighting on the ground was largely carried by the Northern alliance with the help of the US-led coalition. Mulla Omar escaped so did other Taliban and Al-Qaeda leaders. They did not sacrifice their valuable lives for the cause of jihad. Pakistan was sucked into the US-led coalition by the logic of events. If Pakistan had not joined the US-led coalition, it would have been clubbed with the Taliban and Al-Qaeda.

Gen Musharraf realizing the gravity of the situation promptly joined the US-led coalition to protect the interest of Pakistan. It is to be seen whether the Pakistan policy was dictated by tactical considerations. In support of this U-turn policy, he cited two examples of the Prophet entering into temporary peace agreements with the Jews of Medina and Kafirs of Mecca to secure Islam. He was trying to convince his home constituency and the Muslims of the world that U-turn was needed as a strategy to secure Islam in Pakistan and elsewhere. Even during the war on terror he said that it was his policy to protect the Taliban regime.

Musharraf's public posture was not matched by what happened during the course of US-led attack on Taliban regime. As reported in the press there was a reunion of top Taliban militia officials near Peshawar in 2002 with an ISI official allowing them to remain 'unmolested' in Pakistan. Taliban's former deputy foreign minister, Abdul Rehman Zaid amongst others attended the meeting. It was also reported that a personal envoy of Musharraf was also a part of the reunion. This was reported in the Newsweek, a respected paper widely read all over the world.[46] A senior US official then said that 'I am worried that Al Qaeda makes Pakistan its new base'. This prediction came true.

As already brought out, the ISI, Taliban and Osama bin Laden worked together on a high road of global war. Thus, Osama bin Laden's mission and vision in the form of Al Qaeda needs to be focused in the next chapter.

---

46 *Statesman*, 4 June 2002.

4

Al-Qaeda

The concept of Al-Qaeda emerged out of the Afghan jihad, which lasted for 10 years from 1979 to 1989. The Jihadis of all nationalities converged in Pakistan and exchanged notes and views. Dr. Abdullah Azzam, said to be one of the founders of Hamas, settled down in Pakistan. His oratory skill and arguments charmed the jihadis. He built up a Service Bureau in Peshawar, which was the nerve centre of the Afghan Jihad, initially to provide link between the foreign jihadis and their families. Osama knew Azzam from before. He became his chief lieutenant. In 1985 Dr. Ayman-al-Zawahiri of Egyptian Jihad [EJ], joined this core team in Pakistan in mid eighties, which eventually turned into Al-Qaeda after the Soviet troops withdrawal from Afghanistan in 1989.

Al-Kifah (Service Bureau) was established in Brooklyn, US in the late eighties under Mustafa Shalabi a protégé of Dr Abdullah Azzam. It functioned as a recruitment centre for jihadis. American Muslims of African origin and others joined the Al-Kifah. Dr. Abdullah Azzam was allowed to visit 26 states of the US to preach jihad and collected funds for jihad. He was then very close to the CIA, the agency tasked to carry out the proxy war in Afghanistan. Pakistan and its ISI were empowered by US-led secret alliance to act as a frontline state to fight against Soviet troops in Afghanistan. Gen Zia was seen as a liberator of Afghanistan from the Soviet grip.

In February 1989, the Soviet troops finally left the Afghan soil on the basis of Geneva Agreement. In 1989 Al-Qaeda was given a formal structure in a conference at Al-Farook camp in Afghanistan. The participants included Osama bin Laden, Al-Zawahiri, Abu Ubaidah and Al-Banshiri. In all 40 top leaders, mostly Arabs, Egyptians and others attended the meeting. It was decided that the worldwide jihad need to be launched. The gathering was addressed by al-Banshiri whose ranking was just below Dr. Ayman-al-Zawahiri. He said: "We (are) going to make a group and this is the group that is under al-Farook and there is going to be one (leader) for the group and it is going to be focused on jihad and we are going to use the group to do another thing (jihad) out of Afghanistan". Jihadis attending the meeting signed up allegiance oath (bayat) to the new group called Al-Qaeda. Al Qaeda has Arabic root. Basically it means a base or foundation or pedestal. 'Every principle needs a vanguard to carry it forward.' Thus a base is required to reach out to people providing a mode for activism. Without a base or organization nothing is possible to achieve. In democratic states, political parties provide bases for political activities based on a variety of ideas.

It was decided that those who could return to their countries were allowed to go and set up Al-Qaeda cells in their countries of origin. The Binori Mosque in Karachi became the power base of Osama's Laboratory to experiment with Islamic Ummah. The prayer leader of the mosque was Mulla Omar where he reportedly met Osama bin Laden. Then and there was cementing of their relationship, which became deeper in course of time. Thus Al Qaeda was product of evolution, previously known in various names in various countries.

Jihad in America

Soon the loose network affiliated outfits emerged all over the world. The history of creation of Al-Qaeda base in the US is interesting. Ali Mohammed, an ex-Egyptian army officer, settled down in the USA in the eighties. He was associated with Egyptian Islamic jihad led by Dr. Ayman-al-Zawahiri. He joined the US army as an Islamic instructor. He took leave, with the full knowledge of the authorities, to visit Pakistan in 1987 to provide training to jihadis. Not only that, on return he did submit a full report of his activities in Pakistan to his US army authorities. This did not invite any US official reaction as US was sponsor of that covert war. He acted as guide to Dr. Ayman Zawahiri when he visited the USA incognito twice in the early nineties for fund raising and again travelled to Pakistan/Afghanistan in 1991 to handle Osama bin Laden's security arrangements in Sudan. In 1992 he conducted basic explosive training for Al-Qaeda in Afghanistan as also intelligence training.[1]

The Al Kifah was functioning from Farook mosque in Brooklyn's Atlantic Avenue. Dr Abdullah Azzam frequented this centre whenever he visited USA. He addressed the first US Conference of Jihad in 1988. He said: 'The Jihad is not limited to Afghanistan. Jihad means fighting. You must fight in any place you can get to. Whenever jihad is mentioned in the Holy Book, it means obligation to fight. It does not mean to fight with the pen or write books or articles in the press or to fight by holding lectures.[2]

There were reports of differences between Abdullah Azzam and use of fund collected in the USA by Al-Kifah. Azzam was for use of the US fund for consolidation of jihad in Afghanistan, while blind cleric Sheikh Abdel Rehman was for spread of jihad in other countries. Dr. Abdullah Azzam was killed in Peshawar in November 1989 when he was on his way back from mosque after prayer. The explosives were kept in his car and were ignited by a remote control mechanism. All the occupants including his two sons died. This case was never solved by the Pakistani authorities. Some even blame Osama bin Laden for engineering the plot. A month before his murder a meeting was held in which Azzam was asked to account for the funds obtained by him.[3]

The same conflict surfaced at al-Kifah in Brooklyn between Sheikh Omar Abdel Rehman, the blind Egyptian cleric and Mustafa Shalabi over fund use. Shalabi was mercilessly killed in early 1991 for which no culprits could be booked either. Sheikh Omar Abdel Rehman had migrated to USA in May 1990 by courtesy of CIA, although he was on the US watch list. The true story behind the issue of his visa has not yet surfaced. In what way CIA was under obligation to permit him to stay in USA?

---

1   Miller John, Michael Stone, Chris Mitchell, The Cell, Hyperion, New York, 2002, p 145.

2   Ibid, p 70.

3   Ibid, p 64.

Jihad in the USA started in 1987 with formation of a cell consisting of El-Sayyed Nosair, Mohammed Abuhalima, Mohammad Salameh and Alkaisi. Nosair born in 1965 arrived in USA in 1981. He married Carrer Ann Mills who got converted to Islam in 1982 and Nosair soon gravitated to Al-kifah office in Brooklyn. Al Kaisi was serving with US Army's Special Forces' as instructor providing training on survival and surveillance in the Jersey City apartment of Nosair. Nosair practiced hipshot firing. Thus it is clear that the idea and planning to attack targets in USA started during the Afghan Jihad, when US was fighting for a Muslim cause in Afghanistan. Therefore, it is wrong to say that jihad in America started after termination of Afghan jihad in 1989.

The jihadis always seek a cleric to guide them. They soon found blind Omar Abdel Rehman playing that role in USA. Rehman visited Pakistan in 1985 to reach out to forward areas of Afghanistan. He was introduced to CIA allegedly by Hekmatyar, a darling of the ISI. In 1985 the blind Sheikh accompanied by Hekmatyar went inside Afghanistan 'and wept when he heard the sounds of combat that he could not see'.[4] Sheikh Omar Abdul Rehman jumped into Afghan jihad by traveling various parts of the world for fund raising and preaching of jihad. During the honeymoon period between jihadis and the USA such utterances were ignored in the interest of Afghan jihad to inflict severe punishment to Soviet Union to avenge USA's defeat in Vietnam. The objective of Afghan Jihad was different for different countries participating in that covert war.

Nosair was itching for action from before. On 8 December 1989 he lobbed a Pepsi can to Mikhail Gorbachev's car when he was on visit to USA. The Pepsi can did not explode. He was caught and released. The police never examined the Pepsi can stuffed with explosive. His next action again remained undetected when he placed a homemade bomb in metal garbage in Manhattan's west village. It did explode with a mild commotion. He targeted a UN official and put a trail on Egyptian president Hosni Mubarak.

Nosair, Salameh and Bilal Alkaisi thereafter teamed up to kill Jewish Rabbi Meir Kanhane. He was 58 years old, former member

---

4   Jason Burke, Al Qaeda, Casting a Shadow of Terror, I.B. Tauris, 2003, p72.

of Israeli Parliament. He was shot at inside the Marriott Hotel on 5 November 1990. Two shots were fired at Kanhane. While escaping Nosair shot Franklin, a 20 year old Jewish activist and Carlos Acosta, an un-uniformed police officer who came in the way of escape of Nosair. Acosta too fired at them. Two of them survived after treatment and Kanhane died on the spot.

On the insistence of the local Jews Kanhane's body was released without post mortem and sent to Israel for burial. Thus, the embedded bullets could not be extracted from his body. Such bullet recovered from the body was necessary to match the gun with the fired bullets. As a result, the case of Kanhane's killing could not be proved in the court conclusively.

The local New York police released Abuhalima and Salameh, who were a part of the conspiracy for want of evidence and the case was 'solved' by charging Nosair only because he fired the shots. Often the police avoided long investigation to find out the entire conspiracy. The investigating agency refused to unearth the entire conspiracy although 16 boxes of incriminating documents were recovered from the apartment of Nosair. They were sealed but not scrutinized. Nosair, therefore, could not be questioned on various items of seized documents like training manuals of the Army Special Warfare School, copies of various communications, bomb making manuals and maps of locations like the Statue of Liberty, Rockefeller Centre, and most importantly the World Trade Centre and copious notes written in Arabic.[5] They were dumped in a store house. Thus, Nosair's hit list was not even seen and 'unread for nearly three years'. The Kanhane's murder case was not allowed to be investigated by the FBI, again a big mistake which ultimately led to first successful World Trade Centre attack in 1993. In India all seizures are recorded in the form of memo, a copy of which has to be deposited with the jurisdictional court as soon as possible. The Indian system is more transparent as every recovery has to be revealed on paper and scrutinized.

---

5   Miller, Michael Stone, Chris Mitchell, The Cell, Hyperion, New York, 2002, p 45.

The WTC attack of 1993

The gap between Kanhane's murder on 3 November 1990 and the first World Trade Centre blast on February 26, 1993 was the key period when the agencies failed to act inspite of important leads available in the sealed boxes seized from Nosair's house. Thus, there were chances to prevent the first WTC attack if the documents had been scrutinized. The intense anti-US anti-West feelings of the Muslims were never assessed by US intelligence agencies correctly. Each incident was taken as an aberration and not analyzed as part of a global Islamic jihad. Having promoted Jihad in Afghanistan, the US remained under the false impression of having won the hearts and minds of jihadis in particular and Muslims in general. The argument for such a line of thinking was simple. After all the US taxpayers money had been spent for an Islamic cause. How could such US supported jihadis turn against their benefactor? The US did not realise that their enemies were the products of the West.

As said earlier, a dispute grew between Shalabi, Emir of Al-kifah, and others on the question of utilization of funds. Sheikh Abdul Rehman wanted to utilise funds for global Jihad while Abdullah Azzam wanted the funds to be utilised for establishment of a truly Islamic state in Afghanistan. 'A meeting was held in which Azzam was to account for his finances, and shortly afterwards, in November 1989, Azzam and two of his sons were killed by a car bomb'.[6] The ISI which had closely monitored the Afghan jihad and Gen. Hamid Gul, then Chief of the ISI were in a position to unravel the unsolved mystery of this murder of a stalwart of Afghan Jihad. In a similar way Shalabi in early 1991 was 'shot, stabbed and strangled at his home'. Shalabi was under investigation on fund utilization by Abdul Wali Zindani, a Yemeni, who eventually succeeded Shalabi after his death. After this gruesome murder of Shalabi, Sheikh Abdul Rehman's authority became supreme in USA with focus on internal jihad in US as target for attacks.

The credit goes to the US field officers who did smell a rat and did carry on surveillance of the US based Jihadis that included Salameh. Soon they found evidence of bomb material collection by

---

6   Miller, Michael Stone, Chris Mitchell, The Cell, Hyperion, New York, 2002, p 64.

Abouhalima, an Egyptian and a veteran of the Afghan jihad and a close associate of jailed Nosair. Nosair was visited in jail by his old friends about future operations which meant selection of targets and mounting attacks on US soil. Osama bin Laden reportedly contributed $20,000 to the El-Sayyid Nosair Defence Fund collected by Nosair's cousin Ibrahim ell-gabrowny to defend Nosair during the trial. During the trial inspite of oral evidence Nosair was acquitted on December 21 of Kanhane's murder, but convicted for life for shooting Irving Franklin and Carlos Acosta on the basis of oral and ballistic reports. There was no ballistic report on Kanhane's murder as already mentioned. The first jihad trial ended in virtual victory for US Jihadis. They carried the defence lawyer on their shoulders. These signals were significant. Osama however did not appear on US intelligence radar screen as a person to be watched.

Nosair, even in jail, wanted more visible action against US. He was depending on Mohammed Salameh, Nidal Ayyad and Bilal Alkaisi who were acquitted in Kanhane's murder case for reasons already explained. The Joint Terrorist Task Force in New York wisely recruited Eman Salem, an ex-officer of the Egyptian army, who immigrated to USA in the late eighties and worked as an informer working on KGB net in New York for Egyptian police. His under cover activities run smoothly by winning the confidence of Sheikh Rehman, Nosair and his cousin brother. Alkaisi was a bomb making expert who fell with Salameh on leadership issue. He was removed from the action group. Instead, Ramzi Yousef a genius bomb maker was drawn from Pakistan into the conspiracy. Yousef had arrived in New York at Kennedy Airport from Pakistan with a friend Muhammed Ajaj on 1 September 1992. Mohammed Ajaj, a former Pizza delivery man in Texas, left his job and came back to Pakistan. They came to know each other in a camp in Afghanistan. They together flew in 1st class form Karachi to New York on 31 August 1992.[7] Both carried false passports, but Yousef escaped detection while Ajaj was caught and sentenced for six months imprisonment for using a forged passport, but strangely escaped full interrogation in spite of carrying with him all kinds of manuals like bomb making, training manuals and other materials. Ajaj was smart enough to plead

---

7   Jason Burke, Al Qaeda, Casting a Shadow of Terror, I.B. Tauris, 2003, p 99.

for a refugee status from the oppressive regime of Saddam Hussain. He, on release from the airport on bail, immediately met Mahmood Abouhalima in Manhattan's east village. Abouhalima and Yousef were also known to each other from Osama bin Laden's run camps in Afghanistan and settled down in the apartment of Mohammed Salameh. Obviously, Ramzi Yousuf's landing in America was not accidental. It was part of big conspiracy. Mohammad Salameh, a Jordanian managed to travel to USA in 1987 on a new Jordanian passport with US visa which was never issued to him by the USA.[8]

Ramzi Yousuf is said to be an adopted name. He was provided with this new identity on the basis of a genuine Ramzi Yousuf who reportedly died during Saddam Hussain's invasion of Kuwait. His real name is said to be Abdul Basit Karim. He too was born in Kuwait where his Pakistani father worked as an engineer for Kuwait Airlines. Ramzi called himself 'Pakistani by birth, Palestinian by choice.'[9] He met Mohammed Ajaj a former delivery man in Texas, left his job and came to Pakistan. Mother was a Palestinian. His family had moved to Baluchistan. Yousef acquired bomb making skill when he spent several months during 1988 in Laden's training camps in Afghanistan. Researchers, at least many of them, believe that he was sent by some top brain of Al Qaeda to US to help the Al Qaeda's US affiliate Al Kifah to carry out the WTC attack in 1993. All this could not have happened without some one planning and executing this diabolic plot.

All the tie-up arrangements had been made before the D-day. The explosives were arranged by Yousef calling himself Kamal Ibrahim from the chemical companies for delivery of aluminum, magnesium, ferric oxide and nitric acid to the storage shed keeping enough paper trails for eventual successful investigation and prosecution. Rental cars were arranged. The chemicals were subsequently transferred to Yousef's and Salemah's apartment which they were sharing. The duo got into the act of mixing them. After a great deal of difficulty on February 23, 1993 Salameh procured a yellow cargo van by putting

---

8   Cooly, John K., Unholy War, p242.

9   John Miller, Michael Stone, Chris Mitchell, The Cell, Hyperion, New York, 2002, p78, 98.

in a cash deposit of $400 from a Ryder rental office. He made a final survey of the World Trade Centre. On 25 February, he took delivery of three tanks of compressed hydrogen to act as accelerant to his apartment where Yousef and Salameh finally assembled the bomb. To dodge the police Salameh reported to the police on phone that Ryder van taken on rent had been stolen from a parking lot. While doing so he gave false license number. The van was loaded with 1500 pound bomb of explosive mix.

At 12.17 pm on February 26, 1993 the yellow van was parked against a concrete wall in WTC garage at B-2 level. The bomb exploded with a flash and followed by a huge sound. Within a minute some people in the garage were dead or in near death condition. But the Tower didn't collapse the way it was expected. Yousef watching the initial blast, rushed to airport to catch a plane to go out of the US, which he succeeded. It was a rare miracle that only six people lost their lives and not thousands as was calculated by the Yousef's team.

In an investigation of this nature the first priority was to track down the vehicle used as a bomb. The van used in the attack broke into pieces. Some cars in America had provision for hidden VIN numbers on the frames. Such a number could be found by experts only. Hundreds of FBI bomb experts worked at the blast site hunting for material evidence.

The VIN code of the van was decoded at the National Crime Information Centre computer and gave out the name of the Ryder rental van with Alabama Plate No. XA70668, reported stolen on February 25, a day before the WTC attack. From this, the FBI agents could trace the rental company. Mohammed Salameh's name surfaced on record. Salameh kept enough trail behind as he foolishly called the rental company every day even after the WTC blast for return of his cash deposit. He thus out of greed for a small monetary benefit got into a trap of his own creation.

The Indian experience in the Bombay serial blast that happened a month after WTC in 1993 had a similar opening. A central agency on its own provided the names of the persons who had purchased the cars used as car bombs to the Bombay police. The agency's scientific officers visited the sites and obtained the chassis and the engine numbers of concerned vehicles and passed them to higher officers who lost no time in getting the ownership details from the manufacturers. There was a great deal of similarity between the WTC blast and Bombay serial blast cases. The Bombay serial blasts were organised by the ISI, whose chief was Gen. Javeed Nasir, with the help of Dawood, an underworld don sheltered in Pakistan under the care and custody of the ISI. Dawood was not a bomb making expert. The bombing training was given by experts drawn possibly from the ISI.

Salameh was trapped by requesting him to fill up a special form before the company could return the deposit. A form was invented and the FBI detailed a surveillance team at the leasing company.

Salameh showed up inspite of 'FBI big break began to leak out' in the press. He filled up the form unaware of the presence of a FBI man who posed as 'Loss Prevention' man from Ryder. After prolonged bargain Salameh settled for $200 from the Ryder. As he stepped out, he was apprehended by the FBI's disguised surveillance team already in position.

From Salameh's personal search a business card of Nidal Ayyad was found. A search warrant was obtained from the US Attorney Office for search of Salameh's apartment that led to Ahmed Yassin who taught Salameh how to drive the Ryder truck a few days before the WTC attack and also provided the address of the place where the bomb was to be assembled.

Gabrowny's apartment was searched. He was overpowered as he resisted his arrest. On his person Nicaraguan passports with false names and photos of Nosair were found. The plan was to provide travel facility to Nosair in case of his escape from jail. He was charged for assault, resisting arrest and for possessing fake passports.

Salameh's apartment search led to recovery of a letter of Ajaj. Ajaj, who came from Pakistan with Yousef, had already filed a petition for return of his belongings which included bomb-making manuals and videos. The judge of a liberal democracy agreed. Sarcastically the author of 'The Cell' remarked that, 'America is a great country–especially if you are a terrorist'. As already said Yousef and Ajaj came to US together from Pakistan. The obvious link with Afghanistan and Pakistan could not be assessed or analyzed.

On March 10, Nidal Ayyed was arrested who had provided 'hand to get chemicals' to Yousef for bomb making. His computer contained a letter (draft) claiming responsibility for the WTC bombing. This is a typical style of Jihadis. In Indian cases they claim in the name of known or unheard of groups in the name of Islam.

Abouhalima, after the bombing, had escaped to Saudi Arabia by air and then on to Egypt where his family lived. The Egyptian police arrested him and handed him over to the FBI. He kissed and hugged the FBI agents as he was expecting humane and tolerable treatment under the US custody. At that time he seemed to forget the 'hate America' slogan. 'In Egypt he had suffered second-degree burns to his testicles.'[10] He foolishly enquired if Ramzi Yousef had been apprehended. The case stood solved as the FBI had long shadowed the suspects after the Nosair incident. This is a good lesson. Never slacken efforts to chase the suspects who remain unaccounted for. If there is slackening of efforts they again regroup for other attacks as was evident in case of Ramji Yousef who traveled all over the world to organise several attacks.

The terrorist activity did not end even for a brief spell. The next target was Hosni Mubarak who was likely to visit USA in April 1993. The Egyptian intelligence zeroed on Dr. Rashid or Hompten-El. The FBI roped in Abdo Mohammed Haggaz, speech writer of Abdel Rehman, who treated Haggaz as a servant nor did he invite him to Rehman's own wedding. He actually had brokered Rehman's marriage. Haggaz acted as an informant to Egyptian intelligence without FBI knowing about it.

Hampton-El's safe house was bugged and a video camera installed in a building in the vicinity. However, Mubarak's visit to New York was cancelled. The plot thus failed.

---

10 John Miller, Michael Stone, Chris Mitchell, The Cell, Hyperion, New York, 2002, p 109.

Landmark attack conspiracy

Yahya Abu Ubaidah picked up cash of $1,00,000 for Hampton-El from the Third World Relief Agency, an European counterpart of Al-Kifah of Brooklyn. His phone calls were tapped and useful intelligence was received.

Siddiq Ali drew up another plan of organizing bombing of Lincoln, Holland tunnels, the UN building, the New York office of the FBI. If successfully executed America 'would be gripped with fear'. This conspiracy was called the 'Landmark Conspiracy'.

The FBI got Salem to do more than intelligence collection. He agreed to wear a body recorder to capture statements of the suspects from the members of the targeted terrorist cell. Siddiq Ali confided to Salem that he had friends in Sudanese embassy and safe houses for him in Sudan to hide after the proposed attack.

On Salem's request Siddiq Ali provided a safe-house as arranged by the FBI which was equipped with video and sound recorders. The safe house was required for bomb making.

On May 21, 1993 El-Gabrowny took Siddiq Ali and Salem to meet Nosair in jail. Nosair was apprised of the plot. He was delighted and suggested some additional acts like kidnapping Richard Nixon and Henry Kissinger for ransom for his own release. There were also plans to kill 'political figures sympathetic to Israel'. This got leaked to the press, but Salem survived from being exposed. The conspirators did not suspect him as a plant of FBI.

When the plotters were ready, the FBI decided to act. The FBI had the duplicate key of the safe house where bomb making was in progress. On 24 June 1993, the safe house was raided by FBI by making a dramatic entry. Siddiq Ali was apprehended. He had no time to react as the entry of the FBI team was prompt and sudden.

Acting fast on the basis of evidence, oral and documentary, the US prosecutors lined up five defendants for 'waging a war of urban terrorism'. In the meantime, the trial of WTC attack ended against four dependants convicting Salameh, Nidal Ayyad, Abouhalima and Ahmad Ajaj to 240 years prison sentence. Ramzi Yousef and Ahmad

Yassin were still at large as they managed to escape from USA.

Ramzi Yousef

The world attention was focused on Ramzi Yousef. He was evading apprehension. He did not sit idle either. He was a highly motivated operator for worldwide jihad who soon organised terrorist attacks in Southeast Asia after WTC attack. He concentrated his operations from the Philippines.

On 11 December 1994, after 10 months of WTC attack, Ramzi Yousef traveling with an Italian passport declaring himself as Armaldo Forlani managed to dodge the X-ray machine at Manila airport. He was carrying nitro glycerin in a contact lens case and nine volt batteries in the heels of each of his shoes. The same trick was used by Richard Reid when he concealed explosives in heels of his shoe. Yousef was traveling on the Philippines Airlines 434 flight. He disembarked at Cebu's airport. Before disembarking, Yousef assembled the bomb device in the toilet of the plane. He used Casio watch as a timer. He managed to conceal the small bomb device in the pouch of his jacket and left it under his seat undetected by the cabin crew or by passengers. It exploded after two hours on way to Tokyo. The impact killed the passenger Hiraki Ikegani (24) an engineer who occupied Yousef's vacant seat. The impact created a hole in the fuelage and ruptured the cables that controlled the wings of the aircraft. It was a trial run before the real thing to happen in future. This was not lost to those who were tracking Yousef.

He reportedly moved to Bangkok to blast the Israeli Embassy on 11 March 1994. The disaster was prevented providentially as small truck loaded with explosives met with an accident and the driver panicked and fled.

He came back to Pakistan a few months after and organised an attack on a Shia shrine Imam Reza inside Iran on June 20. In this bomb explosion 26 persons were killed and injuring several others. Al Qaeda was all a Sunni outfit and was anti Shia.

The FBI was not able to reach out to contacts for apprehension of Yousef. The FBI man for Pakistan was based in Hong Kong, a far away place. He was also overseeing activities in Delhi. The CIA was proving ineffective in intelligence collection on Yousef. Apparently the ISI under Lt. Gen. Hamid Gul and his successor Lt. Gen Javed Nasir were very close to hardcore Islamists/jihadis in Pakistan. Obviously they would not share intelligence with the FBI or CIA on Yousef.

Ramzi Yousef was located in the summer of 1994 on the island of Basilan, a part of the Philippines, dominated by a sizeable Muslim population. Wherever the Muslims are in majority in a part of a country, they seek separation from the motherland on the basis of the two nation-theories. So is the case in the Philippines. Abu Sayyaf group, an offshoot of Afghan jihad, was aligned with Al-Qaeda. Yousef reportedly trained the locals in the use of sophisticated explosives. In the later part of 1994 Yousef shifted to Manila to join up with his uncle Khalid Sheikh Mohammed who was a high up in the military wing of Al-Qaeda. Mohammed wired about $600 into account of Salameh few months before WTC attack. In Manila two other Al-Qaeda operatives Abdul Hakim Murad and Amin-Shah joined Yousef to set up a cell in South East Asia.

A plot was hatched to blow up by hijacking 12 international flights simultaneously to create a terrible impact in the minds of people living under the shadow of liberal democracies. Yousef decided to prepare powerful micro-bombs to evade security checks. The earlier trial test of a small bomb placed on a flight to Tokyo did not produce enough damage and casualties. The new bomb was tested on ground in November 1994 in a generator room underneath a Manila shopping complex, causing a small fire and little damage. Again on December 1, 1994 another similar device placed under a seat in a theatre caused insignificant damage.

Yousef was hatching other plots also. Assassination plans were made to attack Bill Clinton when he was to visit Manila in November. It was given up because of tight security arrangements. The next plot was to kill Pope John Paul during his Manila visit in January 1995 considering him as a soft target. For this, he took an apartment in Manila for a month in early December 1994 using a false name. The apartment was facing the route to be covered by the Pope. It was to be suicide bombing in the style of a fidayeen attack. He was to be dressed in the attire of a Christian priest. Hakim Murad, a Pakistani being a pilot, an aerial attack on the Pope mobile was also thought of, but scrapped when he came to know that the airspace over Manila would remain suspended during the journey of the Pope.

Yousef's jihadi imagination was stretched to make an aerial attack of the CIA headquarters at Langley by hijacking a commercial plane and crashing the same into a landmark in Washington. All these were revealed by Murad during his interrogation.

Due to bad luck on January 6, 1995, Yousef and Murad faced an accidental fire in the apartment while making bombs in Manila. They hurriedly vacated the apartment leaving behind enough evidence of their evil designs. Yousef's laptop contained files on proposed attacks. Murad, after departure of the firefighters, embarked on a mission to retrieve the incriminating items from the apartment. He was apprehended by the police. The search of the apartment yielded a variety of recoveries like pipe bombs, bomb making materials explosives and explosive chemicals, a photo of the Pope, laptop computer and conspiracy plots were stored in the computer. 12 civil airliners were to be attacked on 12 January 1995. Murad initially identified himself as Yousef before the police to provide enough time to genuine Yousef to escape from Manila.

The CIA was again proving ineffective in tracking Yousef. After the Afghan jihad many competent officers left the CIA. There was growing culture of 'risk aversion' which prevented recruitment of good informers. Partly this culture grew out of a working relationship with the ISI during the Afghan jihad. The ISI did not allow the CIA to operate the Afghan jihad. That task was to be performed by the ISI. The intelligence inputs of the CIA were mostly wrong and to arrange rechecking was impossible due to arrangements between the CIA and the FBI. There was lack of coordination between them.

The CIA, over the years, lost its capacity to build up human intelligence. They preferred to obtain information from other country agencies. In the cold war era the CIA got bad reputation for unethical practices ranging from assassination, overthrow of elected governments and sustaining military dictators. The bright boys preferred to opt for other occupations. As a result the CIA did not anticipate the fall of Shah of Iran's regime in 1979. It was just focused on Soviet Union, which in reality was crumbling due to its internal contradictions. There was total lack of understanding of threats posed by the Islamic fundamentalist groups. The marriage of convenience worked out during the Afghan jihad proved short-lived. This encouraged the fundamentalists to include America as the target and propagate a war on America. The army of clerics like Abdulla Azzam, Sheikh Abdel Rehman was freely allowed to preach hatred against the USA from US soil even during Afghan jihad period. The CIA's dependence on the ISI fighting the Soviets strengthened the capability of the ISI which soon started promoting international Islamic jihad. India's concerns were completely ignored. India was under terrorist attacks from 1989. Afghanistan was kept by the US within the domain of Pakistan. The Pakistanis only favoured Wahhabi fundamentalists to operate in Afghanistan. Tajiks, Uzbeks, Hazaras and Shias of Afghanistan were left out in the 'strategic depth' concept of Pakistan army. Even the President of the US found no time for daily briefing by the CIA. It soon became a bureaucratic organization with 'paper pushers'.

Ramzi Yousef was on the wanted list of the FBI and a reward of $2 million was announced for his apprehension. This was printed on the match boxes and distributed throughout Pakistan. This had no effect on Ramzi Yousef who was moving around the world with ease. He had obtained a new passport from a Pakistani consulate on his declaration of having lost the original passport. This trick is used by terrorists to erase the past travel records. The US investigators soon developed a profile of Yousef on the basis of his application to Pakistani consulate. He traveled to Karachi and melt in the mountainous region of Baluchistan. In Pakistan his 'reputation soured' high and some hardliners engaged him to assassinate Benazir Bhutto, who was then emerging as a political leader to become prime minister again. Benazir admitted about this plot openly. He was injured badly and was hospitalized in Pakistan. All these could not have gone undetected by the ISI as it has presence in all the districts of Pakistan. He was not arrested or questioned by the Pakistani intelligence agencies for obvious reasons.

Coming back to Ramzi Yousef story it may be recalled that the Philippines police made arrest of Murad while Wali Khan, Amin Shah and Yousef returned to Pakistan. Yousef drew up plans to kidnap the Philippine ambassador for release of Murad in association with Istiaque Parker, who reportedly revealed the plan to US embassy in Islamabad. He provided Yousef's whereabouts. On February 7, 1995 he was picked up by a joint team of Americans and Pakistanis from a Su Cas a guest house (said to be Osama bin Laden's safe house) on the outskirts of Islamabad. Islamabad had developed an operational plan not to act till goaded. On its own it refuses to act. Yousef's arrest was because of FBI/CIA'S specific intelligence. Yousef was airlifted to New York. While crossing over the New York, Yousef said the twin towers would not stand there in future. The point he made was that once a target was selected by Al Qaeda, several attempts would be made to attack the target. This assessment seems to be correct. The idea of hijacking civilian planes in 1994 in Manila was not given up. The 9/11 attacks was hatched and executed by the same man Khalid Skeikh Mohammed who gave the idea of Manila attack. The man behind 9/11 was Khalid Sheikh Mohammed. Now he is widely known in several reports as KSM. He too was picked up from Rawalpindi on US intelligence. He was handed over to US without so-called proof of his involvement. This procedure was adopted in many such arrests. For India a different standard is applied. Even Dawood Ibrahim is not being handed over as he is not traceable in Pakistan, when the whole world knows that he is in Pakistan and that he is an Indian citizen. It makes no difference to Pakistan even when he is listed as terrorist financier by the UN or by the US.

Ramzi Yousef faced a court trial for WTC 1993 blast. He was convicted for life long prison term. How could Ramzi Yousef make several trips to all parts of the world which meant a huge expenditure? The world has not been told about the result of world-wide financial investigation of expenditure incurred on Ramzi Yousef's journeys and stays in several places. Such investigations would have linked him to some financiers to promote international terrorism. How did he manage to enter Pakistan and stay undetected? After all there was international hunt for him. His nexus with the ISI has not been exposed. Who prevented full enquiry into his entire Al-Qaeda career and bring out all the facts about him.

1996 Khobar Tower attack, Saudi Arabia

The US used Khobar Tower buildings located near Dhahran, Saudi Arabia. A White Chevrolet Caprice car was found by the US Air Force Observation Centre entering into a parking slot just adjacent to the compound. The car was followed by a large tanker truck driving slowly along the edge of the lot. Two men leaped out of the truck cab and leaped into waiting caprice and just roared away. The sergeant watching the drama radioed a message to his headquarter and rushed down the floors pounding doors shouting "get out, get out". He could reach up to the 7th floor when the tanker blasted with devastating effect, creating a crater of 26 meter and 11 meter deep. The shock wave blew up windows and pulverized reinforced concrete, all of them became burning projectiles. 19 US airmen were killed and more than 50 were hospitalized.

Everyone was expecting as in November 1995 a similar bomb blast attack at US-run training centre in Riyadh, Capital city of Saudi Arabia. More than 40 FBI agents were dispatched to work with the Saudis as they did in last November 1995 attack.

When four young suspects were apprehended, the Saudis needed no help from the FBI. The FBI could not interrogate the suspects "to learn about their organization, contacts, backers and bosses". The four were publicly beheaded on May 13, 1996. The Saudis refusal to cooperate with the FBI was inexplicable. May be it was to hide facts. 'We have no leads whatsoever' said an American spokesman.[11] It was, however, admitted that many opponents of the royal family were drawn from the thousands of devout who fought in Afghanistan along with the CIA-ISI combine's proxy war (1979-89).

To mislead the world, UK based Islamic militant Mohammed

---

11   *Time*, July 8, 1996.

Massari said that Islamic extremist groups were splintered in groups with five, ten or more people.[12] The bodies of US Airmen were flown back to USA along with 58th Fighter Squadron who lived in the building. General Burt Anderson to play down the Islamic onslaught said: "I can tell you my experience in Saudi Arabia. We are welcome. We are welcome as friends. We are welcome as allies".[13]

Southeast Asia

The Al-Qaeda in the US network spread out from Brooklyn from where Al-Kifah was functioning. It covered several states of the US and in such areas where substantial Muslim population was present. More than 40 centers were identified in Western Europe.

In UK, Al-Qaeda had no problem to function. All fugitives from law took asylum in UK. In this category Abu Hamza al-Misri, Khalid al-Fawaz, Yerser al-Siri, Abu Qatada could be included. Many of them were sentenced by their jurisdictional courts with sentences ranging from death to life. UK is known for sheltering all terrorists of all types under a ground rule that no UK law should be violated. Strangely many of them were even given UK citizenship.

Abu Sayyaf emerged in the Philippines to demand a division of the country for establishment of an Islamic state in Southern Philippines. Moro Islamic Liberation Front was formed under Hashim Salamat, a veteran of Afghan jihad, an ally of Osama and fought for separate homeland for Muslims in the Philippines. Their activities were under the supervision of Osama's brother-in-law who was stationed in the Philippines.

Hambali acted as Al-Qaeda's point man in Southeast Asia with a vision to create an Islamic state in South-East Asia by curving out areas from the Philippines, Thailand, together with Indonesia and Malaysia and other areas of Southeast Asia. Such a state was to be called Daulah Islamiah Rayer as one Islamic state based on one religion of Islam with population of 268 million with high growth rate potential. Hambali's destructive skill remained undetected for

---

12 ibid, p 25.

13 ibid, p 26.

more than a decade.

Al Qaeda Cells were in Germany, Spain, Belgium, Chechnya and many hotspots of the world. Most of them remained undetected till 9/11. Some were known but were allowed to operate. Germany, after Nazi rule, wanted to flaunt its liberal democratic views. Germany did not wish to be seen as an oppressive regime.

Global network acted secretly with cutout arrangements. In Somalia the hand of Osama was not found initially till he himself disclosed the facts. He considered the Americans as 'Paper Tigers' when the marine troops were withdrawn after bringing down a US helicopter in 1993 and bodies of killed soldiers were dragged and displayed.

Anti-Americanism in the Muslim world was never taken seriously. Each terrorist act was treated as individual acts of violence. When Kanhane, a Jewish leader was killed in a hotel by Salameh, the case was hurriedly closed treating it as a case of an individual act. A plethora of records were seized but were not analyzed under the orders of the senior officers. This mistake proved too costly. The 1993 tower truck bomb attack in New York could have been prevented if the case documents of Kanhane assassination were fully analyzed and follow up action taken. Since the field officers were aware of the bigger conspiracy, they, however, kept surveillance. As soon as the tower attack was staged in 1993 it took no time for the FBI to nab the culprits as most of them were on the radar screen of the New York unit of the FBI. The FBI had good human intelligence (humint) in USA and that proved useful.

India too faced a serious problem of Al-Qaeda operations. It provided training facilities to Punjab and Northeast outfits. Many of them were trained and sent back for action. Here the ISI played the role of a coordinator. More foreigners were found involved in terrorism in J&K and elsewhere. In India Al-Qaeda functioned through the ISI and Jihadi outfits which are organically linked to Al Qaeda.

Fazlur Rehman of JUI (P) was a close ally of Osama. Secretary of JUI (F) signed up the last Fatwa issued by Al-Qaeda in 1998. The

Taliban-Al Qaeda and a brigade of the Pakistan Army acted in tandem to control Afghanistan. Harkat ul-Mujahideen was an affiliate of Al-Qaeda and the Taliban. It was this outfit that played havoc in J&K in early nineties by inducting foreign jihadis in J&K. Many of them were killed or captured. In 1994 and 1995 kidnappings of foreigners from Delhi and Pahalgam in Kashmir were acts of Harkat ul-Mujahideen. These kidnappings were executed to get Maulana Masood Azhar of HuM released from Indian jail. The Delhi kidnappings could be solved quickly by a brave police officer of UP, Dhrub Lal Yadav who rescued British captives from Saharanpur, a district of UP. The information was provided by Omar Sheikh when he was captured by Dhrub Lal Yadav. This great London School of Economics dropout was literally trembling before Yadav. When Dhrub Lal interviewed Omar Sheikh, he was literally crying and trembling. In the process of rescue Dhrub Lal was killed as he made the mistake by knocking the door of the house where the hostages were kept. There were hardly any Indian commandos in para-military forces in those days. They could have done a better job. Dhrub Lal was honoured by Her Majesty's Government. There is a park in Ghaziabad district of the state of UP in the name of Dhrub Lal Yadav. The author had the opportunity to witness acts of bravery of this officer on many occasions. He earned a number of the highest bravery awards from the Government of India for his daring acts.

The case of Kashmir kidnapping of six foreigners in 1995 from Pahalgam could not be solved as there was a genuine fear of killing of kidnappers. There was lack of real time intelligence also. The Huriyat Conference, in the face of adverse world opinion, was asked to condemn the act. Fazlur Rehman of JUI [F] visited India for negotiation, but the government wisely decided not to yield. One kidnapper escaped, another was beheaded. There was shock wave in the world. Pakistan was under pressure to act. The ISI could have ordered for the rescue of the hostages. After all the Al Faran, which claimed responsibility, was a smoke screen. It was Harkat ul-Ansar the previous name of Harkat-ul-Mujahideen which perpetrated the act. Foreign elements and Harkat were blamed for killing all the hostages and their bodies could not be recovered till date. This case and other cases have been discussed in details in Manoj Joshi's book '*The Last Rebellion*'.

When Kunduz was captured in 1998 by the Taliban-Al Qaeda-ISI combine, maps were displayed in the city squares of Kunduz. In those maps, future targets of Islamic jihad included India, Iran, Central Asian countries and Xingjian of China, USA and Israel.

Maulana Masood Azhar was the secretary general of Herkat ul-Ansar, who was released in 1999 by Indian government after a long negotiation with 5 hijackers of IC 814. The outfit that organised the hijacking of IC 814 from Nepal to Kandahar was Herkat ul-Mujahideen. A brother of Azhar was a part of the hijacking team as revealed to BBC by Muttawakil who was then the foreign minister of the Taliban regime.

Azhar immediately after his release reached Binori mosque of Karachi and declared jihad against India and the USA. He announced the formation of his outfit Jaish-e-Mohammed. Most of the cadre came from Harkat ul-Mujahideen. There were in-fights between Jaish & Harkat on the question of division of assets. This was partly solved by Osama bin Laden who provided Jaish-e-Mohammed with sufficient fund. Azhar also met Osama in Afghanistan for blessing and fund. Azhar was with Osama during his stay in Sudan.

All the jihadi outfits operating in India including Jammu and Kashmir were organically linked to Al-Qaeda ideologically and operationally. These have been even brought out in the press reports of Pakistani journalists. There is nothing hidden about it.

Organisational Structure of Al-Qaeda

Al-Qaeda has pyramidal structure. The same is graphically shown below:

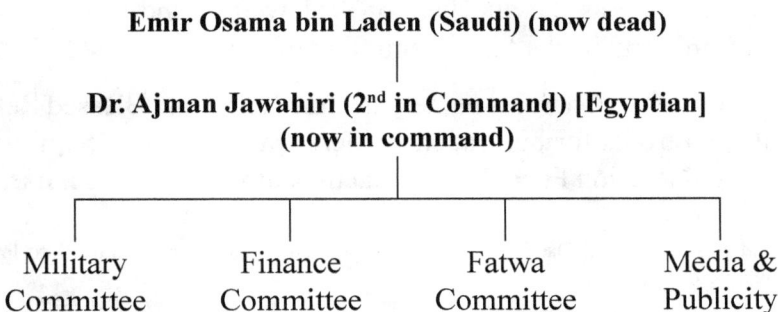

Emir Osama bin Laden (Saudi) (now dead)

|

Dr. Ajman Jawahiri (2nd in Command) [Egyptian] (now in command)

|

| Military Committee | Finance Committee | Fatwa Committee | Media & Publicity |

Military Committee

Military Committee was initially headed by Al Banshiri. He was drowned in Lake Victoria, Kenya in 1995. He was replaced by Mohammad Atef, an ex-police officer of Egypt. Under Osama's guidance he would conceive and organise major plots to attack US and Western interests. He would supervise training and recruitment. Each plan of attack was to be approved by him as revealed from 'The Singapore Government White Paper'. He was aided by Khaled Seikh Mohammed. [KSM as he is called in US reports]

Atef was also helped by 1973 born Abu Zubaidah. He was the rising star and as per some reports he was groomed to take over the charge of the military committee as Atef (1944 born) was growing old. Abu Zubaidah was relatively young to undertake the hard work of the military committee. He was being groomed for a big future role.

Most of attackers involving planning of 9/11 were captured from Pakistan mostly on US intelligence and handed to US authorities without completing legal formalities. Mohd Atef was reportedly killed in US led coalition strike in Kabul on 14 November 2001.[14]

Finance Committee

The task of this committee was for raising of funds from various business and charitable sources. Money was managed well before any organised attack. Money came from hostage taking, contributors, profits from front companies and Saudi Charitable units. Both banking and Hawala routes were utilised profitably to reach out money without keeping any paper trail. Some paper trails are unavoidable as the attackers of 9/11 were found to have used Credit Cards and banks for transmission of money.

Two Islamic Charities namely Islamic Relief and Blessed Relief are alleged fronts for bin Laden.[15] There was transfer of $3 million from Saudi Pension Fund through Saudi National Commercial Bank

---

14   Understanding of Al Qaeda, Mohammad-Mahmoud Ould Mohamedou, Pluto Press, 2007, p 56.

15   Herald Special, January 2000.

and the Chairman of the Bank, Khalid bin Mahfuz was arrested. This happened in 1999.

Fatwa Committee

In Islam Fatwas can be issued by religious clerics. Osama was not competent to issue Fatwas as he had no religious training. Three Fatwas were issued in August 1996, 1997 and lastly in February 1998. Each Fatwa (religious decree), gave legitimacy to lethal attacks in different areas of the world. The 1997 fatwa was to motivate suicide fighters. On February 23, 1998, the final call for 'Jihad against the Jews and Crusaders' was issued with wide publicity. This was signed by al-Zawahiri, leader of the Egyptian jihad, Taha, leader of the Islamic group of Egypt, Shayakh Mir Hamzah, Secretary of the Jamait ul-Ulema-e-Pakistan (JUI) and one Fazlur Rehman, said to be a leader of the jihad movement of Bangladesh. This was a declaration of war on Crusaders (America) and Israel. To strengthen the call of jihad, the Afghan clerics were not far behind. A fatwa was issued under the signature of Sheikh Ahmad Azzam in April 1998.[16]

The formation of The Islamic Front for Jihad against the Crusaders and Jews was a final declaration of a global war. As it was backed by a Fatwa it becomes obligatory for believers to obey the same by waging jihad. The groups that joined were the Jamat-ul-jihad of Egypt headed by Dr. Al-Zawahiri, another Egyptian group led Abu Asim, assumed name of a son of Sheikh Omer Abdur Rehman jailed in US, and two other sons of Rehman. The third Egyptian group was led by Islam Bolo, a brother of Khalid Islam Bolo, one of the assassins of President of Egypt, Sadat.

The Pakistan-Afghan groups are Harkat-ul-Mujahideen and its splinter groups. The Markaz Dawa-ul-Irshad led by Hafiz Mohammed Saeed and his fighting outfit Lashker-e-Toiba. The Sipah-e-Sahaba of Pakistan, an extremist group of Pakistan who are notorious for killing Shias as they consider them as non-Muslims remained associated with Al Qaeda and Taliban.

Harkat-ul-jihad-al-Islami (HUJI) composed of people from many Arab countries. It played a big part in Afghan jihad. HUJI

---

16 Rohan Gunnaratne, *Inside Al Qaeda*, p 47.

based in Bangladesh is quite active with Bangladeshi elements in it.

The jihadis groups active in South East Asia and Central Asia are also part of this front. It may be mentioned that Front's ideology is shared by many named and unnamed groups and individuals.

Media and publicity

Media and Publicity was mostly carried out from Peshawar. This was managed by Al-Zawahiri as he is fluent in English. On major issues of denial and assertion his services were utilised. The powerful London office of Al-Qaeda was managed by 'an old Saudi friend and purported businessman named Khaled al-Fawwz' under the name Advice and Reformation Committee for peaceful reform of the Saudi government.[17] The US had indicted al-Fawwaz as a terrorist in 1998 and his extradition was demanded by the USA. This Publicity department of Al Qaeda was most effective by using modern communication technology with global reach. The statements issued by Al Qaeda, bin Laden, Al Zawahiri were power tools to draw in grass root jihadis or religious minded Muslims into the fold of violent activism. In the absence of these modern day media facilities bin Laden would have been a hero for a mere thousand tribesmen in the Arab World. Modern technology had thus provided a big audience to bin Laden and Al Qaeda.

Strategy

Vertical leadership has been explained. Vertical leadership apart, the horizontal bases have been built up over the years. They were manned by very trusted Lieutenants. They had to go through a screening process. For example, for plotting of the East African twin Embassy blast the principal actor was sent years in advance to create the base.

Some plots of attacks were 'sub-contracted' to use the words of Rohan Gunaratne. The planning was left to affiliates while manpower and money would be provided by Al Qaeda. In this category would fall GIA (Algeria), Islamic Movement of Uzbekistan

---

17 John Miller, Michael Stone, Chris Mitchell, The Cell, Hyperion, New York, 2002, p263.

(IMU), Abu Sayyaf, MILF (Philippines), Jemaah Islamia in South-East Asia under the overall leadership of elusive Hambali. Indian Al Qaeda operation was given to Al Badr, Harkat-ul-Mujahideen, Jaish-e-Mohammed and Lashker-e-Toiba, all organically linked to Al-Qaeda and ISI as evidence would suggest.

O55 brigade was under the full operational control of Al-Qaeda. This brigade was utilised to back up the Taliban militia, which always remained under the control of ISI. The brigade provided the muscle power to Al-Qaeda in Afghanistan and men and officers were drawn from Saudi Arabia and Egypt. Osama, it would appear never trusted Jihadis of other nationalities, may be a hangover of his tribal culture. The brigade was fully financed by Al-Qaeda.

Defence analyst Ashok Mehta said in 2000, 11 corps of the Pakistan Army in Peshawar was dedicated to Afghanistan. It was commanded by Lt. Gen. Said ul-Zafar. His field commanders were Rashid, Shamim and Khanzada. The last two were drawn from the ISI. A Pakistani brigade of 5,000 was helping 50,000 Taliban Militia.[18] This relationship sustained both the Taliban and the Al-Qaeda.

Al Qaeda's operation cells were like commandos or like the Special Delta Forces of the US. After all Al-Qaeda had the facility of long US training. There were mobile strike forces operating during the Afghan jihad (1979-89). The ISI developed mobile training units. The same tactics were adopted by Al-Qaeda. Ali Mohammad, for example, trained jihadis by moving from one country to another and organised protection of Osama in Sudan while serving the US Special Services. This was in the knowledge of many in the US army, but did not raise any alarm.

Al-Qaeda fighting men had one desire to die as a martyr and thereafter reach heaven to have earthly pleasures. During the Afghan jihad a western journalist observed how the jihadis would pitch tents on an open land to attract Soviet bombardment and die as martyrs. People wept if they were not killed by bombs and bullets. Nowhere in the world this type of motivation is available.

---

18 *The Pioneer*, Ashok Mehta, November 25, 2000.

Osama knew how to utilise religious fervor to his benefit. Often he was seen riding on a white horse as was the practice of Prophet Mohammed during his war campaigns. He copied the Prophet in dress and style. This impressed the jihadis.

Al-Qaeda's specific operations

Al-Qaeda, fighting an international covert war with unconventional weapons, devised its own method and style of functioning. Its front offices all-over the world had names other than Al-Qaeda. This was necessary to conceal its operational needs. The operational tasks were largely assigned to shadowy characters that were highly secretive. Many of them did not keep beards and move about in western attire to avoid attraction of the public and police.

For specific operations, sleepers would be planted in the targeted country years in advance, as was found in the Kenya bombing in 1998 or bombing of USS Cole in 2000. The mobile strike team would appear on the scene just a week or two before the actual attack. Before all that, target would be surveyed by a separate team preferably by video as was the case in aborted attempt in Singapore 2001-02. The maps and videos would be shown to the top Al-Qaeda leadership for final clearance of the operation. The video recordings of targeted sites in Singapore were found in Afghanistan by the US forces. Normally Al-Qaeda would undertake one major operation a year. Major events would bear this out. The major attacks on US and Indian interests are given below.

1993	Bombing of the Twin Towers in New York.
1993	Failed plans to attack landmarks in New York.
1995	Manila plan to kill President Clinton, the Pope John Paul II and planning of hijacking and blasting of 11 US airliner's planes.
1995	Attack on US aided Saudi National Guard Training Centre killing seven, including five American soldiers.

1996	Khobar Tower blast, Saudi Arabia, killing nineteen US soldiers.
1998	Bombing of Twin US Embassies in Nairobi and Dar-es Salaam in East Africa, killing 242 people.
1999	Hijacking of Indian Airlines plane by Harkat ul-Mujahideen.
2000	Bombing of USS Cole, off the coast of Aden, Yemen, killing 17 US sailors.
2000	Millennium attacks in Jordan, USA and Paris could not be carried as the operatives were arrested.
2001	Attack on Twin towers and Pentagon on 9 September, 2001, killing 3000 people.
2001	October 1, attack of the Srinagar Assembly.
2001	December 13 attack on Indian Parliament by Jaish e-Mohammad affiliated to Al Qaeda to kill maximum Indian Political leadership.
2001-02	Singapore attacks were foiled by timely action.
2002	A truck bomb exploded on Jewish church in Tunisia.
2002	Blast in front of Sheraton Hotel, Karachi, killing 14 out of which were 11 French engineers.
2002	Bomb explodes in front of US consulates office, Karachi killing 12 people.
2002	Bali Bombings in night club, Indonesia, killing 202 people mostly Australians.
2003	Housing complex for American and UK staff, Riyadh, Saudi Arabia, killing 39 people.
2012	Mumbai attacks by LeT and ISI combine killing more than 166 people and injuring 600.

Indian cases are illustrative and not exhaustive and have been added to show that the jihadi outfits of Pakistan are all organically linked to Al-Qaeda and the ISI. The strategy was to divert attention from Pakistan to India and giving an excuse to Pakistan of its inability to fight on two fronts. These also served to satisfy the jihadis that their cause has not been abandoned.

Al Qaeda fighting manuals

Al Qaeda's jihad manuals seized in Jordan and UK were voluminous. The manuals seized in Jordan were in eleven volumes. They were dedicated to Dr Abdullah Azzam, and Osama bin Laden. There manuals were similar to US manuals prepared for Afghan jihad and handed over to ISI for training purposes. Therefore, the Al Qaeda absorbed the ideas of guerrilla warfare from the Afghan jihad period. The CIA did incalculable damage by providing know-how to the jihadi outfits and the ISI which was responsible for training of Jihadis to fight against the Soviet troops.

Funding for specific operations

Al Qaeda as an establishment had to run the office in Afghanistan and Pakistan. The Taliban were provided with funds as grants from Osama. Maintaining O55 brigade was also costly. The telecommunication setup was worldwide and expensive. Travel expenses of operatives had to be paid. Some estimates have been made to know the extent of normal spending by Al Qaeda. This could have been more than $100 million a year.

For specific operations, a lot of money had to be spent on journeys, stay in hotels, telephone and internet. The key operatives used to be briefed in Pakistan and Afghanistan. The Singapore government's White Paper reveals some such startling facts. Hambali Al-Qaeda's points man in South East Asia, used to visit Karachi to hold briefing sessions with Al Qaeda leadership. This could not happen without the knowledge of the administration and all powerful ISI. After all visas are issued under the control of the government of Pakistan.

Al Qaeda was not a paperless organization as was imagined by many. Facts now reveal that files used to be maintained on operatives with sufficient background materials. Osama used to study such files very carefully. Strike teams used to be selected after in depth study of material on them.

For specific operations special funds used to be raised. The ISI and Al Qaeda operatives were, therefore, allowed to indulge in counterfeiting of currency, smuggling, thefts, frauds specially Credit Card frauds. These have been well documented now. Fake Indian currency of high value is being printed in Pakistan and being pumped into India on a large scale. These are un-Islamic acts but are necessary to lighten the financial burden of Al Qaeda and the ISI.

There are possible links between major kidnappings in India and international terrorist funding. Partha Pratim Burman, a Kolkata based business tycoon was abducted from Calcutta (Kolkata) by Aftab Ansari gang in July 2001. Aftab Ansari and Omar Sheikh came to know each other in Indian prison in 1994. Aftab shifted to Dubai/Pakistan. It is said that for release of Partha Pratim Burman a huge ransom had to be paid and the ransom money reached Aftab by Hawala route. He reportedly gave a substantial amount out of this money to Omar Sheikh and Omar Sheikh reportedly wired $1,00,000 to Mohammad Atta of 9/11 fame. Omar Sheikh was being handled by the ISI. It is now for the US investigators to establish if there were links between Aftab Ansari, Omar Sheikh and transmission of $1,00,000 to Mohammad Atta the team leader of 9/11 attack. This sharing of information is necessary if not done already. It should be made public. Aftab Ansari previously kidnapped Anand Aggarwal, a rich businessman from Mumbai who reportedly paid Rs 22 Crore as ransom. Aftab was cultivated by the ISI and was provided with a false passport. Aftab's connections with the ISI were found in the case of arms smuggling cases in Gujarat. The CBI too intercepted a cache of arms from Gujarat and Haryana states of India where Aftab was found involved.[19] On international pressure the UAE dispatched him to India. He is in Indian jail for trial.

In a similar manner a Pakistani operator assuming a false name Ravi Choudhry managed to kidnap five very rich diamond merchants from Delhi before the New York Twin Tower blast in 1993 and Bombay blasts that happened after a month. The super rich diamond

19 *Hindu*, 25/1/2002.

merchants were released presumably after payment of heavy ransom abroad. Some of these diamond merchants had offices in Europe like Amsterdam. The Pakistani operator's identity was known to Pakistani authorities. The Pakistani ISI operator made the mistake by providing transport in Delhi to some prominent Pakistani politicians who were on way to Ajmer Sharif where a shrine of Sufi saint exists. As was expected the Pakistani authorities did not carry out their investigation. Obviously, this was not possible as the ISI was tasked to raise money for operational purposes. This investigation can now be taken up again by establishing the identity of Ravi Choudhry jointly by US and India. There are indications that Ravi Choudhry had US connections and if the US is genuinely interested to find out how money was provided for 1993 WTC attack on the US soil, this case should not be left unattended. The leads are still available so are the persons in Pakistan who can identify the operator. The case is still alive as will be evident from a press advertisement issued by the CBI in the month of January 2009.

Al Qaeda had support bases all over the world. They generated and kept money in banking system in various names. Reliable third persons were available to hold such money till the money was required for use. The results of the money trail investigations are yet to be made public. This money trail investigations are not taken up seriously as it is worldwide.

Hawala

Hawala route for transfer of money from country to country is yet to be understood by the US and Western countries. These channels work on faith and trust. There is no physical transfer of money. Money collected in dollar terms, for example, from US locals will remain in USA, but the payees will be paid in another country in their currencies. The payee's agent in another country also obtains money from payers to be paid to payees in US. A simple message would be sent to US agent to deliver dollars to US payees. Hawala dealers obtain commission from each deal.

India has detected several Hawala payments to militants in India through this route. Some detected cases ended in conviction from courts. In an Interpol Conference in Paris, held in 1989, the Indian delegate did bring this to the notice of the Western countries and the USA. The USA and the Western countries then termed these as mere 'fiscal offences' and they were unable to deal with the system in the absence of their domestic laws. This is now the opportune time to deal with this problem internationally. This loophole needs to the plugged or else the terrorists will continue to use this route for terrorist funding and operations. It is still happening in India in a clandestine manner and possibly rather openly from the Western world. For smashing Hawala network international cooperation is necessary as it is two-way traffic.

There is a difficulty in Western world, USA and other countries to find out the names of donors for charities and end use of such money. India has a system of monitoring such open donations. The Foreign Contribution Regulation Act provides mechanism to monitor such contributions as such contributions need to be intimated to a government agency. To circumvent this, money is received by Hawala route. All the countries have to device ways and means to tackle this problem. Each country has to introduce a reporting system to keep track of NGOs who receive money or donate money.

Initially, the USA blocked the assets of 26 entities and individuals. Mistakenly or deliberately Herkat ul-mujahideen was shown as a Kashmiri organization when the fact is that it is purely a Pakistani organization. Al Badr, Jaish-e-Mohammed, Lashkar-e-Taiba did not figure in the first list. All these are Pakistan based terrorist organizations with worldwide operation. Al Rashid Trust, which was engaged in terrorist funding, appeared in the first list. It remained under the control of Maulana Masood Azhar, who is the Emir of Jaish-e-Mohammed. It shows how careless was the US authorities in compiling terrorist list. Incidentally, it was reported in press that Gen Parvez Musharraf was the patron of Al Rashid Trust. This did not embarrass him either. Nothing seems to embarrass Pakistani establishment.

Rohan Gunnaratne in his book on Al Qaeda has correctly identified how the Saudi funded International Islamic Relief

Organization (IIRO) was used for funding Al Qaeda in the Philippines, Tanzania, Georgia. He did not mention IIRO's Pakistan chapter had been used for the same purpose. Abu Nasir, a Bangladeshi was initially working with IIRO Pakistan before switching over to the ISI and Lashker-e-Taiba. IIRO was a part of the World Muslim League, a Saudi based organization.

Business and financial committee of Al Qaeda consisted of professionals and bankers to manage Al Qaeda funds across the world. For flow of fund legitimate institutions were built-up, charities and NGOs were infiltrated and funds diverted for Al Qaeda use.

In the management of finance of Al Qaeda the names of businessmen like Sheikh Muhammad Hussain al-Amadi, Zein –al-Abedin (Abu Zubaidah) and Karachi-UAE based Saudi born Mustafa Ahmed have surfaced. Mustafa Ahmed is linked to financing 9/11 operation. He escaped to Pakistan just before 9/11. He is said to be Omar Sheik as revealed by Henry Levy, the authour of the book '*Who Killed Daniel Pearl*'.

Al Qaeda's fund spending was lavish. WTC [1993] bomber Muhammad Salameh had to reclaim his $400 deposit from Ryder International in order to buy a plane ticket to fly out of USA or plan another attack. Ramzi Yousef told the FBI that he needed more money for tower blast in 1993.

Ahmed Ressam arrested in December 1999 on USA-Canada border was found involved in Credit Card fraud or petty thefts and robbery to raise money for Al Qaeda operation in the US. The millennium team for attacks was mostly financed by bank robberies, burglaries and forging of cheques. In the eyes Allah such crimes were pardonable.

It is said that 9/11 did cost $5,00,000 and unspent money was remitted back to UAE. Where money was required, they spent, like high value plane tickets purchased for 9/11 operation as they needed to sit near the cockpit.

Does Al Qaeda represent political aspirations of the Muslims?

In a sense it does. The Muslims with fanatical views have an open agenda to turn the world into an Islamic world. Therefore, all Muslim lands, now in occupation of infidels, need to be reoccupied. In Pakistani books such lands are mentioned. Aurangzeb, the Mughal emperor of India, had officially declared India as Dar al-Islam. Majid Khadduri, an eminent Islamic scholar of USA, has explained the political Islamic agenda. He said that according to Islamic world view the world is divided into two competing jurisdictions *i.e.* Dar-al-Islam and Dar-al-Herb. Dar means jurisdiction. Where Islam is the religion of the state it is called Dar-al-Islam. Non-Islamic jurisdictions are called Dar- al Herb *i.e.* area of conflict which has to be brought under Islamic control. The instrument to be used is called Jihad. Jihad literally means to strive for the glory of Allah. [Islam and International Political order] Jihadis are not preachers and missionaries, but God's soldiers' said Ala Maududi, founder of Jamaat-e-Islam in 1941. Some Muslim scholars have said that killing of innocent people is not Jihad. What needs to be explained is whether the concept of Dar-al-Islam and Dar-al-Herb are still valid. No Islamic scholar of repute has written on the validity of these concepts in context of the present day world.

The two-nation theory in the Indian sub-continent was propelled by this view. Jinnah declared in March 1940 at Lahore that Hindus and Muslims were two nations. His party gave the slogan of Muslim being distinct from Hindu India. The country was divided on this basis as otherwise the British would have ruled the subcontinent for a long time. India did capitulate but did not give up its secular ideology which represents India's world view plural society based on its civilizational past.

The two-nation theory became a driving force in the Philippines, Thailand. Creation of such Muslim states would lead to one Islamic state in Southeast Asia, which would include Malaysia, the Philippines, Thailand, Brunei, Sarawak, Indonesia, and Sulawesi. This was the dream of Al Qaeda. MILF, Abu Sayyaf and Jemeeh Islamiah were working on this idea. What appears to be impossible can be possible within a short time. This is borne out of Indian experience.

'Muslim India' was vaguely conceived in 1930 by poet Iqbal. Jinnah made the call official in 1940 and in April 1947 Pakistan was created. An idea can grow faster than some analysts can imagine. Integrative factors just collapse if the idea grips the masses at the grass root level. This was fully shown by Indian general election results before partition in 1945-46. Jihad call was finally given and implemented in August 1946 by a call of Direct Action, which was unleashing of violence. Indian secular leadership just capitulated to gain independence from Britain.

Under Osama the idea of one nation of Islam was again taking shape more vigorously than before. Chinese are pragmatic. They have managed to keep the Islamic states in good humour by keeping close relationship only to save Xinjiang and Tibet from being separated from the middle Kingdom. China, Pakistan and North Korea nexus has been in position for more than 40 years. One reason is the Xinjiang factor.

Gen.[retd] Hamid Gul claims loudly that Pakistani army is pro-Islamic. All the terrorist outfits have the blessings of the ISI, which is a part of army. Such outfits are the force multiplier. Army rule will continue in Pakistan directly or indirectly. Institutional interests are too heavy and lucrative to be sacrificed. Zulfikar Ali Bhutto conceived the nuclear bomb as 'Islamic bomb'. Pakistan will continue to aid and abet terrorism all over the world by proxies, an art of warfare taught by the Chinese and lately by the Americans during the Afghan Jihad.

The next war may he launched from Asia. The target will be the USA for destruction of the US economy and plural democracy. Sleepers will be activated to strike at the opportune time. Dr. Zawahiri has survived this war on terror, the inevitable can happen. Pakistan needs watching along with the remnants of Al Qaeda, the Taliban.

The spirit of Jihad has taken roots in various parts of the world. Some such trouble spots needs to be mentioned.

Bangladesh

Bangladesh was created in 1971 out of Pakistan. Bangladeshis fought for independence when its elected majority leader Mujibur Rehman was denied the post of prime minister of Pakistan. That was the only fair election in Pakistan after its creation.

In 1972 Bangladesh adopted a secular constitution with a dose of Bengali nationalism. Mujib, the tallest leader of Bangladesh, was killed by a group of junior army officers, one of whom subsequently became an ISI operative for launching unrest in the Northeast India. The army rulers in Bangladesh like Zia-ul-Rehman and Ershad made the Bangladesh constitution Islamic.

During partition of the sub-continent in 1947, the minority population in Bangladesh was 39 percent. Pakistan adopted a programme to drive out minorities. The process was halted briefly during the Bangladesh Liberation struggle and during the period of administration of Mujibur Rehman. He was killed on 15 August 1974. Now the minority population has come down to less than nine percent. Analysts believe that the minority population would be reduced to 2 percent in another 10-15 years. Pakistan's minority population including Christians is less than two percent.

Bangladesh situation was in focus due to rise of fundamentalist forces abated by the ISI. ISI's big presence in Dhaka was observable. ISI's anti-Indian activities were observed by Northeastern states like Assam and Tripura, Manipur, Meghalaya. Bangladesh became a hotbed of fundamentalists. Those who opposed the Liberation War were enjoying powers aligning with Bangladesh parties. Jamaat-e-Islam, Bangladesh, secured 17 seats in a house of 300 members in the election held in October 2001. Much of this success was due to 9/11 attack on US. Two of the Jamaat leaders were in the Begum Zia's ministry. Jamaat vehemently opposed the US-led coalition's war on terror and said so openly.

Maulana Ubaidul Haq, who was a rabble rousing cleric, had united a dozen radical groups often called Bangladesh Taliban. The slogan raised was 'Amra Musalman, Amra Hobo Taliban' (We are Muslims, we will become Taliban). The drift was alarming because the Bengali Muslims are basically moderate and are proud of Bengali nationalism. Tagore's songs are very popular. The national song of Bangladesh is one composed by poet Tagore.

After 9/11, Maulana Ubaidul Haq declared: 'President Bush and America are the most heinous terrorists in the world. Both America and Bush must be destroyed. The Americans will be washed away if Bangladesh's 120 million Muslim people spit on them' (Far Eastern Economic Review, April 4, 2002). Thousands of Bangladeshi Islamic militants took to the streets in anti-US demonstrations with Osama's posters and banners.

There were reports filed by foreign journalists that some Al-Qaeda operatives had taken shelter in Bangladesh in and around Cox's Bazaar, which was denied by the government. Cox bazaar has been the traditional route for gun running.

Four members of Jamaat-ul-Mujahideen were arrested in Naogaon in Bangladesh on May 30, 2003, for possession of a football sized package of uranium of Kazakhstan origin sufficient to make a dirty bomb. A document showing how to make such dirty bombs was also recovered from them. 17 others were arrested for distributing papers, posters and tapes of Osama bin Laden. Many were found praying for his survival when the US led coalition launched war on terror in Afghanistan.

Bangladeshis were also found to be fighting along with the Taliban in Afghanistan. The US authorities did not officially release any such information. However, the Northern Alliance had such information on them and made it public.

The ISI's game plan is to annex Bangladesh again by a popular support movement. When Bhutto framed the Constitution of Pakistan in 1972, he had included Bangladesh as part of future Pakistan after vacation of aggression. This was dropped when Bangladesh was recognized by Pakistan in 1974. Bangladesh had by design fallen in the orbit of China-Pakistan axis. Bangladesh purchases its arms and planes from China as a part of grand strategy of Pakistan. When situation is ripe Bangladesh may join Pakistan in some sort of federation. This possibility can not be ruled out in the event of capturing of power by the fundamentalist forces. As of now things have changed after the regime change.

Tablighi Jamaat, Lashker-e-Toiba had good presence in Bangladesh. It was said that Hafiz Mohammed Saeed, Amir of Markaz-Dawa-wal-Irshad and its fighting outfit Lashker-e-Toiba and Azam Cheema, a top functionary of the Lashker-e-Toiba had visited Bangladesh and recruited Jihadis. One of them was Abu Nasir on whom much has been written elsewhere. This information came from Abu Nasir.

The nexus between Pakistan and Bangladesh was exposed by Bangladesh by nominating a die-hard fundamentalist Salauddin Qader Chowdhary, to the top post of the OIC. He was known for expanding terror networks and arms twisting terror tactics. Like his father Fazlul Qader Chowdhary, he too was sold out to Pakistan. Father and son perpetrated in conjunction with the marauding Pakistan Army in 1971 blood-curdling horrors. Details of their horror tactics are well documented by Bangladesh Liberation War Documents and by the People's Commission appointed by the Committee for Elimination of the killers and Collaborators of 1971 in Chittagong district. 'These include gruesome killing of 71 year old principal Nutan Chandra Singha and assassination of Farooq, a student leader and Dayalhari Biswas, another college student'. After Liberation they attempted to flee but were arrested. Under the general amnesty offered by Mujib government, they were released. Chowdhury reportedly maintained a private army of terrorists called Aziz Bahini.

Salahuddin Chowdhary had venom against India. He was involved in many acts of Hindu cleansing in Chittagong area. He was a diehard Muslim Leaguer and served as a Cabinet minister in Gen Ershad's Cabinet and acted as advisor to Begum Zia. He was aspiring to become secretary general of the organization of the Islamic countries. His nomination has been criticized by the press. It is alleged that he was nominated at the instance of Pakistan 'to increase the leverage of the Pakistan-Bangladesh axis in the Islamic world' 'to discomfit and disturb India'. On the floor of Parliament in July 2003 he eulogized Anup Chetia, now in Bangladesh jail, as an Indian freedom fighter. BNP-jamaat dispensation only exposed its true colour.[20]

There was ever proliferating Islamic terrorist network in Bangladesh. B B Nandi, who was in Research and Analysis Wing (RAW) for years, has been a watcher of events in Bangladesh. He had been watching the linkage between Bangladeshi Islamic network, which functioned under the ISI. For example Moin Khan, leader of Herkat ul-Jihad-islam [HUJI] was fired from the army during the Awami League government for his jihadi links. He was an explosive expert in the Bangladesh army. He reportedly worked under his officer Inayat alias Honda Shaheb, a Pak based Pakistani diplomat. He trained ULFA and other insurgent groups at Dudh Pukur Para in Sylhet district of Bangladesh. In July-August 2003 he clandestinely visited Mumbai and Kolkata with six kg of RDX. For his inward and outward journeys, two officers of the Bangladesh Directorate General of Forces Intelligence posted in Kolkata on cover assignments arranged Moin's transit accommodation in a private guest house in Kolkata and railway tickets for Mumbai and return journeys. He was said to be involved in the bomb attacks in Mumbai on 25 August 2003 and seizure of 25,000 rounds of AK-47 seized in Kolkata on 3 September 2003 bound for Kashmir. In July 2003 a truck arriving from Bogra district of Bangladesh was seized carrying 1,10,000 rounds of AK-47 and 10 kg of RDX. The rounds bearing no markings were believed to have come from the Bangladesh Ordinance Factory at Jaydevpur.

Bangladesh had a number of Islamic terrorist outfits. Two of them had been very active namely Jamaat-ul-Mujahideen and Sahadate-al-Hikma. These organizations were bent on Islamization of Bangladesh. They targeted secular parties and individuals. They chiefly operated from districts bordering West Bengal. They belonged to madrassa trained students and many belonged to Jamat-e-Islam and its student wing Islami Chhatra Shibir (Islamic Students Front).

Two Bengals at one point of time were drifting. Muslims are absolutely safe in West Bengal. They occupy important positions in

20 *The Statesman*, dated 5 August 2003, Bibhuti Bhusan Nandy's writeup on Salahuddin

politics. In Bangladesh, Hindu minority had no space. In the name of Islam, Bangladesh became a fundamentalist state. Bangladeshis intellectuals with liberal views were marginalized. All efforts were made to make it a prototype of Pakistan to create trouble in the neighbourhood in the name of Jihad.

Sahadate-al-Hikma's top leadership was in the hands of Freedom Party floated by assassins of Sheikh Mujib. Hikma's convener Kaissar Hossain Siddiqui reportedly revealed that Dawood Ibrahim, the underworld mafia don, had funded the outfit. The Bangladesh government had to ban these two organizations to save its skin. The ISI has created a new base in Bangladesh to export terror to India via Bangladesh. Dawood works for the ISI which is not hidden from anybody.

11 terrorist outfits were active in Bangladesh. Herkat ul Jihadi Islam (HUJI) is top on the list. HUJI participated in Afghan jihad. HUJI also participated during the Taliban regime. It remained a part of Jamaat-e-Islami. The principal and clients took part in religious cleansing as part of total Islamisation of Bangladesh. The 11 outfits were working under an umbrella organization called Islami hands. Its declared goal was to establish a transnational Islamic state comprising Bangladesh, the Muslim majority areas of the Northeast India, Arakan hills of Arakan, Myanmar. It was thus attempting to do what the Jemaah Islamiya was doing for Southeast Asia. The declared programme was to create an Islamic state in Southeast Asia by grouping Islamic dominated areas into one state. Much has changed after the regime change with a new dispensation in place now. It is being led by the daughter of Mujibur who was the founder father of Bangladesh.

The West Bengal is vulnerable. The ISI and Islamic terrorist outfits have been using West Bengal as the launching pad. The political climate in West Bengal suits the ISI. Mujahideen outfits use West Bengal as a base for terrorist attacks all over India. Al Qaeda as an ideology is knocking at the door of West Bengal.

Singapore

A Singaporean source provided information to the Internal

Security Department that one Mohammed Aslam bin Yer Ali Khan, a Singaporean of Pakistan origin, had claimed to have taken part in jihad in Afghanistan. On 4 October 2001 just after 9/11, Aslam again left Singapore on a flight to Pakistan. Between 13 October and 16 October 2001, a close friend of Aslam, Mohammed Ellies son of Mohammed Khan was in contact with Mike (Fathur Rehman) and Sammy. In mid October 2001, Ellias was found trying to procure ammonium nitrate and converted US $3500 into local currency required for reconnaissance of the US and Israeli Embassies.

On 3 December the press published a report of Aslams's arrest by the Northern Alliance in Afghanistan. That prompted the ISD to take a quick action against the network in Singapore.

On 9 December 2001, ISD detained 6 persons and searched their houses and offices. On 15, 16 and 17 December 2001 many more were arrested. The last person was arrested on 24 December 2001. In all 23 persons were picked up for questioning.

On 14 December 2001, the US provided a videotape of the Yishum Mass Rapid Transit (MRT) station found in Afghanistan along with a debriefing note.

13 out of 23 were found to be active members of Jemaah Islamiya (JI). JI was involved in briefing and surveillance of targets, in the procurement of logistics for bomb construction. Targets selected were the US Embassy, American club and commercial buildings, housing US nationals. The members of the JI made out observation reports and video recordings of the targeted places and submitted them to the foreign terrorists who were in control of the operations.

In September 2002, 18 more persons were detained out of which 17 were confirmed JI members, one was MILF member. The later group had conducted surveillance of many other strategic installations like water pipelines and Changi Airport of Singapore.

Plan I was to mount multiple Truck bomb attacks against the US related targets sometime between December 2001 and May 2002. In preparation of that Malaysian JI leader Faiz bin Abu Bakar Bajana then contacted the Singaporean cell to assist a friend called Mike

(Fathur) which he did and instructed the Singaporean to assist an Al-Qaeda operative called 'Sammy'. Sammy arrived in Singapore in October 2001 and met the Singaporean Fiah Musa members near a hotel. Mike along with 3 Singaporeans physically checked the targets. Mike (Fathur) told one of the locals to obtain 17 tons of ammonium nitrate (AN) in addition to stockpiling four tons of AN in Malaysia and a quantity of TNT already available. A safe home was to be located for bomb making.

Mike gave a local operative a total of US $5500 in cash to cover expenses. Six trucks were to be used loaded with 3 tons of AN each. Actual bombing would be carried out by outsiders as suicide bombers. All of them were believed to be Arabs. They would arrive a day before the planned attack. This was the peculiar style of Al Qaeda operations where only a fidayeen team can be involved in attacks. Locals were used as foot soldiers.

The terrorist plan was disrupted by timely arrests. But that did not deter them. On 13 December 2001 Hambali met with Singapore and Malaysia JI members in Johar, Malaysia, to mount the attacks on a smaller scale. Mike @Fathur continued with his scheme and procured 6 tons of TNT to be smuggled by sea from Minadano to Indonesia and then to Malaysia and Singapore via sea route. Mike was arrested in January 2002. He is an Indonesian whose real name is Fathur Rehman Al-ghazi. He was a bomb maker trained by the MILF. He was involved in the bombing of a light Railway Train in December 2000 which killed 22 persons.

Singaporean ISD informed the Philippines authorities and he was identified. His capture led to the recovery of 1.2 tons of TNT, 300 pieces of detonators as well as six rolls of detonating coils all meant for Singapore blasts. If not arrested the plan would have been pursued and developed into a fruitful action.

Australia

Australia has not faced any terrorist attack so far. This country of 19 million people has half a million Arabs. Before 9/11, a man with a video camera was captured in 2000. He had video recorded the Israeli Embassy building in Canberra. This arrest was kept secret but now made public.

Jade Roche, a British immigrant in Australia embraced Islam and married an Indonesian Muslim. He was assigned the mission to operate cells on behalf of Al Qaeda and Jemmah Islamiya, an Al Qaeda affiliate in South East Asia. Intelligence community believed that Jemmah Islamiya cells operated in Sydney, Melbourne and Perth.

This view is reinforced by the fact that Abu Baker Bashir, Amir of Jemmah Islamiya reportedly visited Australia eleven times from 1991 to 1998. His mission was significant and mission oriented.[21]

Conclusion

Most of Al Qaeda network had been disrupted in many countries. The Bali bombers have been hanged. Many operatives were arrested and are convicted or facing trial. The US has not faced any major terrorist attack since 9/11. Some were arrested before they could mount another attack. Those arrested had links with Pakistani jihadi organizations. Same is the story with UK where arrested people were those who had Pakistani links. So is the case of Spain where many attacks have been foiled by timely action. It is the cherished dream of terrorists to re-establish Islam in Spain.

Al Qaeda's present top leadership has been neutralised. The planners of 9/11 have been apprehended from Pakistan. The chief architect of 9/11 attack Khalid Sheikh Mohammad [KSM] was apprehended from Rawalpindi. He was planning 9/11 attack since 1995-6. Now US agencies have sufficient inputs on Al Qaeda network. Many new leaders are on the radar. What is surprising is that the US took a long time to eliminate Osama bin Laden. Al Zawahiri still operates despite all the inputs it has on him. There are reasons to believe that he is hiding in Pakistan as he has no other safe place in the world to hide. The emergence of neo-Taliban in Federally Administered Tribal Area and their inroads into eastern parts of Pakistan is a matter of deep concern. This stronghold area of neo-Taliban is the most secured place for Al Qaeda and its top

---

21 Report filed by Reymond Ronner and Jane Perlez, International Herald Tribune, December 17, 2002.

leaders to function. The Pakistan Army is not interested to deal with them. The army has made peace deals with the neo-Taliban leaders that provided space to neo-Taliban and Al Qaeda to operate stealthily. The primary objective of Pakistan Army is to gain back Afghanistan for gaining their age old held 'strategic depth' concept.

Al Qaeda as an idea will survive for a long period as long as the basic Islamic concepts are not revised in the light of the realities of changed world. This can happen only when the soul of Islam is found out by scholars of repute. There are some indications of that happening. Contrary to popular belief some scholars believe that Islam provides space for discussion and interfaith coexistence. Sufi Islam which is dominant in South and South East Asia will prevail in future. In the last chapter; *The Future of Al Qaeda*; all matters relating to this area of concern will be discussed.

5

9/11

Black Tuesday, 11 September 2001 Attack on The World Trade Centre and Pentagon

Introduction

The United States of America, the sole global superpower, witnessed helplessly one hour of terror and hell in cloudless early morning of 11 September, 2001, the like of which was never witnessed before. The method of attack was unconventional, unique in conception and execution. There were plane hijackings in plenty in the seventies and eighties. The hijackers in the earlier cases bargained for release of their comrades in jail and other political gains. "Hitler, the Japanese and the Soviet Union could not do what Al-Qaeda has been able to do" on 9/11.[1] Thus, there was a sense of acute insecurity in America as the fun loving Americans never had faced such devastating terrorist attacks on the soil of America, unlike India which has been a victim of Pakistan sponsored terrorism for the last three decades. The images of collapse of twin towers with engulfing fire and helpless people jumping out of them will haunt many in the world for generations to come.

On the same day of 11 September, Pakistan observed the 53rd death anniversary of Mohammed Ali Jinnah, a leader for creation of Pakistan. It was pure coincidence. On the same date in 1973 General Augusta Pinochet Ugarte staged a military coup to oust

---

1   K. Subramaniyam, *The Times of India*, 5.11.2001.

the democratically elected President of Chile Salvador Allende. The Camp David Accord was signed on the same date and again on this date the senior Bush made his fateful speech announcing war against Iraq. In the coded language of Al-Qaeda the date was called 'two sticks dash cake with one stick down' *i.e.* 9/11.

On this day in 1893 Swami Vivekananda addressed the Parliament of World Religions at Chicago with vibrant soul stirring message to the world spreading the message of interfaith tolerance for universal peace. "We in India believe not only in universal tolerance, but we accept all religions as true". He quoted Gita; "Whosoever comes to me, through whatever form I reach him; all men are struggling through paths which in the end culminate in me". This eternal message needs to be conveyed to all the suffering souls of the world. The full text of Swami Vivekananda's address should be made available to those seeking help of god in solving world's religious crisis.

Planning and attack

The sequence of hijacked plane attacks on US targets looked like movie action pictures. Two days before that day, on 9 September, the legendary Ahmad Shah Masood, the most prominent anti-Taliban Leader of the Northern Alliance, was killed by two Moroccans posing as journalists carrying explosives in a video camera. Obviously, there was a link between these two major events. Now the Scotland Yard had arrested an Egyptian exile Yasser al-Siri, 39, from his West London residence. Al Siri had reportedly provided the assassins of Ahmad Shah Masood with a letter of introduction which enabled them to get visas for coming to Britain. The hit men thereafter secured visas for Islamabad from Pakistan High Commission in London. As will be seen hereafter there are too many Pakistani links with Al-Qaeda and its allied groups in terrorist activities all over the world. The result of investigation in Britain in respect of Masood killing is yet to the made public. It is too sensitive a case in which Britain and Pakistan are involved for providing safe visa passage to assassins of Masood. Masood's case should be fully investigated by all the concerned countries and results made public.

Al-Siri allegedly was running an Islamic radical organization in UK since the last 8 years after fleeing Egypt where he was sentenced to death by an Egyptian court for a bomb blast. His extradition to Egypt was reportedly turned down by the UK.[2] UK has a bad track record of harbouring terrorists of all nations. The Indian experience is no better in the matter of terrorist funding through Hawala network from UK. Terrorists of all nations were allowed to function from Britain if they followed an unwritten ground rule of not committing any crime in Britain.

One hour of terror and hell

American Airlines Flight 11 carrying eighty one passengers and a crew of eleven took off from Boston at about 8 a.m and crashed into the World Trade Center's north tower at 8.45 a.m. The flight-path was Los Angeles International Airport. A hijacker told the pilot, overheard by the air traffic controller at 8.28 a.m, that "we have more planes, we have other planes. Don't do anything foolish, you won't be hurt" After that plane's transponder was already disconnected. The pilots did not enter a four digit code indicating a hijacking as the system was neutralised.[3]

Belty Ong, Flight attendant of flight no AA 11, made a call to an American reservation supervisor describing hijacking in progress. This was communicated to Craig Mosques, manager–on–duty at American's operation centre in Fort Worth, Texas. Ong also told that hijackers had stabbed two flight attendants, one already succumbed to injury. She further informed that the hijackers had slit one passenger's throat and stormed the cockpit. Throat slitting was Al-Qaeda's operational speciality. The same technique was used in Indian Airlines hijacking of IC814 in December 1999. One passenger was killed in the same manner.

Craig Marquis verified Ong's employee number and the hijacker's seat positions. The air traffic frantically tried to track the hijacked plane's changed flight path, but failed.

---

2 *Hindustan Times,* 24 October, 2001.

3 *Hindustan Times,* quoting from Christian Monitor newspaper Web Site, 13/09/2001.

The American Airlines flight 11 had already turned south over Albany in the direction of New York City. Further tracking was impossible as the hijackers had turned off the flight transponder, a special device that would allow controllers to distinguish the radar image of a particular plane from hundreds of other blips on the screen. Really speaking the controllers had no idea where the plane was really heading for.

Another flight attendant of AA 11 Marry Amy Sweeny, 35, called up Michel Woodword, flight services manager at Logan and calmly described how 4 hijackers with middle eastern looks, some wearing red bandanas, were carrying box-cutters and hijacked the plane.[4] On being asked about the location of the plane, she said she saw water and buildings there after the plane swerved and began descending. Her last communication was "Oh my God, Oh my God", just before the Tower crash.

The United Airlines Boeing Flight 175 took off from Boston at about 8.14 a. m and crashed into the World Trade Center's 1362 foot south tower at 9.03 a.m. It had 56 passengers and a crew of nine. The flight-path was again for Los Angeles International Airport. The twin towers with 110 storeys were just reduced to a pile of dust in no time. 'Oh my God' was the common cry of all those who witnessed the event in New York.

In case of United Flight 175, the pilot radioed a message that someone had made an announcement from the cabin intercom that every one should 'stay in their seats'. Later the plane changed the flight path and shut down the communication between the pilot and the controller.[5]

After two successive crashes on WTC towers there was no confusion on the nature of Ariel attacks on US targets. Orders were issued for total evacuation from police headquarters, City Hall, the UN and Empire State building. By 8.52 am two American Air Force F-15 of 1977 vintage took off to cover 70 miles *i.e.* 8 minutes

---

4 John Miller, Michael Stone, Chris Mitchell, The Cell, Inside 9/11 Plot, Hyperion, New York, 2002, p 9.

5 John Miller, Michael Stone, Chris Mitchell, The Cell, Inside 9/11 Plot, Hyperion, New York, 2002, p 12.

away from flight No. 175 which crashed into the second tower at about 9.03 am. Realizing the gravity of the situation by 9.30 am all international and domestic flights were grounded.

Each of these two planes was roughly carrying 37,000 litres of aviation fuel sufficient to destroy the steel structure of the WTC in a raging inferno. The towers were targeted at their weakest spot.[6]

American Airlines Flight 77 [Boeing 757] took off from Washington's Dulles International Airport and crashed into the west wing of the Pentagon at 9.43 a.m. The flight-path was also to Los Angeles International Airport. There were 58 passengers and 6 crew members on board. At about 8.56 am just few minutes after the first WTC crash the plane 'double back' toward Washington, shut off its transponder and did not answer repeated calls from the controllers.

At about 9.24 am three more F16s took off and were on the sky by 9.30 am and headed towards New York not knowing the changed flight path of American Airlines flight 77. Just before 9.30 a controller on duty observed a fast moving primary target about to move into the restricted airspace above the Capitol. On being alerted the secret service got the White House evacuated. At 9.36 the plane was identified as a Boeing 757. First the plane crossed over the Pentagon and then turned 360 degree to bring it to ground level and at 9.38 the plane slammed into the west side of the Pentagon. All on board were killed.

United Airlines flight 93 took off from New York International Airport and crashed into a field near Shanksvilk at 10.10 a.m. which is south-east of Pittsburgh of the state of Pennsylvania. There were 43 passengers on board. The plane could not hit the selected target as the passengers, who came to know about the three previous cases on cell phones, decided to give a fight as they knew their fate would be no different from other three flights. All the four hijacked planes were on internal flights as selecting international routes would have attracted a greater security checks.

There was a lot of real time drama on flight 93. Just before 9.30 am air traffic controllers had heard someone in the cockpit say 'Hey,

6   Towering Inferno, *The Week*, p 42, 23 September 2001.

get out of here'. Another voice with Middle Eastern accent told the passengers: 'this is your captain. There is a bomb on board. Remain in your seats. We are returning to the airport.'

The hero of this flight was 38 years old Tom Burnett. He was 6'2" tall and a former college football player. Deena, his wife, had already known about the WTC crash on TV. She and mother of Tom were worried about the safety of Tom. Tom and Deena spoke to each other on cell phone. That makes an interesting reading.

Deena	:	Tom are you OK ?
Tom	:	I am not.
Deena	:	They just hit the Pentagon.
Tom	:	Pray, Deena just pray we are going to have to do something.
Deena	:	I love you.
Tom	:	Don't worry I will call you back.

The last call was around 10 am that was the fourth call from Tom. He said: 'A group of us are going to do something. 'No Deena' was the answer when she asked for restraint. He said "if they are going to run the plane into the ground, we have to do something'. He told Deena to pray.

Like Tom other passengers called up friends and loved ones. The Passengers had taken a vote and then decided to storm the cockpit. The war cry of passengers was 'are you ready' 'let us roll'. Yes, the passengers of this flight will be remembered forever for giving a real fight to hijackers. A thriller film can be made out of this fight to show human courage against all odds. The cockpit recorder picked up the sound of a violent struggle.

The United Flight 93 crashed in an uninhabited field near Shanksvilk, Pennsylvania, 80 miles southeast of the Pittsburgh and 163 miles from the Capitol; which was believed to have been its target. Both Pentagon and Capitol were surely on the crash-list of the hijackers. 35 passengers, 7 crew members and 4 hijackers perished. The hijackers failed to achieve success and victims stood out as heroes that prevented Capitol Hill being attacked.

Thus, in all 264 innocent passengers including women and children were victims of terror and death for no fault of theirs. All the flights were for long distance destinations providing enough aviation fuel to cause devastating fire on impact. The sequence of hijacking shows very high degree of prior meticulous planning and several rehearsals. As a new lethal method of terrorist attacks it was 'just simple and brilliant'. These were 'bombless attacks' brilliantly executed by dedicated zealots for a cause unworthy of acceptance in the first year of the new millennium. In the 80's when hijackings were common, people used to carry little tear gas spray or pepper spray. The use of spray would have incapacitated the hijackers. Use of these was banned with the decline of hijacking cases.

The first crash (WTC tower) could have been taken as a mere accident. After the second crash, all the flights should have been grounded for search and seizure of other possible conspirators who might have planned more such attacks. That would have prevented two more strikes. Such a drill was apparently lacking. This shows that the air traffic control system did not react promptly after the first crash.

The whole world witnessed the horror caused by a group of terrorists with total disbelief and deep anguish. Said CNN cameraman: 'I thought I had woken up in a nightmare. It felt like a very bad horror movie'.[7] 'Our lives won't be the same again' said one of the BBC news editors. The scale of tragedy and utter humiliation of the United States could have sparked off an immediate war against the suspect nations harbouring terrorists. As aptly said by Jayant Mathew,[8] the enemies "are well trained idealists, flushed with unlimited resources and a large following, who have repeatedly shown their utter contempt for human life." Decidedly these 'freedom fighters' as often described by Gen Musharraf, were targeting innocent civilians and not combatants. This is what has been happening in Kashmir where innocents are being killed by

---

7   *Hindustan Times*, dated 13.09.2001.

8   *The Week*, September 22, 2001.

Pakistani sponsored terrorist groups. As was expected an attempt was made to blame the Jews for the attack. The same technique was used to describe dastardly killings of people in India by terrorists by blaming Indian intelligence to damage the image of Pakistan and Jihadi outfits. All terrorist organizations and their sponsoring states play the same game of denial.

Panic reaction

Such an outrageous attacks caused wide spread reaction in USA. A war cry was raised by 150 students in Berkeley, California urging the US to 'whip terrorism'. 'I want justice' said President Bush. New York Mayor Giuliani rejected $10 million for WTC relief from a Saudi Royal who linked the WTC attack to US foreign policy. 'Wage war on those nations, that harbour terrorists, one at a time, wrote a reader to Time magazine. Another wrote that 'some one has killed a part of me'. When some civil liberty activist raised some question on breach of privacy law, a protesting writer said: 'If the civil libertarians don't like the idea of the federal government monitoring more e-mails or requiring a national identification card, propose they move to Afghanistan'.[9]

The terrorists achieved their objective of creating terror in the minds of the Americans. Manhattan's Empire State building was evacuated several times in September 2001 following a rumour that a hijacked plane was about to strike it.[10] So was the case of Sears Towers in Chicago. The White House was vacated and family members of President Bush were shifted to safe haven. Vice-President Dick Chiney went into a nuclear proof bunker. Panic gripped the Americans of all walks of life.

Americans were not accustomed to deafening explosion of a suicide or car bomb, towers collapsing like a pack of cards, a hail of glass and debris and the screams of the innocent victims. In February 1993 the World Trade Centre Truck bomb attack could do nothing of this kind as the towers did not collapse. "Terrorism seemed like something that happened somewhere else and somewhere else a safe

---

9   *Time*, 22 October, 2001.

10   *Time*, October 1, 2001.

distance over the horizon".[11] All that changed. After all 'the World Trade Centre represented economic machismo and cultural hubris of America'. 'The Americans will never be the same again'. Said Kofi Anan: 'We are all traumatized by this terrible tragedy'.

Reaction in the Muslim Community

Bin Laden's supporters in Tihar jail in India celebrated the September 11 attacks. Many fanatics lodged in Asia's highest security jail where in celebration mood,[12] a story filed by Neeta Sharma and Munjal Dubey. The most happy jail inmate was Abdul Rauf, (Hawash) a Sudanese national nabbed on June 16, 2001 along with three associates arrested by Delhi police. They were suspected to be working for Osama bin Laden. Rauf had 6 Kg RDX and a detailed layout of the US embassy building in his possession at the time of his arrest. His plan was to attack the US embassy in New Delhi.

Yasser Arafat was horrified, but thousands of Palestinians celebrated chanting 'God is Great'. Some distributed candy to passersby. Who would share grief of Arafat at this hour of victory? Some even said that the next attack would be launched against Tel Aviv.[13] Some honked their car horns and flashed victory sign. Some such visuals were shown on TV.

Syed Ahmad Bukhari a cleric of Jama Masjid of Delhi, said: 'If the Ulema announce Jihad, it is obligatory for each and every Muslim to support it.[14]

The Muslims saw Osama as 'our Robin Hood'. Vendors were hawking bin Laden shirts and posters in many parts of the world. America was seen as a bully. Girls appeared in classrooms in hijab, the Islamic head-scarf and even donned head-to-toe burqa. Even educated signed up with the Taliban and vowed to fight for bin Laden.[15] Some Muslims did condemn these attacks but did not

---

11 *Time*, September 24, 2001.

12 *Hindustan Times*, September 13, 2001.

13 *Hindustan Times*, September 12, 2001.

14 *Time*, October 8, 2001.

15 McGrick, *Time*, September 9, 2002.

receive much of attention.

Public reaction

The response to this unimaginable 21ˢᵗ century Pearl Harbour should be as simple as it is swift-kill the bastards. Reactions like a gunshot between the eyes, blow them to smithereens, poison them were heard. As for cities and countries that host these worms, bomb them into basketball courts[16] and quoted by Along Long Kumar in second opinion.[17] US Muslims changed their names to escape suspicion as all the hijackers were Arab Muslims. A Pakistani-American Tariq Hasan, 35, changed his name to Jery Hasan. Most students were going to court to change their names sounding less Muslim and less Arabic. Muslim carried the stigma. 'Oh, you are one of them' when they announce their first name. Mohammed Khalil went to court two days after September 11 to become Michael. In California, a man called Badr become Mark.[18]

Introspection

Said a writer: 'What is it in US behaviour that drove them to such hatred?' Said another: 'What it is about our way of life and policies that make people hate us so much?'

For the first time the Americans realised that it was wrong giving refuge and financial support to IRA. For the first time the US administration banned target assets of more then 60 terrorist entities. For the first time the US declared Lashker-e-Taiba, Jaish-e-Mohammed and a host of other terrorist organizations as Foreign Terrorist Organizations under its own two laws which they had refused to do earlier for geopolitical reasons. Indians were demanding this minimum action as per the domestic laws of USA. Every thing changed. The Americans realised that terrorism was not that happens elsewhere. So far terrorism was seen as a local affair arising from local disputes. It was not seen as global tidal wave of political Islam spreading all over the world and the US was

---

16 Steve Dunleavy, *New York Post*, September 12, 2001

17 *Pioneer*, India dated 23.04.2002.

18 *Indian Express*, dated 23.03.2002 reporting from Washington.

responsible for creation of this deadly phenomenon, a fact of history which can not be ignored.

For the first time the US realised that after Soviet withdrawal of troops in 1989 from Afghanistan, a mistake was committed by not ensuring a transition to a moderate and tolerant regime. That task was left to Pakistan. The ISI guided the Afghan policy and created Taliban in 1994 for which credit was given to Gen (retd) Nasirullah Babbar, then interior minister in Banazir's government. The Geneva Agreement provided a mechanism for peaceful transfer of power through the instrumentality of Loya Jirga of the Afghan tradition. All that did not happen.

The US and the Western World, for reasons of expediency, ignored terrible terrorist activities in India, including Kashmir, Chechnya, the Philippines, Myanmar, Africa and various other hot spots. They were not treated as part of a global jihad.

The expatriates of Punjab and Kashmir were allowed to use the soil of America and Europe for fomenting terrorism in South Asia. The ISI sponsored terrorism in India was tolerated in the eighties as Pakistan was fighting a proxy war in Afghanistan on behalf of the US. The fugitives from law were in USA and extradition requests were dragged on only to delay the due process of law. Thus, 'by perpetuating the cycle of violence we (US) are breeding a new generation of terrorists' said a commentator.

Rescue workers heroic deeds

More than 300 firefighters, who jumped into action, were found missing. Many died including high ranking members of the fire fighting department. One of the fire department's chaplain Mychal Judge had just rushed to the scene to comfort victims, only to be killed in a rolling wave of concrete chunks that buried him. By early evening the Trade Centres were reduced to dust. Many brave fire fighters even raced up stairways to rescue trapped people on the upper floors. They were found missing subsequently and died in a heroic act of rescue. It was 'less of a fire-fighting operation and more like a war'. O'Neil, who was in FBI looking after terrorism, joined a security firm a month ago after retirement died while engaging himself in rescue work. O'Neil was a legendary figure in the New York branch of the FBI. He became a victim of the attack which he was expecting in any case.

Loss from attacks

More than 2996 people were killed in these four attacks that includes 19 hijackers. 125 people were killed in the attack on Pentagon. Only 291 bodies could be found intact in WTC. No survivor could be rescued from ground zero. Debris removal posed a big problem. Some 108444 truck loads could remove them. Steel worth 190568 tons could be salvaged. For 69 days underground fires continued to burn. Such was the impact of aviation fuel loaded crash effect. 21 billion dollars worth of the property were lost due to attacks. One hundred thousand people lost jobs in Manhattan area alone.

The psychological and sociological effects of the attacks can never be estimated. More than four hundred thousand New Yorkers suffered from Post Trauma Stress Disorder. 600 incidents of violence or discrimination against Muslims were noticed. Even Indian Sikhs with turbans were targeted as their turbans looked similar to Osama's headgear.

The purpose of terror as a weapon for jihad has been explained by a Pakistani Brigadier S K Malik in his book on 'Koranic Concept of War'. Gen. Zia had written the preface and the book was recommended for cadets undergoing military training. Terror has been advocated as weapon of war quoting scriptures. 'Huge number of American – as many as nine in 10 – felt symptoms of stress after the attack of 9/11'.[19] The lethality of these attacks caused severe distress to forty percent of the population in America. In the defence services of the US there were reported cases of stress and killing of wives who got separated from their husbands. The terror practiced by the terrorist groups in India under the patronage of the ISI, which are fully documented, can now be better appreciated by the world community. But the Indians have the tremendous capacity to live with stress. Their spiritual outlook helps them to overcome the trauma of incidents of death and disorders caused by the terrorist

---

19 *The Herald Tribune*, 9 September, 2002.

groups over the last three decades. Despite of all provocations India never declared a war on terror the way the US did after one incident of 11 September 2001. Hats off to Indians for their endurance level. Now after 26/11 Mumbai attack, Indians are demanding action saying 'enough is enough' with no response from Pakistan establishment.

Could US prevent the 11 September strike?

The South Asian Law on Conspiracy is rather well defined. The object of conspiracy has to be defined by direct evidence or by providing circumstantial evidence. In Islam a Fatwa is to be obeyed. A part of the fatwa issued by the blind cleric Abdul Rehman in 1998 read as under: "Destroy them (read USA) thoroughly and erase them from the face of earth. Ruin their economies, set their companies on fire, turn their conspiracies to powder and dust. Sink their ships, bring their planes down. Slay them in air, on land, on water. And (with the command of Allah) kill them wherever you find them. Catch them and put them in prison. Lie in wait for them and kill these infidels. God will support you against them and will cure the afflicted hearts of the faithful and take all anger out of their hearts". Copies of the fatwa were available in all central madrassas in Pakistan and these were in great demand.[20] All the subsequent attacks on US interests followed this fatwa guideline. It is of interest to know whether the CIA and the FBI had analyzed the fatwa for intelligence gathering and building up cases against terrorist organizations. Rehman's fatwa were read out from mosques all over the world.

In hindsight it would appear that the two powerful agencies of the USA, *i.e.* CIA and FBI, had before the incident, several bits of information and intelligence on the phenomenal increase of activities of Al Qaeda operatives. Most of these operatives, however, could not be linked with Al Qaeda in the first instance for want of surveillance, follow up enquiries on leads, search and interrogation. The existing U.S. laws and procedures proved totally inadequate to deal with the emerging threats on the soil of America. This always happens in a free democratic society which allows freedom and nourishes pluralism. As per survey, 54 percent of Americans feel

---

20   Nation, Pakistan, 29.08.1998.

FBI/CIA should have been able to prevent attacks.[21] Though Sheik Abdul Rehman has been locked up tighter than a drum in solitary confinement at the US Bureau of Prisons, Federal, Medical Centre outside Rochester, Minnesota, where he is being treated for diabetes and poor heart condition. If this is true, he should not have been kept out of loop. If he was still active, there was something terribly wrong with prison administration. It is not clear if his 'fatwa' was taken up for investigation to prove its genuineness.

There was a secret planning meeting of Al Qaeda in January 2000 attended by Hawaf Al-hazmi in Kuala lumpur, Malaysia. After attending the meeting, Al-Hazmi flew to Los Angeles. Although he was being tracked by the CIA, his entry to USA was really puzzling and did indicate a devastating intelligence failure. The Kuala Lumpur meeting was even confirmed by Prime Minister of Malaysia Mr Mohathir and video recordings were provided to CIA. The FBI was not informed about the Kuala Lumpur meeting by the CIA. He figured in USS Cole attack which was under investigation by the FBI.

Another hijacker Khalid Al-Midhar had easily obtained a multiple entry visa for US, but the intelligence and enforcement agencies did nothing to keep track of him. The question that remains to be answered whether such persons got their visas by manipulation or by sheer lack of application of mind. Does FBI/CIA have the right to give clearance of visa applications? Was there any system of computer check of persons applying for visa? Khalid-al-Midhar had also reportedly participated in the USS Cole attack. He was the son-in-law of Ahmed Mohammed Alia al-Hada, a Yemeni who had participated in Afghan war and a close confidante of Osama. He had received 221 calls from Afghanistan until 1998. His second son-in-law was assigned a suicide attack on US soil after 9/11 with a team of 13 others but was foiled in 2002. He lost his two sons for Al Qaeda in Afghanistan and Yemen.[22]

Al Qaeda, which carried out these strikes, proved too smart for U.S. intelligence operatives. All the increased activities of

---

21 Sunday, Times of India, September 8, 2002, p16.

22 Rohan Gunaratne, Inside Al Qaeda, p 141.

fundamentalist elements were seen as possible attack on July 4, 2001, which is celebrated as Independence Day in the United States. Nothing happened on that day. There was perhaps a strong feeling that the possible attack had been aborted. That assessment of the counter intelligence activities of the FBI and CIA proved to be wrong. This presumably led to complacency on the part of these agencies.

The last threat issued by Osama bin Laden was in January 2001 at the time of the marriage of his son with the daughter of Mohammed Atef, his chief operational commander. Osama clearly indicated a possible strong attack on US soil, purportedly to rescue or take revenge for lifelong imprisonment of Sheikh Abdur Rehman in 1993 World Trade Centre attack and for planning of more such landmark attacks. The Al-Jazeera video recording of bin Laden's outburst in January 2001 against the United States was perhaps treated lightly. Such utterances of bin Laden were legally valid evidence to prove that Osama bin Laden had knowledge of the conspiracy and or guiding the conspirators. The object of conspiracy was defined by Osama bin Laden on several occasions.

It is a New York Federal Court, New York that passed the order of imprisonment of Sheikh Omar Abul Rehman was also the venue of trial of twin African embassy bombing cases. On the 12 September 2001, the trial court was to pass judgment of the case which was delivered on 19 October, 2001. Is there a link between the two?

The CIA has to explain a lot as to why the same Sheikh Omer Abdul Rehman, the blind cleric, was recruited by it for mobilizing jihadi recruits and why CIA sent his two sons to fight Afghanistan jihad.[23] Sheikh Rehman's background did not warrant recruitment by the CIA. It was because of his close CIA connection that he could manage to slip into America despite restrictions imposed on him. Independent researchers can now record Sheikh's statement to know how the CIA had used him. He was Jihadi hero in the eyes of the USA in Afghan jihad (1979-89) who become a villain after the WTC bombing in 1993.

---

23   John K Cooley p 64.

In the month of August 2001, the US intelligence had some reports on Laden's focused interest on US targets on U.S. soil. But the said reports did not specify the targets to be attacked. Possibly the intelligence inputs were more based on intercepts, which are always vague in language and contents. No fool would speak on targets and other conspiratorial details on phone, cell phone or on internet E-mail. Obviously, the CIA and the FBI had no human intelligence [humint] to penetrate into the cells of Al Qaeda. In 1993 WTC case the 'humint' got all the evidence on tape-record which proved useful to unfold the conspiracy during the trial. The lack of 'humint' was a palpable deficiency in the US system of counter-intelligence operation.

Again the FBI failed to unearth the big conspiracy even when a French citizen of Morocco origin Zacarias Moussaoui was arrested on immigration charges on 17 August 2001, just a month before the 11 September. On him a big lead also came independently from a flight school in Minnesota. The flight school informed the local police authorities that one Moussaoui undergoing training was behaving strangely. He only wanted to learn how to fly aircrafts without learning take off and touch down lessons, which are more important than flying an aircraft.

On FBI's request the French intelligence reported that Moussaoui held 'extremist beliefs' with some 'troubling connections'. The French reported that he had traveled several times to Pakistan and Afghanistan. That itself should have been a cause for worry and subject of in-depth investigation. Since the French intelligence did not link him with Osama or Al Qaeda, this piece of vital intelligence was not taken up very seriously and dealt with casually. In 2001 Pakistan was being ruled by Gen Musharraf. His regime could have been approached to check antecedents of Zacarias or through their sources abroad. Even the French intelligence could have been asked to give more details about his 'troubling connections' and his possible Jihadi connections in Pakistan or Afghanistan.

The FBI's interrogation methods should have been enough to confront Moussaoui with his Pakistan and Afghanistan visits. The suspect would have given some cock and bull story as that is always the case. The story could have been cross-checked with Pakistan authorities or again independently. That he told all lies would have been known and that would have been a good enough ground for his further in-depth interrogation. This confrontation tricks always force a suspect to reveal the truth. A suspect comes out with truth only when he imagines that the interrogators know all the facts about him and bluffing would not be useful. This is an elementary trick of any scientific interrogation.

The inability of the CIA to gather information on this man who was rightly spotted as possible suspect was perhaps overlooked. May be there was lack of real time intelligence sharing between the agencies. The initial background material on him was enough to build up quickly his deep financial and terrorist relationship. For flight training one has to pay a princely sum of $ 8000 if not more. If that type of money was paid by cash, an unusual thing to happen in the USA. A cash transaction enquiry was called for keeping his fundamentalist background in view. Perhaps, as is the case elsewhere, there was lack of coordination between the CIA and FBI. Often the internal and external agencies are faced with jurisdictional issues in the absence of a coordinating unit which has the power of tasking. In India a tasking unit was created in the case of terrorism in Punjab. That gave good results.

The USA has a system of reporting on substantial cash transactions that includes banks, financial institutions etc. If money was paid from a bank account, inland or overseas, a further lead was available to explore his possible links with terrorist outfits. It appears that these elementary exercises were not perhaps carried out even after his arrest a month prior to September 11 incident. It was a case of a 'missed chance' to prevent a deep conspiracy. His polygraph test would have exposed the falsity of his statement.

Legal wire tapping law is available in the US, unlike India, where such wire-tapping intercepts were to be made as piece of legal evidence. Such facility is now available in India. It has been reported in the US press that no such 'intercept warrant' was obtained against Moussaoui for wire tapping on the ground that the judge of the Foreign Intelligence Surveillance Court had previously complained to the Attorney General John Ashoroft about some previous 'FBI request for them'. The fear of the USA privacy law appears to have prevented the FBI to undertake such a vital exercise even when the suspect hailed from another country with doubtful antecedents as revealed from the alleged French intelligence report. This was a serious lapse on the part of the FBI.

Only after 11 September, the FBI thought it prudent to search his computer which strangely disclosed that the said suspect Zacarias Moussaoui had collected information on crop-dusting aircraft. This surely indicates that the terrorists had a plan to initiate bio-terrorism also. The US soon witnessed anthrax terror surfacing in USA in a big way. More terror can be created by bio-terrorism than bombing or attacking a few prominent targets.

Press Trust of India (PTI) filed a damaging report from its London office on 8 September 2002 on US failure to pick up a good piece of intelligence provided by an aide of Wakil Ahmed Muttawakil, the then Taliban foreign minister to the US consul general, David Katz in Peshawar in the third week of July 2001. The story came from the Independent Daily from London. "Muttawakil learnt of the planned attacks on America not from other Taliban leaders, but from the leader of the Islamic Movement of Uzbekistan (IMU) Tahir. IMU had relationship with Al-Qaeda in its fight against the Uzbek government. The aide was in Kabul and disclosed that Muttawakil ordered him to alert the USA and UN about what was going to happen. Muttawakil was desperate to reach out to the US and UN and wanted prevention of such massive planned attacks on the US soil. Apart from David Katz another official was also present possibly from the US intelligence services. It is now learnt that this piece of good intelligence was not passed on to superior officers as the aide purposely did not reveal that the warning came from Muttawakil. The vital information was thus downgraded locally. The emissary pleaded to mount pressure to drive out foreigners out of Afghanistan and stop Pakistan supporting the Taliban.[24] Katz was subsequently posted at the American Embassy in Eritrea. He reportedly declined to talk about this meeting with the aide of

---

24 *The Statesman*, 8 September, 2002.

Muttawakil. The American intelligence service was suffering from "warning fatigue".

There is said to be an intercept before 11 September between Osama and an associate located in Pakistan. Osama reportedly praised the scale of operation and also praised the jihadis for planning the operation.[25]

Missed early warning signals

The possible Link between IC 814 hijacking and WTC attacks is based on a report that Omar Sheikh, now sentenced to death for murder of Daniel Pearl, a US journalist, had reportedly sent by wire or otherwise $100,000 to Mohammad Atta, the principal architect of 11 September attacks.[26] Omar Sheikh had to be released from Indian prison in exchange of release of captive passengers of IC 814 in December 1999. His possible role in funding the 9/11 will be discussed as we proceed with the unfolding of events.

On 10 September Mohammad Atta and three others wired $5000 each to UAE and the man who collected the money left for Pakistan. The press reported his name as Mustafa Ahmed with strong connections in Pakistan. Much has not been heard about these financial transactions nor there are reports of confirmations or denials of such transactions. Any possible Pakistani links are not highlighted by the US media possibly for political reasons.

A Srinagar resident Nadeem Khatib was killed in an encounter on February 21, 1999. Khatib had obtained pilot training at Karnal, Haryana, India. He could only complete 17 of the 300 hours of flying. He then left for the South East school of Aeronautics in Georgia where he obtained 700 hours of flying training and a license. He returned to India in 1995 and again left for the US to complete a jet aircraft flying course from Atlanta. He reportedly served with terrorists units in Bosnia, Chechnya and Afghanistan. Was he being trained as a pilot for air attacks? It is said that the US intelligence authorities showed no interest in Khatib affair. A little probe in the

---

25 *Asian Age*, 8 October 2001.

26 *Asian Age*, 8 October 2001.

USA would have opened some leads to terrorist network that funded his costly training and reasons behind the pilot training without seeking placement for career promotion. This was unusual.

When Syed Abu Nasir, a Bangladeshi Lashker-e-Toiba was apprehended in Delhi in January 1999 for organizing attacks on US interests in India, the theory of the Indian police was reportedly brushed away by the US agencies. Nasir had foreigners with him who managed to vanish. He was tested by FBI official on lie-detector and found his involvement to be true. Such casual approach of the FBI is rather amazing.[27] In the same way when Howash, a Sudanese, was caught and was found to be planning to bomb the US embassy in New Delhi, no great interest was shown to follow the leads provided by Howash. He even named Al Safani as another conspirator, who according to Hawash, took part in USS Cole operation that remained untraced. On the basis of evidence, the Delhi police (India) had charge sheeted the case naming Osama bin Laden and Al-Safani as absconding accused.

There is an interesting report that the FBI's field office in Phoenix, Ariz, had reported last summer that an unusual number of Arabs were taking flight lessons.[28] The US border management was really porous as the US believes in freedom and open society. There is nothing wrong in that. In another case the CIA had apparently intimated the Immigration and Naturalization Service barring entry into the US of two men called Khalid Almihdhar and Nawaf Al-hazmi. The CIA action was based on certain valid reasons. Almihdhar had attended a meeting in Malaysia in January 2000 with people who were later implicated in the bombing of USS Cole. The Immigration Service on Computer Search reported that both these men had already landed on US soil. The FBI, responsible for internal security of the United states, could not unfortunately trace them. This failure proved costly as they boarded the flight 77 and crashed into Pentagon. The US visa regime was porous and benefited the terrorists.

One missed signal was the militant activities in France that

27 *Frontline*, October 12, 2001.

28 *News Week*, October 29, 2001.

came too late and much after the event. The story revolves round Djemal Beghal, an Algerian born Frenchman. He had months of terrorist training in Afghanistan. He was instructed in July 2001 by Abu Zubaidah, operational expert of Al Qaeda and ranked next to Mohammed Atef, to return to France and organise a suicide bombing of the US embassy in Paris. His first task was to shave his beard, and put on western clothing and behave like a non-Jihadi. He even received gifts from bin Laden that included prayer beads. He was fully baptized for the Islamic cause.

Fortunately on July 28, Beghal's plan just collapsed at Dubai airport where he was apprehended for possession of a forged visa extension document. After weeks of interrogation he poured out of a wealth of information on Al-Qaeda. The address of the Hamburg cell of Al Qaeda was obtained, but Mohammed Atta and his associates had already slipped into USA and were within days of carrying out their diabolical mission.

As per operational plan Beghal was to visit Morocco and Spain for fund raising and make tie-up arrangements. In 1997 he visited London where some of the Muslim clerics had been preaching and teaching Jihad. Three plots were hatched, namely WTC attack, blasting of US Embassy in Paris and assassination of Ahmed Shah Masood in Afghanistan. London was the common point for meeting of terrorists of all these three plots. In London Abu Qatada, a Palestinian from Jordan, a fugitive from his native state, was given asylum by the U.K. His London mosque was frequented by Beghal, Zacarius and Abu Walid, right hand man of Abu Qatada. They were often seen together.

It may be said without hesitation that Islamic militancy took deep roots in Europe during the eighties and nineties and the European governments just failed to understand the depth, the danger and the gravity of the militant groups hopping from one country to another. It became the 'forward operating base' for world wide Islamic terrorism. Britain was used as 'a way-station' for those sent to Afghanistan for arms training and briefing. France was the base for foot soldiers and Germany was used for 'notching conspiracy'. London became the forwarding operating base for many non-

Muslim outfits also like LTTE and the Punjab terrorists also..

The UAE authorities realizing the gravity of the situation after the US blasts, handed over Beghal to the French authorities only on 23 September 2001. Before that Beghal had signed 32 documents in Arabic with 16 questions that summarized his confessions, which he quickly retracted before the French authorities.[29]

Beghal was meticulous in his planning. He had already recruited Kamel Dondi for US embassy blast in Paris. They roped in a French man Jerome Courtailler who got converted to Islam, and Abu Dahdah, bin Laden's chief Lieutenant in Europe. Abu Dahdah made at least 20 trips to London. His cell number was found in Mohammad Atta's papers. From Madrid residence of Abu Dahdah videotapes of airports and a CD-ROM on the infra-structure of an American airport were also found. Beghal recruited a soccer player Trabelsi, a Tunisian living in Brussels, as van driver for the suicide mission. In other words the tie-up arrangements were almost complete for Paris attack.

The most significant disclosure was that Beghal intended to open a cyber cafe to communicate in code with Laden's operatives in Afghanistan. Most codes were hidden in pictures transmitted over the internet. The final approval always came from Afghanistan. The same technique was used by a Pakistani who opened a cyber cafe in Delhi before the Red Fort attack by the Lashker-e-Toiba. The bin Laden and his extended outfits used profitably the modern means of communications in a secured way.

Nanci Peloosi, a member of the US Joint Intelligence Committee, was truly right when she said that 'people talk about connecting dots' as if the intelligence analysis was that very easy and simple. The last nail on the coffin was hit by Senator Richard Shelby, another member of the Joint Intelligence Committee. He said: 'they don't have excuse because the information was in their lap and they didn't do anything to prevent it'.[30]

19 out of 20 hijackers reached and settled in the US blending

---

29   International Herald Tribune, December 29-30, 2001.

30   *The Statesman*, 4 June 2002.

'seamlessly into suburban America'. It is estimated there was 18 months of preparation for New York and Washington attack. Out of 10 trained pilots only six were used. The names of the four others are yet to surface. The six took leadership roles. They were separated by thousand of miles and remained in the US undetected for the longest period. Out of 20 only Zacarius could he caught who refused to spill the bean. The FBI could not extract any information from him as they did not confront him with his dangerous antecedents or searched his computer in the absence of a warrant for search.

As it would appear now the conspiracy was hatched in Germany with support base in Britain, UAE, Afghanistan and Pakistan. For reasons of political necessity, the names of Pakistan and ISI are never mentioned as Pakistan was then a close ally of the US. None of the hijackers brought their wives or families. Seven of them comfortably obtained Florida's driving licenses posing as US citizens. The same technique was used by the LTTE operatives in India for proving their Indian citizenship. It is the rough estimate that some $500,000 was received from overseas for 9/11 attack. Mohammed Atta, 33 then, son of an Egyptian lawyer, is considered as the 'axle of the plot'.

The US intelligence community after the September 11 attack, took the stand that the attack could not have been prevented. Now we have the version of a senior FBI lady officer Coleen Rawley who becomes the first 'whistle blower' claiming a cover up operation. She could not stay silent. In early May 2002 at 3 am she rushed to her office to write her version of the story. After fine-tuning the draft she dispatched a 13 page memo to FBI Director Robert Muller and she flew to Washington for hand delivery of copies to two members of the Senate Intelligence Committee and also met with committee staffers. The FBI 'classified' the memo, which in India means a 'top secret' document.

Her arguments were that despite a good and reliable report on Aquarius, no wiretap or warrant to search computer of Zacarius could be obtained by the FBI. The FBI headquarters, instead acting fast, sat over the report raising silly questions by the desk officers. No enquiry was conducted to find out who all had taken flight lessons and obtaining reports on their antecedents. Such an exercise would have blocked the attacks. Muller and his senior aides omitted, down played, glossed over or mischaracterized her office investigation of Moussaouri Zacarius.

Bin Laden's extended family stayed at various places in the US and Europe. It was said that a report did indicate that a member of Osama bin Laden's family was told to move to safety. This was another early warning signal missed by the agencies.

In India people with knowledge have been advocating for stricter visa regime with on-line computer facility. This has been advocated as anti-national and anti-social characters of neighbouring countries beat the Indian visa system by producing fake visa at the point of entry. In the USA all the 19 hijackers were believed to have entered the USA with valid visa documents. Out of 19, 6 visas were to be traced. The USA has all the facility of visa computerization. Even if 6 visas are traced, it does not help in the investigation of the case. For Indians visiting America even on tourist visa, hundreds of questions are asked. Visas are not delivered on a platter. The fear of the Americans was that the Indians visiting America may ultimately vanish and settle down in America by a variety of methods. The fear of terrorists visiting the USA was not on high priority.

How strange it was that Mohammad Atta and Marwan Al-Shehhi entered USA on 'tourist visa.' The duo crashed two planes into the twin towers of the WTC. Their visa status did not entitle them to go in for a flight training course as they did not obtain 'student visa'. The flight training school authorities just failed to detect this anomaly nor did they apparently inform the authorities. It appears that there is no system of intimation of enrolment of foreign citizens to US immigration authorities to check their travel and visa status. Once a visa holder enters the US, he melts into the crowd.

It is said that Ahmed Ajjaj landed in the United States in 1992 with a Swedish passport under 'visa waiver' system. Even his passport was fake as it contained his photograph super imposed on another photo. He was merely jailed for a passport fraud. That was fine for him as he reportedly plotted the 1993 WTC bombing from his safe haven in prison. He came to USA along with Ramzi Yousef. The tendency to quickly dispose off cases with minor offences was proving counter productive. A quick check-back on his antecedents by the CIA/FBI would have yielded leads which could have prevented the first WTC blast in 1993.

A Joint Congressional Panel has been tasked to review the performance of the CIA, FBI and other intelligence agencies to find reasons for not anticipating the September 11 attacks and also recommend steps to strengthen these agencies. During the panel hearings reports appeared in newspapers about two vital intercepts recorded by the National Security Agency on September 10, 2001. The intercepts were in Arabic. These were two snippets of conversion, one stating 'the match is about to begin' and the other saying 'tomorrow is Zero Hour'. These intercepts were translated after 11 September precisely on 12 September.[31]

Same was the case of Rajiv Gandhi murder. The LTTE's wireless intercepts between Jaffna and Madras (Now Chennai), giving enough information on the impending murder of Rajiv, could be decoded only after Rajiv Gandhi's death on 21 May, 1991. Such bureaucratic delays were noticed all over the world. The quick dissemination of useful intercepts is necessary if terrorist crimes are to be prevented. This is possible if bureaucratic delays are reduced.

Investigation

Now the chairman of the Senate Intelligence Committee Sen Bob Graham told reporters in the month of May 2002 that some requested documents were not being turned over to the committee nor did they receive interviews of potential witnesses. In India such interviews are called statements of the witnesses. CIA spokesman denied the charge. Graham said that the Committee may exercise its subpoena power to force cooperation. On Intelligence, the US spends more than $ 30 bn a year.

In the absence of definite leads, the first step the investigators took was to embark upon interviewing Muslim non-citizens who entered the US post September 11. In the first phase 5000 were

---

31   International Herald Tribune, August 3-4, 2002.

interviewed. Only a few could lead to terrorist groups. 3000 more were interviewed subsequently. The FBI could net in only one person who had sighted one of the hijackers and the address of another person who was linked to one of them. Of the 20 taken in, most of them were charged with immigration violations. This exercise was highly criticized as a stunt by the Arab American Institute.

In Rajiv Gandhi assassination case a slightly different exercise was carried out by interviewing of persons who had links with LTTE in a significant way. There was enough building up of a list of such persons on the basis of linkage evidence. The exercise yielded good results by way of recovery of documents and disclosure of facts. Perhaps the US did not build up a list of persons who could provide material evidence on the basis of hard facts.

Now US army is teaching its officers how to interrogate suspects already in the custody of the US. Staff Sgt Siersdorf, who was said to be a veteran intelligence operative, was teaching new recruits how to extract information. The Pentagon now calls them 'human intelligence collectors'. They are authorized 'not just to lie' but to find out prisoner's ethnic stereotypes, sexual urges, religious prejudices, fear for family safety, or resentment of his fellows.

The US was then facing a shortage of experienced interrogators as also intelligence officers with knowledge of Arabic language Posthu, Urdu and other languages of the troubled region. Al-Qaeda and Taliban prisoners were fanatics who had deep hatred against the United States. It was difficult to extract information from them. For each information provided by the prisoners there has to be substantial corroboration which require assistance from the concerned countries. Even in small cases the developed countries insist on 'Letter Regotary' to be addressed to jurisdictional magistrates or courts of competence. It is the experience of the requesting countries that such exercises are delayed and fruitless as a magistrate has no training in interrogation nor is he expected to do a policeman's job. International judicial assistance needs revamping. Interpol system is more useful as it allows investigators to visit other countries and obtain documents and interrogation reports. The requested country offers police assistance for carrying out such exercises in terms of their domestic laws.

All these techniques are elementary known to all police officers in the world. A new recruit is incapable for good interrogation. It requires years of experience to become an expert interrogator. The trouble is that Al Qaeda and Taliban operatives are held as prisoners of war and are required to be treated as such under the Geneva Convention of 1949. The best course would be to segregate these prisoners who had committed criminal offences prior to 11 September and hand them over to FBI. Abu Zubaydah falls under this category. The former Taliban Foreign Minister Muttawakil, who did not like Arab involvement in Afghanistan, may be too willing to disclose the relationship between Al Qaeda and Taliban, how the ISI helped to build up Laden and Taliban. He was under the US custody. But then how can the US do this as that goes against the interest of Pakistan.

Planning of the conspiracy

The theory of Al Qaeda conspiracy for the US attacks on September 11.

This has now been explained by two top Al Qaeda leaders to a reporter of Al-Jazeera, Yosri Fauda who was the Bureau's Chief of London office. He met Khalid Sheikh Mohammed and Ramzi Binalshibh near Karachi. Binalshibh is a suspect of bombing of USS Cole. Ramzi Binalshibh was also a former roommate of Mohammed Atta, the ring leader of the 11 September hijack group. Yosri Fauda claimed that he was taken to a location near Karachi blind-folded.

According to them the plan was plotted in Kandahar. Ramji Binalshibh described himself as head of Al Qaeda's military committee. They described the US attack as 'Ghazwah' which means a raid against enemies of the Prophet. It took two years to plan the attack. US Nuclear targets were the first choice which was ultimately given up.

The hijackers were recruited from Al Qaeda's 'Department of Martyrs'. Atta was a sleeper recruited in 1992 and so was Nawaj Al Hazemi. Binalshibh wanted to be the twentieth hijacker and applied for visa for flight training three times but failed. Both Binalshibh and Khalid were subsequently arrested in Pakistan on the basis of US intelligence.

Leading hijackers, names not mentioned, were summoned to Kandahar for a 'shura' or council meeting. Four advance reconnaissance units were sent to America.

The plotters used internet extensively to communicate with Binalshibh who remained in Germany. The messages were in German address to 'Jenny', a fictitious girlfriend of Atta. Each target had a code name. WTC was 'the Faculty of Town Planning', Pentagon was the Faculty of Fine Arts and Congress was the Faculty of Law. The final date of attack was communicated by telephone. The date was communicated in a coded language, 'two slicks, a dash and a cock with a stick down'. The news of the proposed attack reached Osama on 6 September.[32]

This damaging disclosure of Khalid Sheikh Mohammed and Binalshibh forced Pakistani foreign office spokesman Aziz Ahmed Khan to deny the existence of Al Qaeda office in Karachi and the report was described speculative. The point to be considered as to why the Al Qaeda should take the credit for the attack which they have been denying so far. Much of the story can be cross checked by the FBI which is investigating the case. How was it that the suspects of the 11 September attack had managed to escape the dragnet inspite of Interpol's red alert notice? Why the ISI could not apprehend them in the first instance immediately after 9/11.

US released photos of 19 men suspected of orchestrating the attacks on the WTC and Pentagon said AFP, Washington on 28 September. Said Attorney General John Ashosoft: "It is our hope that the release of these photos will prompt others who may have seen the hijackers or been in contact with them to contact the FBI with any information they may have that would be helpful in the investigation".[33]

The FBI was said to be pursuing 200,000 leads and considered

---

32 *Statesman*, Tuesday 10 September, 2002 quoting: Times report from London.

33 INT.com dated 28-09-01.

the case as the largest probe in the US history. The Indian experience in Rajiv Gandhi assassination was similar. The photographs of the principal suspects including of one-eyed Sivanasan were flashed all over Tamilnadu. Hundreds of information flowed in and some were useful to identify the suspects, their whereabouts and location. Once the persons were identified it was not difficult for the tracking teams to apprehend them dead or alive.

FBI Director Robert Muller said: 'our primary focus was on preventing potential future attacks. We are working hard to identify and locate associates of the hijackers who may pose a threat to this (US) nation'.

ABC News reported, Laden planned another attack to free Sheikh Omer Abdel Rehman. In an interview an Al-Qaeda operative, known as 'max', said while 'it would be very difficult for them to do this release, they are trying, even now, just looking for a chance'.

A doubt was raised by a French writer Thierry Meyssan in his book 'The Horrible Fraud'. He claims that the whole episode is 'a loony fable', patched together by the White House and the US Department of Defence. His theory was based on the following reasonings:

(a) The American Airlines flight neither 77 nor any other aircraft crashed into Pentagon on September 11. The explosion was supposedly detonated on the ground. There is no film footage on Pentagon air strike.

(b) The planes that struck WTC were 'Pilotless planes' directed by remote control.

(c) Story in the May 27, 2002 in Time magazine referred to Meyssan's theory without denial from the right quarters.

(d) The beneficiaries of the war on terror were the military industrial lobby whose dreams have been fulfilled.

(e) The theory of Mossad (Israeli Intelligence) involved in the act as no Jew employed in the World Trade Centre turned up for work on that fateful day.

Added to this is Gen Musharraf's theory that Osama bin Laden might not be responsible for the attack and other brains loyal to Osama might have staged the attack. He said: 'I did not think it possible that Osama sitting up there in the mountains could do it.'

Musharraf's statement did not invite any comments from the US or the allies. In fact, he was kept in good humour by providing financial and military aids. As a result the foreign exchange reserve of Pakistan had gone up to $ 7 bn from less than 1 bn in 2000. Gen Musharraf had good idea of Taliban and Al Qaeda. Where were Mullah Omar and Osama? Are they teamed up or working separately. Gen Musharraf should know better. The USA and Musharraf were silent. This was intriguing. How was it that USA was being misled by Musharraf without raising any eyebrow? One Vazeershuddin repeated the story of the French author, which was reproduced in the National Herald of 9 September, 2002 (an Indian newspaper). The writer is a Hyderabad based senior journalist. This story did not click in view of the overwhelming evidence unearthed during the investigation.

Funding

Terrorism is sustained by two factors. There has to be a sanctuary for training and hatching conspiracy. Some states, which are called 'rogue states', give protection and shelter to principal promoters of terrorism. The second factor is to raise fabulous amount of money and to provide financial infra-structure for flow of terrorist money to desired destinations.

Taliban and Pakistan provided the safe sanctuary to various terrorist organizations. Prominent researchers like John K. Cooley had termed the area as 'hub of international terrorism'. There was a plethora of open reporting on terrorist training facilities in Pakistan and Afghanistan by the international and Pakistani press. All the terrorist groups in Pakistan and Afghanistan were under the control of Taliban and Al Qaeda. They worked in tandem. From 1998 onwards the Jihadi groups like Lashkar-e-Toiba in Pakistan openly claimed to have dispatched Jihadis to Chechnya, Dagesthan, Bosnia, Myanmar and the Philippines. Of course India was included as the prime target to be attacked. 'Al Dawa', magazines of Markaz Dawa-Wal Irshad, the parent body of the Lashker-e-Toiba, periodically reported the names of such terrorists who sacrificed their lives fighting against the 'infidels'. These did not cause any alarm to the USA and its Western allies. Indians have been victims of terrorism for the last three decades. Every year more than thousand policemen are killed in anti-insurgency operations. The Indian army casualties are quite substantial. These signals were ignored on the ground that no US and Western targets were attacked. Few killings of Western and American hostages were considered as of no firm indication of Jihad against them. US anti-terrorists analysts worked under a syndrome that no terrorist would dare attack the USA on its own soil for fear of massive retaliation. This was a wrong estimation of the developing situation. In terrorism there is always an escalatory ladder of violence and attacks. The last rung of the ladder is yet to be reached. More serious and devastating strikes are expected by serious analysts, after 9/11.

There have been too many compromises with the terrorist groups. One blatant case is of Lashker-e-Toiba. In 2000-01, the Lashker-e-Toiba and its parent organisation Markaz Dawa Wal-Irshad had obtained legal opinion from Pakistan lawyers to beat the US system of declaration of a Foreign Terrorist Organisation by a backdoor pleading with the US authorities that no US targets would be attacked and non-combatants to be spared in Jammu and Kashmir. The US President, who has now waged a 'war on terror' in all its form, initiated a laudable campaign against the 'evil'. He often says that 'make no mistake' of US determination to deal with all forms of terrorism. His hit list of 27 entities and enlarged to another 37 did not include Lashker-e-Toiba which operates not only in India, but also elsewhere. The US authorities did not scrutinize the annual convention reports of LeT from the year 1997 onwards. In their annual conventions the US, Israel and India had always been openly declared targets to be attacked.

Funding of terrorism was neglected for a long period. Now there is a talk of starving of funds available to the terrorists. This is not an easy task as all leads will lead to regimes who are allies of

USA now to fight against international terrorism. More than 4000 investigators of the FBI were hunting for evidence world over.

The USA for years neglected the Hawala networks that operate from the US without any official hindrance. In 1989 this matter was brought to the notice of all countries by the Indian delegate in an Interpol conference with documentary proof of US soil being used for this purpose. The US and the Western world treated this as a fiscal offence and not a conduit for terrorist funding. Now Hawala has emerged as the main route for terrorist funding.

Maulana Masood Azhar, Amir of Jaish-e-Mohammed, was a close ally of Osama bin Laden. Jaish-e-Mohammed operated bank account with ANZ Grindlays Bank in Sadar Branch of Rawalpindi. Cheques flowed into this account from all over the world. Several other bank accounts were yet to be traced.[34]

Douglas Farah from Freetown, Sierra Leone reported that Osama bin Laden operatives dealt with gems business with the rebels *i.e.* Revolutionary United Front by buying gems at below the market rate and selling them at a huge profit in European markets. Gems can easily be converted into cash. Sierra Leone's diamond fields are said to be richest in the world and have remained largely under the control of the rebels. The Liberian government was accused of providing safe houses for secret transactions. The report had identified one Bah Ibrahim Bah, a Libyan as RUF's diamond dealer.[35]

Ahmed Rashid, who is considered an expert on Taliban and Al Qaeda, said in October 2001 that "External financial loyalties and their methodical preparation would allow their leaders and fighters to survive at least for six months". Over the last 7 years, the Taliban had built up extensive links with external groups, religious parties and smugglers. It was difficult to shut this down internationally.[36] The reality is that Al Qaeda could sustain itself by hawala system of funding and this route of money transfer has not been smashed by the

---

34 *Pioneer*, October 31, 2001.

35 *Indian Express*, November 3, 2001.

36 *Herald Tribune*, 27, 28 October, 2001.

international community by imposing a ban on them. Such money transfers are carried out openly in the US and the US Treasury was aware of it.

This war against terrorism is not only limited to military strikes against the fully armed terrorists, but also a war against the "highly complex financial network that nourishes terrorism world-wide is the real enemy to vanquish".[37] The money flow is global, without money trail, pumping money into terrorist network through thousands of legal business entities, dubious charities, welfare trusts and substantial individual contributions. What is required is to disrupt the staging points, chock the flow, identify the evil entities with legal backup to freeze and confiscate the terrorist money world-wide. So far they have managed to escape from the clutches of law as the laws are inadequate and insufficient. The scale of terrorist operations in Jammu and Kashmir and elsewhere in India will require more than what a state like Pakistan can financially afford. Financial sleuths have to be inducted and trained to look for evidence of flow of money into terrorist outfits. This element of global attack on financial network is lacking as many state actors are helping this evil financial network. This is a serious matter, which cannot be just wished away.

19 hijackers of 9/11

Nationalities of these 19 hijackers were as follows:

- Saudi Arabia   15
- United Arab Emirates   2
- Egypt   1
- Lebanon   1

Investigation so far conducted, and as found from press reports, has been able to piece together the participatory roles of the 19 hijackers. The principal actors have to be those who got training in flying civilian aircrafts knowing that they would be killed when they would crash against the targets. They formed the core group of the

---

37 Cover story, Financing Terror, Business World, 15 October 2001.

suicide squad determined and highly motivated to act the way they did. It was a part of a powerful force which had a long term goal of expelling the US forces from the whole of the Middle East. It was a coalition of groups whose tentacles stretched from Gaza, the West Bank through Egypt, Iran and Iraq, Pakistan and Kashmir up into Central Asia.[38] Incidentally, Hawksly is the author of 'Dragon Fire' a futuristic study of nuclear war between India, Pakistan and China.

Profiles of hijackers

1. Mohammad Atta, (a trained pilot), Abdulaziz, Alomari, M. Alshehri, Satam Al Suquami, boarded AA flight 11 which crashed into the north tower at 8.45 a.m. Marwan Al-Shehhi, and Ziad Jarrah, Fayez Rashid Banihammad, Mohand Al Sehri, Hamza Al Ghamadi, boarded United Airlines Flight 175 which crashed into the WTC south tower at 9.00 a.m.

2. Khalid Almihadhar, Majed Moqed, Nawaf Alhazmi, Salem Alhazmi, Hani Hanjour (Pilot) all boarded AA flight No: 77 dashed against the Pentagon at 9.43 a.m.

3. Ahmed Alnami, Ahmed Ibrahim Al Haznami, Ziad Samir Jarrah and Saeed Al Ghamadi which boarded AA flight 175 crashed in the forest area of Pittsburgh at 10 a.m.

Trained pilots commandeered the controls of the planes and tough 'minders' took control of the passengers and crews. There should have been five hijackers for each plane making a total of 20. One of them Zacarious Moussaouri was arrested a month before on a fake passport case. He was to have been included in the Pittsburgh case by way of simple logic.

As all the 19 hijackers were dead and gone. Thus, in the absence of living hijackers, it was a difficult task to find out other conspirators who planned the operation in a copybook manner. The hijackers needed a superior brain to work out the details of the operation, needed enough money to execute the plan. They also needed visas to enter USA. The back-up team members have been finally located and apprehended. In hijacking of IC 814 by Pakistani

---

38 Hamphrey Hawksly, *The Week* September 23, 2001.

Jihadis in December 1999, the back team was located in Mumbai (Bombay). On the basis of intercepts they were promptly located and apprehended which opened up the case.

The US system provides surveillance by secret video recording at important places. In one such video recording Lofti Raissi, an Algerian pilot living in the United Kingdom was found flying with Hani Hanjour from Las Vegas to Phoenix in June 2001. Raissi had previously lived in USA with a social security number of a dead woman. His extradition to USA from the UK to answer a variety of questions was rejected on the basis of inadequacy of evidence. How can evidence be collected in the absence of custodial interrogation of the suspect?

The other person who could possibly prove the existence of the principal planner was in US custody namely Zacarias. He successfully dodged the FBI investigators before 9/11. He was key to a successful break through in the unfolding of the conspiracy. Apparently the FBI had failed to elicit enough information from him on 11 September incident. He was subsequently charged in a court of law for 9/11 attack.

The hijackers were surely guided by a master mind. In such cases the principal actor or actors remains far away from the scene of occurrence. In the case of Rajiv Gandhi murder case the conspiracy was hatched in Jaffna or in the area under the control of LTTE. That could be proved by oral evidence backed up by documentary evidence in the form of letters addressed to LTTE headquarters but due to difficulties of travel such letters could not be delivered to him. The fingerprints on such letters matched with the finger-print of a female body of the LTTE who committed suicide when the group was trapped by the police at the outskirts of the Bangalore city of India.

Where the conspiracy was really hatched in September 11 case? One theory was that the whole conspiracy was executed by Mohammad Atta, who had in spells visited Pakistan and Afghanistan. Facts of such visits have to be proved by documentary and oral evidence mainly from Pakistan. Enough light can be thrown if each of his visa applications was critically scrutinized. That type of investigation would lead to Pakistan. He made numerous calls. Can FBI build up an extensive analysis of telephone calls to locate his contacts and handlers? This is perhaps not possible as Pakistani link will be exposed.

Such thinking is based on Atta's long stay in Hamburg in Germany. He had frequently visited the US, Spain in the critical period in 2001. His contacts in USA and Spain will have to be located by scrutiny of hotel records, cell phones records, car rental agencies and payment particulars. All his contacts need to be checked and searches organised for unearthing of evidence. For this to happen international cooperation is necessary. His visit to Spain is rather intriguing.

Atta's German contacts were important. Rajiv Gandhi case opened up due to folly of the photographer Hari Babu who took 10 vital pictures showing the location of the hit squad positioned at different places in a public meeting to be addressed by Rajiv Gandhi. The photographer died in the blast and the camera with the roll was retrieved wisely by the police. These photographs, shown on TV and newspapers, enabled the people to cooperate with the investigation team and good evidence could be collected on each of them.

It is claimed that four hijackers received military training in Osama bin Laden's training camps in Afghanistan. If this was established by evidence, in a way it proves Al Qaida's involvement with the hijackers. It is clear now that this type of evidence has been really unearthed to show such linkage. This again leads to Pakistan as four hijackers might have transited through Pakistan. How did they receive visa from Pakistan?

The FBI could trace one Herbert Villalobos, a witness valuable to prove how he helped Ahmed Saleh Al-ghamdi and Armory and another to obtain Virginia state ID cards on August 2, 2001 by a so called their chance meeting with him near the office of the Virginia Department of motor vehicles in Arlington. He and his friend reportedly signed up papers to prove their identity as residents of Virginia. Alomori on paper was shown as Oscar Diaz. Vallalobos was perhaps booked for helping some accused to obtain false identity to obtain false driving license. It is said Vallalobos did not work for Al Qaida and perhaps never heard of bin Laden. Why the licensing authorities failed to check social security numbers which were available on line computer?

In Rajiv Gandhi assassination, on CBI's public request, some 3000 callers provided information on some of the accused still escaping the CBI's dragnet. Out of 3000 odd information, only couple of inputs was found to be true. In a similar way the FBI received response flooded with phone calls and E-mails.

It is claimed that within hours of these attacks, the agencies were able to intercept phone calls from known Osama bin Laden's supporters boasting **'we have hit the targets'**. All these intercepts must have been proved by voice matching and tracing the individuals. The task was stupendous, may or may not provide further leads to prove the conspiracy and involvement of Osama bin Laden and lieutenants whoever they may be.

All possible suspects and members of Al-Qaeda were arrested in the USA and elsewhere for possible clues in the investigation of the September 11 case. The FBI was looking for one Nabil al-Marabh. On September 17, he was not found at 2653 Norman Street, Detroit. Instead three others namely Karim Kourbriti (23), Ahmen Hannan (33), and Youssef Himimssa were found at that residence. From the residence some notes were found indicating an American base in Turkey. They have been charged for commission of fraud. However, Marabh was eventually arrested on 19 September in the subway Chicago. He had a valid license to haul hazardous materials.

The FBI had rounded up 800 people perhaps on suspicion. Out of 800, only 10 were said to have links to hijacking. Strangely each of these ten was 'not talking'. Under law a suspect can refuse to talk. This makes the job of the FBI harder.[39] The list of suspects will increase further. Three Germans and one Australian were arrested by Pakistan authorities when they tried to enter Pakistan after visiting Afghanistan. Within 48 hours one German was extradited to USA

---

39 Newsweek, 29 October, 2001.

and the other three might also have been extradited.[40]

Any straight forward investigation will ultimately lead to Pakistan, Saudi Arabia and UAE. This is bound to happen as Taliban and Osama bin Laden was the test-tube babies of Pakistan and its ISI. The rumour was that General Mahmood, the ex-ISI Chief, was close to Omar Sheikh, a 27 year old British national who was one of the kidnappers of three British tourists from India. He was apprehended by a chance encounter with Ghaziabad police of the state of U.P., India. Inspector Drub Lal Yadav of Ghaziabad Police Station, after interrogating him, found that two Britons were holed up in another district called Saharanpur of state of U.P. Omar Sheikh was subsequently arrested for murder of Daniel Pearl, a journalist. On ISI - Taliban link the best judgment has been given by Ahmed Rashid "Such parenting could not be severed overnight".[41]

Dhrub Lal Yadav lost no time in locating the house where they were kept. He launched a frontal attack at midnight by knocking the door. The door was slightly opened by the terrorists who opened fire on Dhrub Lal Yadav and his constable. Both died on the spot. The terrorists managed to escape under the cover of darkness leaving behind captive British nationals.

Dhrub Lal Yadav had worked under the author in Jhansi range at police station Kalpi of district Jalaun, U.P. He became a local hero in Bundelkhand when he organised a series of daytime encounters against the dreaded gangs like Phoolan, Mustaquim, Balwan, Ram Avtar and many others. He had earned a number of gallantry awards for extreme bravery. The demand of the kidnappers was to bargain for the release of Masood Azhar. Ultimately Azhar and two others were released in exchange of captive passengers of IC 814 which was hijacked by terrorists belonging to Harkat-ul-Mujahideen, an affiliate of Al-Qaeda. The headquarters of Harkat-ul-Mujahaideen is in Raiwind near Lahore, the place where the Prime Minister of Pakistan Nawaz Sharief lived. Raiwind is also the headquarters of Tabligi Jamaat, an organization devoted to spread of pure form of Islam and said to have played a big role in recruitment of Jihadis

---

40 *The Friday Times*, October 26, November 1, 2001, Salman Hussein.

41 *International Herald Tribune*, 27-28 October, 2001.

from all over the world during 1979-89 Afghan jihad.

There are common features of hijacking of Indian plane IC 814 in December 1999 and hijacking of four planes in USA on 11 September, 2001. Some of the hijackers of IC 814 knew how the plane functioned. They also spoke highly of Osama bin Laden to pilots. They even threatened to dash against any target in the event of failure in the exchange deal. The five hijackers of IC 814 are now safely residing in Pakistan and there are no efforts to trace them and extradite them for trial in India. This is in violation of international conventions on terrorism. Gen Musharraf joined the US-led coalition to fight against terrorism in all its forms. He could have proved his credibility by arresting the hijackers of IC 814 which he refused. One hijacker Ibrahim is brother of Maulana Azhar.

At the very initial stage of hijacking of IC 814, some of the conspirators, local and foreigners, providing ground support were quickly picked up in Mumbai. Perhaps intercepts made that possible. All the hijackers have been identified by name and address. The trial of these absconding hijackers has been blocked by Pakistan by not providing assistance as Harkat-ul-Mujahideen have links with ISI for its Kashmir operation and have deep links with Taliban and Al Qaeda. In Khost missile attack on August 20, 1998, many Mujahideen of this outfit were killed. Now again in October 2001 Jihadis of Harkat were killed by US bombardment in Kabul. This is in the knowledge of the whole world. Evidence of hijacking of Indian Airline planes were found from Harkat's Kabul office.

After release from Indian prison Omar Sheikh took shelter in Pakistan. Investigation done so far is leading towards him as he is suspected to have arranged transfer of $ 100,000 to Mohammad Atta. It is not known whether the money was transferred by wire or by 'Hawala' which is the underground banking system in the sub-continent. This lead has possibly blocked by evasive reply from Pakistan. It is a major embarrassment for ISI which may have known about the 11 September attack on US targets from before. The ISI chief was in the USA on 11 September. Omar Sheikh and Masood Azhar reportedly met bin Laden who gave enough money to Azhar to form the Jaish-e-Mohammed on January 31, 2000. Most of the members of Jaish have been drawn from Harkat ul-Mujahideen. Omar Sheikh subsequently found to have murdered Daniel Pearl, a US journalist in Karachi. He has since been sentenced to death by an anti-terrorists court. Interestingly, he surrendered before an ex-ISI officer who was secretary of Interior of the Sindh Government.

How did Omar Sheikh receive that kind of money? There is a story that Omar Sheikh and Aftab Ansari (Indian Mafia don) developed friendship while they were lodged in Indian jail. Aftab mafia group organised a lot of kidnapping to raise substantial ransom. In case of Partha Burman's kidnapping from Kolkata (Culcutta) reportedly crores were received for his release. The ransom money was sent to UAE through Hawala channel. Reportedly Aftab shared the money with Omar Sheikh. Sheikh was said to have sent $1,00,000 to Mohammad Atta out of this kidnapping. Thus, if true Indian money was used for 9/11 attacks.

This story is now getting confirmed. John S. Pistole, Deputy Assistant Director of the FBI's Counter-terrorism division told the US Senate Governmental Affairs Committee on 31 July 2003 'that investigators have traced the origin of the funding of 9/11 back to financial accounts in Pakistan.' For obvious reason Pistole did not elaborate on the details of funding jihadis. This was made known to the US authorities by India immediately after 9/11. Gen Mahmod Ahmed, ISI Chief was forced out of the ISI. Even Sheikh's mobile numbers were reportedly provided to the FBI. Pistole was silent on these vital elements of conspiracy. It was, however said that money flowed to the hijackers through associates in Germany and UAE and the contact point was Khalid Sheikh Mohammed [KSM] who was really the brain behind the attack from Pakistan. As a part of secret and unwritten understanding the US authorities are reluctant to rope in Omar Sheikh and Lt. Gen. Mahmood Ahmed for interrogation. Thus, there is a reasonable feeling that 9/11 investigation will reveal less and hide more.[42]

Omar Sheikh is a UK national. So was Mohd. Bilal alias Asif

---

42 *The Times of India*, dated August 2, 2003, carrying a report filed by Manoj Joshi who has good understanding of terrorism in South Asia. He is the author of local 'Last Rebellion' which brings out Pak ISI's proxy war in Kashmir.

Sadiq, the suicide bomber of 15 Corps Headquarters, Srinagar. He was initially recruited by the Harkat-ul-Ansar from Birmingham in 1994. The UK links are important in the investigation of 11 September case. Intercept recorded by the UK authorities are yet to come to surface. It is most unlikely that UK will not share such intercepts with other agencies. They rarely do that. India has never benefited out of the India cooperation on terrorism before 9/11.

UK quickly took a U-turn to avoid embarrassment. Tony Blair joined the US-led coalition, visited various countries with a report on Osama's involvement in US attacks. Margaret Thatcher told Mullahs to condemn terrorism as 'the people who brought down these towers were Muslims and Muslims must stand up and say that is not the way of Islam. Passengers on these planes were told that they were going to die and there were children on board. They must say it was disgraceful.[43] Britain was on the defensive as it did nothing to disallow terrorists entering into Britain. It was acting as 'stage for international terrorism'. The track record of Britain was allowing terrorism to grow.

Time, not to be left behind, said if moderates wanted to defeat hatred preached by the ignorant mullahs, 'they must do more to stop the recruitment of boys from Birmingham or Finsbury' and to explode bombs in Yemen and Kashmir'.[44] How can one believe that M15 and M16 were totally in the dark about the enhanced activities of fundamentalist elements within Britain and abroad?

Mohammad Atta (33) an Egyptian received maximum attention as one of prime movers behind the September 11 attacks. His father Mohammad Hassan Attiya is a lawyer by profession. His two daughters, one is a professor and the other a doctor respectively. Mohammad Atta the youngest sibling was a much pampered child of her mother. "He used to sit on the lap of his mother until enrolling at Cairo University." Atta was affluent.

Egypt has a long history of religious fundamentalism starting with Hasan al-Banna's creation of Muslim Brotherhood in 1928,

---

43 *Asian Age*, 5 October 2001.

44 *Asian Age*, 5 October 2001.

while Nasser's nationalism with a mix of socialism was the political colour of the regime. The clash of these two forces, nationalist and Islamist, exploded in 1981 when President Anwar Sadat was assassinated by Al Jihad elements which included Dr. Ayman al-Zawahiri, now in command of Osama bin Laden's Al Qaeda.

President Anwar Sadat's fault was that he made peace with Israel. The fundamentalists called him a puppet of the West and a traitor to Islam. The Arab nationalism and the Muslim fundamentalism thrive on permanent hostility with Israel but have a separate agenda of pan-Islamism.

Mohammad Atta was the product of this situation of turmoil and crisis. He became religious at the age of 12/13 years, the same way Osama bin Laden became religious after witnessing Israel's victory over Syria and Egypt in 1973 and civil war in Lebanon in 1975. Atta graduated from the Cairo University's engineering department in 1990. He got a job with a German company in Egypt, but on his father's insistence he went to Hamburg's Technical University for further studies in Urban Planning. He wanted Mohammad Atta to be an achiever.

Hamburg has substantial Turkish, African and Arab Muslims with three mosques in the vicinity of the university, two Turkish and one Arab mosque. He chose the Arab mosque as Turkish Muslims are considered less devout. Imam Ahmed of the Arab mosque often preached that "America was an enemy of Islam and country unloved in our world!" This must have influenced Atta's world view. After some time he returned to Egypt but again came back to Hamburg in 1996.

Atta's return to Hamburg and living with two hijackers Al-Shehhi (UAE) and Ziad Samir Jazzah in an apartment at 54 Marienstrasse looks strange. This became clear when Atta disappeared from Hamburg in November 1997 and reappeared in early 1999. He however submitted his thesis in August 1999 and earned a degree. During 1997-1999 he reportedly stayed in Afghanistan and Pakistan.

In 1999 one Said Bahaji got married in Hamburg which Atta attended. Out of many guests two deserve special mention. Mamoun

Darazanli, a Syrian businessman was one of them. He was a suspected financial conduit of bin Laden's Al Qaeda. The second guest was Marwan Al-Shehhi who crashed against the second tower of the WTC. The intimacy of two tower crashers is now fully established. Said Bahaji is a German citizen. Against him an international arrest warrant was issued.

Mohammed Atta arrived in America in June 2000, nearly 13 months before the September 11 attack. He disembarked at New York International Airport in New Jersey. He spent most of the time in 'perpetual motion', earning a pilot's License in Florida in the last 6 months of 2000. In between he travelled extensively in the USA and made at least two trips to Europe. All these must have been very expensive. While undergoing flying training in Venice, Florida, he received $ 100,000 by wire transfer from one Mustafa Mohammed Ahmed from UAE. It is believed that his other name is Shayak Said, a finance chief of Osama bin Laden.

On April 8, 2001 Mohammad Atta reached Prague, the capital of Czech Republic. He was reportedly received by Ahmed Khalil Ibrahim Samir al-Ani, Iraq's consul posted in that country. According to Israeli intelligence al-Ani handed over a vacuum flux of anthrax to Atta in a cafe in Prague. The strain of anthrax detected in the USA was mixed complex chemical additive that only three countries are capable of manufacturing *i.e.* America, Russia and Iraq. On April 22 al-Ani was expelled from Czech Republic. It is also said that Atta made trips to Prague in May and June 2000. Atta reportedly met Habib Faris Abdullah al-Mamouri in Rome. Al-Mamouri had meetings with Atta and others in Hamburg and Prague. Al-Mamouri was said to be a general in Iraqi secret service. In Rome he was given a cover appointment as headmaster of an Iraqi school since 1998. He just vanished in July 2001. Reportedly he had specialized in forging links with fundamentalist groups in Pakistan, Afghanistan, the Gulf and Sudan.[45] This line of investigation did not yield result. Otherwise the USA would have used this link-up to show Saddam in bad light.

Mohammad Atta's visits to several places are perhaps being

---

45 John Stock, London, The Week, November 11, 2001.

looked into. He visited the naval base at Norfolk, Va, twice in February and April in 2001. Each visit requires focused investigation for collection of evidence on Al-Qaeda network and its involvement in 11 September case. There were several instances of Al Qaeda operatives working in the USA for years. Ali Mohammed moved to USA from Egypt in 1984. This is the period when the USA was encouraging Jihadis for taking part in Afghan Jihad (1979-89). He served as an instructor in US Special Forces at Fort Bragg, N.C. At the same time, perhaps with the permission of the U.S. authorities, he was imparting training to Islamic terrorists in Brooklyn, N.Y. and Jersey City, during the week ends. Later on he was found involved in bombings of two US embassies in Africa in 1998. Reportedly his links with Osama bin Laden was established on his own admission.[46]

Atta started meeting with other conspirators. His travel to Spain twice does raise a question mark. All these happened between January and July, 2001. He made hundreds of cell phone calls. Two days before the attack he returned his rented car to a car rental agency in South Florida. If his telephone/cell phone calls are analyzed on computer, a pattern will emerge giving a complete picture of his linkages. This Steven Emerson an independent journalist did after 1993 WTC attack. He got details from court exhibits and made contacts with persons who received the calls from America. He got valuable clues to build up his book called 'The American jihad'.

Atta's luggage was found at Logen airport in Boston. Containing many other things, his 'will' was also found. It now appears that Atta was the principal actor in all the four hijack cases. Scrutiny of Atta's bank accounts revealed that remittances were mostly received from some bank accounts in the Middle East and Pakistan.[47] The FBI is yet to disclose publicly the details of such transactions nor has it disclosed or completed list of conspirators for their apprehension. Interpol Red Alert notices would have given the world a fair idea of all the characters involved in the attack. There was hesitancy on the part of the US authorities to name Pakistanis involved in the

---

46 *Newsweek*, October 29, 2001.

47 Chris Blackhurt and Paul Lashmar, October 14, 2001. The article was originally published in the Independent Sunday.

conspiracy. Even the US publicly never demanded for arrest and extradition of Omar Sheikh who reportedly had sent $ 100,000 to Mohammad Atta. Because of this strange behaviour, Sheikh Omar could kill Denial Pearl in Karachi. Was Sheikh Omar close to former ISI chief Gen Mahmud? Was it a mere coincidence that Gen Mahmud was in the USA on 11 September? Did not Pakistani press report that this General has pro-Taliban and pro Osama leanings? If nothing was wrong with him, why did Musharraf remove this General from the ISI? It was beyond the capacity of a single individual to collect a group of 20 hijackers, motivate them, and organise money and other logistics. 'The people behind them need to be identified by hard evidence'.[48] This was the principal task to find out the involvement of other actors behind the scene. Apparently, the FBI has miserably failed to identify by evidence the involvement of other actors or else such evidence would never surface as the principal allies of the US-led coalition are those who had shamelessly supported Osama bin Laden and the Taliban regime.

Omar al-Bayoumi who claimed as an Assistant to Director of a Saudi based aviation Services Company was arrested by the Scotland Yard as he helped pay the rent of two hijackers Nawab Alhazmi and Khalid Ajmihdhar for their apartment in San Diego. Al Bayoumi is well educated and may be privy to many secrets.[49] Lotfi Rassi, an Algerian pilot was seen on videotape flying from Las Vegas to Phoenix in June 2001 with hijacker Honi Hanjour, the pilot who crashed into the Pentagon. The UK court refused his extradition to USA as US failed to provide more clinching evidence against Raissi. It is not known whether Raissi's account were checked and his home searched for evidence. That he made frequent visits to USA was perhaps not backed up by evidence of his deep conspiratorial intimacy with Honi Hanjour and other members of the group. It is not known how he could finance his frequent trips to the USA. The US failed to gather evidence against him.

In a case of conspiracy, as understood in India, the object of conspiracy has to be established. All the conspirators may not have

---

48 Jim Yardley, The Making of Atta, Asian Age 16 October, 2001.

49 Newsweek, October 29, 2001.

the full knowledge of each others in the conspiracy. They are like train passengers who participate in the conspiracy by entraining the train at one point of time and detraining when they have completed their tasks. There are a number of good case laws in India which has settled a number of intriguing questions of a case of conspiracy. Conspiracy is largely established by a chain of strong circumstantial evidence leading to one conclusion of guilt.

The object of conspiracy is determined by direct or circumstantial evidence. A conspiracy case is built up brick by brick. In a very rare case that direct evidence of ordering of tower crashing would be available. It is the most difficult case of this century. In contrast the WTC case of 1993 was much simple. Direct evidence was available to link the principal accused with the crime as the FBI could organise a 'sting operation' on Sheikh Abdur Rehman. There was a willing FBI plant to tape-record evidence against Rehman and others.

The main thrust area of the investigation should have been to capture the terrorist money flow evidence and evidence captured by NSA of conversations world wide. It is doubtful if such secret intercepts can be cited in evidence in view of USA's stringent law on wire tapping.

Evidence against bin Laden – leadership hierarchy

The best evidence has already surfaced by capturing the key figures of Al Qaeda. Key figures were Osama bin Laden, Al-Jawahiri, Mohammed Atef, Abu Zubaidah. After bombing of US targets in Kenya and Tanzania on August 7, 1998, Mulla Omar immediately denied Osama's involvement. But with the arrest of Mohammad Sadiq Howaida, arrested in Pakistan, a link was found between Al-Qaeda and the blasts. Howaida joined the team two years ago and described Osama as 'our leader'. He admitted to have provided technical, engineering and logistical support for the bombing of the Nairobi US Embassy. He is a Palestinian and travelled to Pakistan on a forged Yemeni passport. He was a part of seven member team that included Egyptians and Lebanese sponsored by Osama. He was apprehended on 14 August 1998 and six others who travelled to Pakistan just managed to vanish. They were on their way to

Afghanistan where Osama was to greet them personally. He received military training in Afghanistan during the Soviet occupation.[50] He was also in a select group dispatched to Somalia to support Somali Leader Gen Farah Aideed in his hit and run operations against the US army in 1993.

The Taliban and Osama bin Laden were inseparable. It was reported that the Taliban movement would not be confined to Afghanistan but would be exported to neighbouring countries. The Taliban had displayed maps in all the main squares in Kunduz city how the Islamic movement would be pushed into Iran, India and Central Asian Republics. On the maps Bukhara, Tashkent, Dushanbe, Isfahan and Delhi had been clearly shown as future targets of the Islamic militia.[51]

Omar Abdel Rehman's Fatwa

Omar Abdel Rehman, jailed for WTC blast of 1993 managed to issue a Fatwa while in prison, which were read out from mosques all over the world. A part of the Fatwa said: "Destroy them (USA) thoroughly and erase them from the face of earth. Ruin their economics, set their companies on fire, and turn their conspiracies to powder and dust. Sink their ships, bring their planes down. Slay them in air, on land, on water. And (with the command of Allah) kill them whereever you find them. Lie in wait for them and kill these infidels". Copies of this Fatwa were widely available in madarsas in Pakistan.[52] Omar Abdel Rehman's sons were with Osama bin Laden. The irony is that Omar Abdel Rehman was picked up by CIA for recruitment drive for jihadis from all over the world.

The leadership of Al-Qaeda was primarily made of Saudis, Palestinian's and Egyptians. The leadership was bonded by marriage alliance. Dr. Ayrman Zawahiri is from Al-Jihad of Egypt. This group had openly claimed responsibility for a series of attacks in Egypt. This group finally merged in 1998 with the International Front for Jihad of Osama bin Laden which is a part of Al-Qaeda. Born in

---

50 Frontier Post, Pakistan, 18/8/98.

51 The Muslim, 26/8/1998.

52 Nation, 29.8.98.

1951, he is 6 years older to Osama. The bespectacled Dr. Jawahiri lacks Osama's charisma and prefers to avoid limelight. He is a veteran of Afghan war (1979-89). His knowledge of Islam is more profound than bin Laden. The Egyptian Jihadis after assassination of President Anwar Sadat in 1981 fled Egypt because of crackdown. They had no other place to go except Afghanistan and Pakistan and work for Osama bin Laden and the Taliban. He is alive and operates from Quetta as per several reports.

Mohammed Atef

Mohammad Atef, born in 1944, was a former Egyptian police officer. He was Al-Qaeda's military brain for training and planning targets to be hit. He was credited to have organised attacks on US interests world over which included Somalia, twin embassy blasts in Africa and USS Cole. As per trial records of 1998 blasts, Atef was in touch by satellite communication with the conspirators. He acted as an intermediary between Laden and the Al-Qaeda operatives. When Tony Blair said, he knew the key aide of bin Laden, he was possibly referring to Atef.[53] His daughter was married to a son of Osama bin Laden which was solemnized in January 2001. He was reportedly killed in Tora Bora by the US army.

Abu Zubaydah

The third man involved in September 11, 2001 attack was Abu Zubaydah, a Saudi national born in 1973. He emerged as a successor of Atef. His area of responsibility was to recruit hard-core terrorists and organise overseas operations. This was revealed from the statement of Ressam recorded in a U.S. Court. Abu Zubaydah was apprehended by a US task force from Faislabad, Pakistan in 2002 and shifted to Cuba Island. His interrogation must have provided the FBI & CIA more details than known before.

For success in the investigation capture of core group of Al-Qaeda has been completed. The ISI officers had long association with Osama bin Laden. Thousands of Pakistani, serving or retired officers of the Pakistan Defence Services, were with the Taliban

---

53 International Herald Tribune, 8 October, 2001.

militia. Pakistan's ISI had detachment offices functioning in major cities like Kabul, Herat and Kandahar before 11 September. It was doubtful if the ISI after 9/11 would ever pass real time intelligence on Osama bin Laden to the US.

Osama bin Laden was not 'a visible trophy available for a quick grab'. To track him down was difficult. The ISI did not play any role in liquidation of Osama bin Laden. It played a negative role by misleading the US. Who could have provided intelligence to the Taliban when Commander Haq was launched by US for organizing anti-Taliban elements in Pasthun area. Haq was captured and killed ruthlessly. Osama was personally known to various ISI operatives for the last 20 years. How was it that a Pakistani journalist could meet Osama even on 7 or 8 October 2001 and the ISI was unable to locate his hideouts. One can change the ISI chief, as was done, but the ISI cadre, officers and men, were deeply under the spell of right elements. Gen (Retd) Hamid Gul who was the ISI chief during the crucial period of Afghan Jihad (1979-89) publicly stated that he had friends in the ISI. The US had to build up its own network of sources for capture of bin Laden. After all Musharraf was an unwilling ally conscripted by the US administration.[54]

Jamal Ahmed Fadl, a former middle level operative of Al-Qaeda gave out a lot of information in his deposition in early 2001 in New York Federal Court. He exposed Al-Qaeda's world-wide operations in Turkey, Algeria, Syria, Chechnya, Jordan, Eritrea, Tajikistan, the Philippines and Lebanon.[55]

Abu Dahdah is a cleric living in Madrid. He received a significant coded call on 27 August 2001. He and seven others were arrested in Madrid in November 2001. He visited London and met bin Laden twice in Afghanistan and visited training camps in Indonesia, Sudan, Yemen and various Gulf states. Atta met him in January and July in Spain. Dahdah visited London 10 times to meet with Abu Qatada and other Osama agents.[56]

---

54 Mubashir Zaidi, *The Hindustan Times*, November 4, 2001.

55 International Herald Tribune, October 1, 2001.

56 Daniel McGrony, Statesman, November 21, 2001.

Abu Qatada was said to have been a member of Al Qaeda's Fatwa Committee and lived in London with his wife and six children. He is nicknamed as Al-Qaeda's European Ambassador. He was granted political asylum in 1993 after he was sentenced in absentia by a Jordanian court for series of blasts in that country. His assets were frozen estimated to be pound 1,80,000 after 9/11. This was found from his London bank account.

Future terrorist attacks

The September 11 attacks are the beginning of a new series of terrorist attacks all over the world. Osama's declared aims, announced over the years, were to liberate the Middle East from the clutches of Israel, drive out American troops from the Gulf region and finally overthrow the Saudi Royal family. He said in 1998 that 'if the present injustice continues, it will inevitability move the battle to American soil, just as Ramzi Yousef and others have done'.[57] He said: 'This is my message to the American people'. Now there is an acute sense of vulnerability in every country of the world. Every country now knows that the tentacles of Al-Qaeda have deep penetration for possible terrorist attacks.

The contours of the future terrorist attacks have already surfaced in the form of anthrax, a biological agent that kills people by inhalation or by contact. Cholera can be another biological agent. The US is free of cholera for years. All these would escalate tension and may lead to a world war like situation. Surely the situation in the world is grim.

Nuclear capacity

There were some apprehensions that Al-Qaeda had some sort of nuclear capability. Enriched uranium reached tribal areas of Pakistan in tins in 1996. The going rate was Rs. 3, 50,000 per tin of 1 kilo of uranium. Hawash, an arrested Sudanese, accused attempting a bomb blast of US Embassy in New Delhi, reportedly confessed to have been engaged for locating nuclear scientists. Three Pakistani nuclear scientists were probed for possible link with Al Qaeda. In

---

57 Lukose Mathew, The Week, September 23, 2001.

1998 President Clinton apprehended higher technological capability of Al-Qaeda for mass destruction. Therefore, a couple of terrific terrorist attacks in future are not ruled out. No security alert can prevent such attacks. The terrorists retain the tactical advantage of selection of target and timing of attack. All these can possibly be prevented by a frontal attack on terrorist network, crippling their financial resources, recruitment and training. During the course of war against terror what would be the American response if a nuclear device is set off by a terrorist in any of the major cities of America. The enemy is now shadowy and elusive.

The banning of terrorist organizations is the first element in this war against terrorism. The tax haven countries should be compelled to fall in line with the international community to spot, locate and freeze terrorist funds. They should be declared rouge states if they fail to discharge their international obligations. Crime and terrorist money are flowing to such jurisdictions. Apart from being tax haven country, Switzerland was visited by Al Qaeda operatives including Dr. Ayman-al-Zawahri.

High treason – British Act of 1351

Several hundreds of British youth of Muslim origin had gone to Afghanistan to fight alongside the Taliban. Many of them fought proxy war in Kashmir. In terms of an Act of 1351 they were committing a high treason as the British Law provides that any British citizen giving comforts to the enemies of the Queen and fighting British soldiers anywhere in the world would qualify the definition of high treason. The British Government has since issued a circular to the effect that if the British citizens fight on the side of the Taliban they would commit high treason. This was a clear warning to Al-Mahajiron as they were in the recruitment of Jihadis for Kashmir and Afghanistan. There is a joke in Britain that holy warriors should be given free tickets to Afghanistan out of the British defence budget.[58]

---

58 Farrukh Dhondy, British Jihadis and the definition of war, *The Times of India*, November 5, 2001.

Manual to kill – Al Qaeda style

Nick Fielding writes from London on Al-Qaeda's killing manual recovered from the home of Khalid Deek when he was arrested in connection with an alleged plot to bomb Jordan's main airport in Amman on the eve of the millennium. On the basis of intelligence gathered a similar bombing in the US was foiled. What was of interest was that Al-Qaeda had produced an 'Encyclopedia of Jihad' with eleven volumes containing 7000 pages in book form and CD-ROM. The encyclopedia is dedicated to Osama bin Laden and Abdullah Azzan, Osama's guru during the Afghan war (1979-89). 'It provides guidance on how to inject frozen food with biochemical agents to create mass panic, rig up a door lock to explode when the handle is turned, and bring down a plane with a missile.'

The eleventh chapter of the encyclopedia deals with bio-terrorism, explaining how to disperse potentially lethal organisms and poisons, ranging from botulism and viral injections to anthrax and resin. It mentions a training camp in Pakistan where toxins are manufactured.

The volume dealing with security and intelligence says that long term planning is required with creation of 'sleeper' cells setup years in advance so that he can start the mission 10 years before the start of Jihad. How to turn cameras into bombs is explained. In case of assassination of Ahmed Shah Masood this technique was used.[59]

There are speculative reports that Osama bin Laden had obtained nuclear capability. Such a report was filed by Philip Webster and Ronald Watson in the Times, London. If not nuclear device, he might have obtained radio active material to contaminate a small area and hundreds could die and thousands more exposed to radiation poisoning. Such a possibility is made out from the previous contacts of bin Laden. In 1993 Jamal Al-Fadi met a senior Sudanese Military Commander in Khartoum to procure enriched South African uranium at a price of $ 11.5 million. The deal perhaps never went through.

A separate attempt was made to buy weapon grade nuclear

---

59 *Times of India* - November 5, 2001.

material through the Russian Mafia which was foiled by Czech Authorities. This was revealed by a German T.V. Report in the month of October, 2001.[60]

The arrest/detention of two retired Nuclear Scientists in Pakistan raised concern. Sultan Bashiruddin Mehmood and Abdul Majid were questioned to know their links with Mulla Omar and bin Laden. After retirement Bashiruddin formed an NGO called Ummah Tameer-e-Nau (Reconstruction of Muslim Ummah). This NGO was affiliated to the Al-Rashid Trust, which was linked with Al-Qaeda. His NGO consisted of nuclear scientists and retired military officers. Michael Krepon of Henry Stimson Centre believes that 'it is easy to get fissionable material, but difficult to make a bomb'. Al Qaeda could have the capability to mix nuclear material with RDX to create a big impact.[61]

Such a dreadful scenario can only be prevented by the moderate Muslims in the Muslim states. The voiceless silent majority Muslims are the natural targets of the fundamentalist group. They are incapable of organizing themselves as they lack muscle power. One way is to press for democratization of such regimes. Even this prescription may be dangerous as is the case in Algeria. Even democracy can be hijacked by fundamentalist groups. Indonesia has been largely secular with proud tradition of liberalism and tolerance to other faiths. The Hindu mythology is still popular in Indonesia. The civil airlines emblem is 'Garuda'. Hindu names mixed with Islamic names like Sukarno or Sukarno Poutri (daughter of Sukarno) is popular in Indonesia. Indonesia has sizeable Hindu population in Bali.

The world leaders have to have a long session on civilization conflicts. Inter-faith reconciliation is the answer to this crisis of fundamentalism. A big movement has to be launched. A world declaration on inter-faith reconciliation has to be drawn up on the lines of Human Right Declaration. In this UN has a big role to play. Iran has suggested such a debate under UN sponsorship. Even regional debates can defuse the situation. India has already

---

60 *The Statesman* - October 27, 2001.

61 *The Statesman* - 26th October, 2001 and the *Hindustan Times* - 26th October, 2001.

organised such a civilizational debate in 2003. Under domestic and international pressure Saudi Arabia is now attempting to bring in a dose of liberalism. It is contemplating to allow all the four schools of Islam to function. Pluralism is a check on fundamentalism.

Conclusion

There was massive intelligence failure. Persons of doubtful antecedents were allowed to enter the US. One case was of Khalid al-Midhar and the other was of Zacarius. There was obviously lack of coordination between the agencies. The US neglected the epicenters of terrorism radiating from the Taliban regime of Afghanistan and Pakistan. The CIA–ISI relationship was cold. There was no wrest while human intelligence capability with the CIA externally aided the FBI internally. The hijacking of the Indian Airline flight IC 814 was not evaluated. It was read in the light of India-Pakistan relationship. It was actually a trial of dry run for 9/11 hijacking of four US aircrafts.

6

Osama bin Laden

"God said Islam will spread until every person in the world becomes Muslim"

Dr Fateema Nassef, Rabiat Islam, Saudi Arabia.

Osama bin Laden became a household name in most of the world and an icon of jihadis all over the Muslim countries so much so that many parents adopted 'Osama' as the name for their sons. Bin in Arabic means son. Thus Osama is son of Laden, the pictures of this Saudi multi-millionaire holding an AK-47 assault rifle, which he claimed to have removed from the body of a Soviet General reportedly killed by him. This picture adorned many homes in the Arab World. In Peshawar, in the North-West Province of Pakistan bordering Afghanistan, there was a market place named 'Osama Bazar' from before. Pakistani cops demanded that the name be changed fearing backlash from certain quarters. Propaganda cassettes and tapes, bloated with fiery speeches and discourses of this iconoclastic godfather championing the cause of jihad are available, both readily and discreetly, in several countries including India. In UK they are still being sold and the joke is London now can be called Londonistan. Needless to say that his name figured in the list of 10 most wanted fugitives of Federal Bureau of Investigation (FBI) much before the 9/11. American intelligence dossiers described him as the leader of terrorist organization by the name of Al-Qaeda – meaning "The Base" in Arabic. He was declared the most wanted in the watch list of FBI after 1998 USS Cole attack and of two US

Embassies attacks in two cities of East Africa. A sketch fact-file of bin Laden prepared by the FBI at one time would read as follows:

Date of birth	:	1957
Place of birth	:	Saudi Arabia
Height	:	6.4" to 6.6"
Weight	:	160 lbs.
Build	:	Thin
Hair	:	Brown
Eyes	:	Brown
Complexion	:	Olive

Osama bin Laden was born on 10 March 1957. His mother Hamida Alia Ghanoum was neither a Saudi nor a Wahhabi. She was a daughter of a Syrian trader. Osama was seventeenth son of his father.[1] People described Osama bin Laden as a reclusive billionaire who had launched a massive ideological onslaught against the enemies of Islam. Beside non-Muslim countries which opposed Islamic fundamentalism, the adversaries in this holy war which included liberal Muslim regimes as well, because he believed that any form of acceptance of western models of governance, social growth and development violated the fundamental tenets of Islam. The movement, therefore, was aimed at scuttling any move towards dilution of orthodox Islamic tenets. Strangely, this Islamic hero had a 'melancholic smile and soft voice' and 'slightly high, with a raspy quality that gave it the texture and sound of an old uncle giving good advice.'[2] Mostly he was seen in green army field jacket with a shawl over it.

Islamisation of Osama bin Laden

Osama bin Laden's initiation to the Islamic fundamentalism was not an overnight development. His indoctrination occurred at

---

1   Al Qaeda, Casting a Shadow of Terror, Jason, I.B. Tauris, London, 2003, p 44.

2   The Cell: John Miller, Michael Stone and Chris Mitchel, Hyperion, New York, 2002, p 185.

early impressionable age. His hatred towards Western regimes accumulated gradually over the decades of history which he was a witness. It is widely believed that bin Laden's metamorphosis began in 1973, when as a teenager he often accompanied his father, Muhammad bin Laden, to the construction sites in the holy mosques of Mecca and Medina. Osama was said to be one of the 52 children of his father Muhammad bin Laden who had a number of wives. His father, who became a construction magnet, was entrusted with the task of refurbishing the two holy mosques, the two most sacred places of Muslims in Saudi Arabia. The subsequent Lebanese civil war attributed by the orthodox mainstream Islamic school of thought was often referred to as another turning point in shaping bin Laden's personality. As a teenager he had visited Beirut in 1975 and the University education from 1974-1978 at Abdul Aziz University in Jeddah, where he studied Management and Economics,[3] Osama bin Laden's young mind struggled hard to absorb the rationale behind the agony of innocent Lebanese during the hostilities and completely buried himself in the thought that it was punishment from God as said by the Islamic scholars. The Islamists argued that deviation from the path of Islam was the real cause for agony in Lebanon, an argument which left a deep mark on bin Laden's state of mind. He had education at various places including Egypt's Al-Azar University and till the time Lebanese civil war broke out there was nothing unusual noticed in this computer literate young man. Like any youth at younger age he too was fun loving and often visited Beirut for fun and games when he was in school and college. He often found himself in the center of drunken brawls during one of the several nights. This version of his early fun loving life has been refuted by Jason Burke.[4]

Osama bin Laden's lineage can be traced back to coasts of Hadramaut. Hadramaut is in Yemen, east of Port Aden. These Yemeni Arabs were traders of international repute for centuries and Hadrami merchants of this area often migrate to Saudi Arabia. Originally they were said to be Jews converted to Islam.[5] Osama's

---

3   Laden a cult figure, PTI Feb 20, 2000.

4   Jason Burke, I.B. Tauris, London, 2003, p 44-46.

5   World Affairs April-June 2002, Vol 6Ho2, Come Carpentier De Gourdon, P.108.

father Muhammad bin Laden migrated to Saudi Arabia where he worked as a bricklayer for a company called Aramco. He earned one Riyal a day only and kept a part of his earnings in a tin-box. As luck would have it, he built up his own construction company. For reasons not known it is said he killed himself by crashing his own aircraft. Osama joined his father's business and grew from strength to strength.

The turmoil in the Middle East in mid 70's was another major factor that shaped the psyche of this cult figure engaged in the war against the world's most powerful nation. The Arab world had virtually slipped into a collective sense of demoralization during the Yom Kippur War in 1973. In this war, Israel turned the tables on Egyptian–Syrian Combine who had launched a surprise onslaught on Israel. The subsequent oil embargo imposed by the Arab world did not yield the desired results as the US and the West did not adopt anti-Israel policy inspite of oil embargo.

Besides these states sponsored developments, importantly, the Arabic hoi polloi was finding it increasingly difficult to cope with the Royal family of Saudi Arabia, which reaped financial benefits out of oil. Supplementing this was the affluence and exposure to West, which was injecting a sense of identity crisis among the rich Arab Muslims. The seeds of sociological discontent were thus planted as opulent Arabs found themselves in a state of cross cultural conflicts within, after being thrown open to evils as well as personal freedom and liberalism.

The assassination of Saudi King Faisal, in March 1975, by his own Western-educated cousin, Prince Faisal-bin-Musaid, was nothing but a manifestation of this cross cultural tension. Prince Faisal killed his cousin after his visit to the US and Europe where a diametrically opposite culture virtually pushed him into a state of nervous disorder. Consequently, a process of reverse indoctrination was taking place through which many Arab Muslims were beginning to plummet back into the fold of Islamism.

Around the same time in the mid 70's President Anwar Sadat of Egypt courted the West in an abortive attempt to bring peace with

Israel, an act which attracted hostile response from the orthodox Islamic intelligentsia. The Egyptian scholars like Wail Utham, who is portrayed as the ideologue of the militant branch of Islam, called for bringing back of the rule of God with his fiery publication, 'The Party of God' where it was said that "the Party of God was in struggle with the 'the party of Satan (West)' and urged for the adoption of militant methods to arrest the erosion of Islamic culture from Western aggression. The situation was already assuming volatile proportions under an apparently serene surface and in 1977 the visit of Anwar Sadat to Jerusalem and subsequently recognition of Israel by Egypt provided the final thrust of blowing up the lid from its top. Without any loss of generality, it may thus be said the tentacles of revolt spread far and wide from its rudimentary beginnings in Egypt.

A few years later Ayatollah Ruhumullah Khomeini wrested power in Iran on February 1, 1979 after the ouster of Shah of Iran. The establishment of an Islamic Republic of Iran by Khomeini provided an instant source of pride for the Muslims, which later was severely dented when President Sadat provided asylum to the dethroned Shah of Iran in Egypt.

Storming of grand mosque of Mecca

It was only natural that more upheavals were to follow and the Wahhabi Sunni uprising witnessed in Egypt and Saudi Arabia was nothing but a manifestation of collective angst among a sizeable section of the Muslims in the Arab World. On Nov. 20, 1979 the Grand Mosque in Mecca was seized by 400 armed Wahhabi followers under the leadership of Juhayman-ibn-Muhammad-ibn-Sayfal-Utaba, a former Captain of Saudi's White Guards, who declared himself the Mehdi, chosen one of the Koran, who will appear before the end of the world.[6] He announced that the House of al-Saud deviated from the true path of Islam and called for overthrow of their apostate ruler with the backing of the Western powers. A series of bomb blasts rocked Saudi Arabia. It turned out that the rebels used Laden's company trucks to smuggle their weapons into the mosque. The Saudi security forces failed to gain control of the mosque. The crisis finally ended only with the arrival of a detachment of the French

6   Price of Honour, Jan Goodwin Little, Brown and Company, US, p213.

paramilitary Special Forces, Pakistani forces sent secretly. The French Special Forces was headed by Paul Barril equipped with sten-guns, grenades and chemical weapons.[7] It is said that elite French Commanders staged an assault 'through the underground Labyrinth of the holy city' the maps of which were made available by the Laden Construction Company. Mahrous bin Laden, a brother of Osama, was then in change of the Mecca branch of the company. He was held guilty of negligence and awarded punishment of a few months of captivity. However, the Laden family continued to enjoy the trust of the Saudi royal family. The reason was that the Royal family and Sheikh Mohammed Laden got connected through 'marriage and business associations'. Barring Osama, all other brothers kept close rapport with many of the Royal princes and act as reliable advisers 'in matters of trade, finance and diplomacy'.[8] This is how Osama bin Laden came into the picture directly for the first time and provided open support to the social issues raised by Juhayman. Utabi and his 62 followers were subsequently beheaded. Osama felt that 'the men who seized Mecca were true Muslims and that they were innocent of any crime and they were killed ruthlessly'.[9]

Gen Zia as president of Pakistan turned this event against the US. While he was on a cycle ride in Islamabad he was questioned by people as to how this could happen in Mecca. He blamed America. As a result a crowd of people stormed the US embassy in Islamabad and killed a few people there. This situation was ultimately controlled by Gen Chisti, a Zia protégé at that time. Anti-Americanism runs in the blood of Pakistanis inspite of US government's aid and support to all military rulers of Pakistan right from the very birth of Pakistan.

Osama bin Laden having finished his high school in 1974 did join Management and Economics at Abdul Aziz University in Jeddah. He did not follow his brothers who were educated abroad. At the age 17, he got married to a Syrian girl related to his mother. He graduated in 1979. He heard the speeches of Abdullah Azzam and Mohammed Qutb, brother of Syed Qutb, who inspired

---

7   Ibid, p54.

8   World Afairs, April-June 2002, Vol 6 No. 2, Come Carpenter De Gourdon.

9   Jason Burke, Al Qaeda, Casting a Shadow of Terror, I.B. Tauris, 2003, p55.

Islamists by his publications while he was in jail. Syed Qutb was executed in 1966. Such Islamists got shelter in Saudi Arabia to counter the atheist socialism in the Middle East. Both of them were members of Muslim Brotherhood, founded by Al Banna in 1928 for transformation of Muslim countries into Islamic states. Banna was assassinated allegedly by the Egyptian secret service in 1949 in retaliation of the killing of prime minister by a member of the Muslim Brotherhood a year ago.[10]

The real emergence of Osama bin Laden as an icon can actually be traced to Soviet induction of troops in Afghanistan. When the jihad call came for fighting the Soviet troops which entered Afghanistan on 25 December 1979, to protect the leftist regime in Afghanistan, bin Laden was the first Arab to reach the trouble-torn country and formed the core group of mujahideen, which was ostensibly receiving financial, material and logistical support from the CIA, Royal family and the ISI. What has not been said loudly that Prince Turkie picked up Osama and arranged to send him to Peshawar to explore the possibilities of raising an Arab mujahideen force.[11] Perhaps it was Prince Turkie, Intelligence Chief of Saudi Arabia and the CIA, who agreed to pick up Osama as he was already baptized for a jihadi mission. This part of Osama's life is rather based on circumstantial evidence rather by any direct admission from bin Laden. Even if it is true he did never make an open admission of it. Osama bin Laden arrived in Peshawar in early 1980 for a month or so. He on his return to Saudi Arabia canvassed for jihad and persuaded his family, relatives and friends for support in terms of money and men to fight jihad in Afghanistan. Some time in 1984, he finally settled down in Peshawar at 61 Syed Jamal-din Afghani Road on rent. The house became his service Bureau called Beit ul Ansar. Ansars were the first group of converts to Islam made by Prophet himself in Medina after the Hijra.[12] Osama bin Laden spent much of his time in the publication of an Arabic news paper called al- Jihad of Abdullah Azzam which mostly reported on the progress of jihad in Afghanistan. The news paper was distributed free of cost

10 Jason Burke, Al Qaeda, Casting a Shadow of Terror, I.B. Tauris, 2003, p47.

11 Cooly, John K., Unholy War, page 225.

12 Jason Burke, Al Qaeda, Casting a Shadow of Terror, I.B. Tauris, 2003, p56.

throughout the Muslim world. This was possible as it was funded by wealthy Arabs. The staff was all Arabs.[13]

Bin Laden used his expertise in construction industry to counter the Soviet forces and used material and financial resources to build trenches, bunkers, caves and roads in the mountainous terrains of Afghanistan. All this was in the knowledge of the CIA and the ISI. In return bin Laden received precious lessons in artillery and overtime achieved finesse in using sophisticated weapons such as Stinger missiles and recoilless guns. Such lessons were imparted exclusively by the ISI. Interestingly, it is said that he attacked the Afghan government forces frontally and never got injured. This act of fighting enhanced his image. He enhanced his image by show of man management by visiting injured jihadis in hospitals and each family of the deceased jihadi received cheque. This he inherited from his father who always used to carry wad of notes to give to poor people. Not only these acts of humanism and charity, he used to participate in group discussions with Arabs and narrate stories of past Muslim heroes of their unique battle achievements like Salahaudin, who united the Islamic factions to defeat the Crusaders of the 12th century. Often he did not forget to the Surah ya Sin, the 36th verse, which is said to be the heart of Quran. This verse it speaks of 'problems of human moral responsibility and certainty of resurrection and judgment.'[14]

It was true that his lifestyle was really Spartan. His modest diet was mostly honey, date and bread. He exercised regularly, practiced martial arts and loved horse riding. His simple habits, humility and commitment to the cause of Islamic purity impressed people and mujahideen leaders and commanders. He never sided with any of the Islamic parties fighting the Afghan war (1979-89) and thus remained politically non-controversial.

---

13 Ibid.

14 Jason Burke, Al Qaeda, Casting a Shadow of Terror, I.B. Tauris, 2003, p57.

Osama in Afghan War (1979-89) and creation of Al Qaeda network

Rapid transformation of Osama bin Laden as the most powerful fighter for Islamic jihad was the outcome of his long involvement in Afghan War. During the process of the war he came in close contact with Islamic groups all over the world directly and through his trusted aides. He organised a recruitment drive, paid for travel expenses of the Arab volunteers and set up Ma'sadat Al-Ansar, a centre for Arab mujahideen in Afghanistan.[15] It is now widely believed that he was providing support to rebels in Chechnya, Central Asian Republics, Kashmir and Muslim dominated erstwhile Soviet Republics, and the Philippines. The support-ideological, material, logistical and financial-is prompted by the objective of Laden to include these jurisdictions in his proposed larger Islamic Ummah. The idea is to create an Islamic state dismantling all territorial boundaries and the Islamic world to be governed by the ultra-orthodox Sharia law.

Laden's links with Pakistan military establishment

It is often said that Osama bin Laden was the test-tube babe of Pakistan's ISI-CIA combine. Osama knew all the Pakistan players in the Afghan jihad. What is now revealed is that Osama was courted by the Pakistani army for destabilizing the elected regime in Pakistan. Benazir Bhutto took over the reigns of the country after 1988 election which happened after General Zia's death in a plane crash. The ISI and Pakistan army were opposed to her. The Pakistan army and the ISI created a political front called IJI under Nawaz Sharif which failed to secure majority in the National Assembly. To destabilise her government a serving corps commander called a secret meeting, where Osama and Nawaz Sharif were present. Osama was told that a woman in the position of head of the government was against Islam. Osama was requested to provide money to overthrow Benazir Bhutto from power. Nawaz Sharif promised Osama 'to bring Islam to Pakistan'. Osama reportedly paid $10 million to finance the no-confidence move against her. This story was revealed by Benazir Bhutto to the Herald in January 2001, much before the 9/11. The

---

15   Yussef Bodonoskey, p 10.

story has not been denied by the Pakistan army or a defamation case filed against her by any of the players. She insisted these secret deals should be investigated for wider awareness of the public and expose underhand dealings of the Pakistan's security establishment.[16]

Abdullah Azzam

Osama came in personal contact with his spiritual guru Abdullah Azzam in Pakistan. Osama was greatly influenced by the personality and teachings of Azzam, who was a former guerrilla, and founder of the Hamas in Gaza in the West Bank. He was born in north Palestine in 1941. He was good in studies from his school days. As a child he joined the Muslim Brotherhood. He obtained a degree from an Agricultural college and later joined Shariah College, Damascus University and obtained BA degree in Shariah in 1966. While studying for his doctorate at Al Azzar University in 1973, he came in contact with the family of Qutb and Sheikh Abdel Omar Rehman, a spiritual leader of al-Gama al-Islamia, the blind cleric who subsequently played a big role in promoting jihad in America.

After the Jews captured the West Bank in 1967, Azzam migrated to Jordan where he got involved in jihad against Israeli occupation and also pursued studies by obtaining MA in Shariah from the University of Al Azahar. In 1970 he took a teaching job in Cairo University and obtained PhD in Ussulal-Fiqh in 1973. In 1979, he was expelled and moved to Pakistan for a teaching assignment in the International Islamic University in Islamabad. Osama heard him speaking on jihad from before when Azzam was in the Middle East as a young lad and he was greatly fired by his fiery speeches. He found a teaching job in Saudi Arabia in Jeddah in 1978. In 1980 he left for Pakistan to join jihad and got a job at the International Islamic University funded by Saudi money inaugurated by President Zia a year ago.[17]

Azzam left his teaching assignment in Pakistan to join the Afghan mujahideen war. He was recruited by the CIA for recruitment

---

16 The Herald Annual, January 2001, Interview of Benazir Bhutto.

17 Jason Burke, Al Qaeda, Casting a Shadow of Terror, I.B. Tauris, 2003, p 68-69.

of jihadis from all over the world.[18] He was sponsored by CIA to visit 26 states of the USA for recruitment of jihadis. He was close to several officers of the ISI who were directly dealing with Zia-ul-Haq. His recruitment drive was aired on ABC News 'Day One' magazine programme on July 12, 1993.[19] These are matters of record.

Osama bin Laden too came under Azzam's spell. The duo teamed up for organizing various activities. Azzam's spiritual sermons had lasting effect on Osama.

Azzam's visit to America led to opening of Al-kifah Refugee Services centre in Booklyn's Atlantic Avenue, a branch of Peshawar (Pakistan) based 'office of services'. The organization that later become al-Qaeda.[20] The Al-kifah office became the head quarter of jihad in America. There was nothing secret about it as the CIA was promoting jihad to fight the Soviets in Afghanistan. Such was the obsession of the CIA against the Soviet Russia. Azzam was not an original thinker like al Banna, Mahududi or Qutb but he could fuse his oratory with the past thinkers' ideas with Quranic verses to his spell bound audience mostly jihadis to inspire them to fight for jihad.

Azzam created in Peshawar Maktab-al-Khidmat (MAK) to receive, supervise, and organise the benefits of Arab volunteers and managing private funds received from private donors from abroad. This flow of money was separate from the CIA and Saudi Arabia's official funding. His thinking was totally focused on jihad. He said that 'right now fighting is compulsory on each and every Muslim on earth'. This he again said in his 'last will' written in 1986. His best book was said: 'Defending the land of the Muslims is each man's most important duty.' In this book he wrote some thing worth noting by those who study the reasons of the present tidal wave of Islamic terrorism worldwide. He wrote that 'this duty (jihad) will not end with victory in Afghanistan; Jihad will remain an individual obligation until all other lands that were Muslims are returned to us so that Islam will reign again; before us lie Palestine, Bokhara, Lebanon, Chad, Eritrea, Somalia, the Philippines, Burma, southern

---

18 Cooly, John K., Unholy War, p204.

19 Cooly, John K., Unholy War, p88.

20 The Cell, Miller Stone and Mitchell, Hyperion, New York, p49.

Yemen, Tashkent and Andalusia (Spain).[21]

Osama's commitment to the cause of Muslim Ummah was discernible from a battle in 1987 where he fought in a hand-to-hand fight during an attack on the Soviet-DRA forces in Shaban in the Paktia province of Afghanistan. The mujahideen suffered heavy casualties before they withdrew, but Osama's stature grew manifold among the rank and file of the mujahideen. He used to carry a Kalashnikov, which he claimed to have captured from a dead Russian General in Shaban. He became even much fearless after Paktia and he intended to "die in glory". "He was a hero to us because he was always in the frontline, always moving ahead of everyone else" recalled Hamza Muhammad, a Palestinian in Afghanistan who now manages Laden's construction projects in Sudan.[22] In 1986, bin Laden participated in the battle of Jalalabad as part of Arab contingent. He dug in at 'Jaji' against repeated assault from the forces of Democratic Republic of Afghanistan (DRA). Such assaults did not yield any result as mujahideen attacks were repulsed by the DRA forces.

Laden returned to Saudi Arabia after the mysterious death of his spiritual guru, Abdullah Azzam, in a car bomb blast in Peshawar, Pakistan in 1989. His mission in Afghanistan seemed to have ended and decided to return to his native place after withdrawal of Soviet troops. He returned to Saudi Arabia as a great hero, became a role model amidst wide ranging media coverage. Gaining from Afghanistan experience, he told that a true commitment to jihad could surmount all obstacles of the super powers. He became a much sought after celebrity.[23] After all the Soviets had to retreat. The home of al-Saud benefited out of his preaching. There was no turf war between them till then and he devoted time to his construction company, lived in a modest apartment and practiced the Islamic way of life. Then came 1990-1991 Iraq-Kuwait war and the differences surfaced between him and the Saudi Royal family.

---

21   Jason Burke, Al Qaeda, Casting a Shadow of Terror, I.B. Tauris, 2003, p 69 and Cooly, John K., Unholy War, p7.

22   Cooly, John K., Unholy War.

23   Bodonosky, p28.

The Iraq-Kuwait war transformed US as the most hated enemy of Osama as he could not tolerate "the infidels walk everywhere on the land where Muhammad was born and where Koran was revealed to him by Gabriel. The rulers had become powerless". The metamorphosis of Osama bin Laden appeared to have come full circle. So far as the US was concerned, CIA-ISI's infant, Osama, now appeared to have grown up and positioned as USA's Frankenstein's monster. In other words, as an observer said, the USA "having sown the wind is now reaping the whirlwind".

The seeds of hatred towards US, however, were visible much before the Iraqi invasion of Kuwait. On the night of April 24-25, 1980 the US attempted to rescue its hostages from Iran and failed in that secret mission. For a superpower, such as the US, this was utter humiliation. This gave them a view that super powers are vulnerable and can be defeated by jihad. The strength of jihad was thus overestimated in the light of the Afghan jihad experience. The reality was that Afghan jihad was fought on the strength of US-Led supply of money, arms including Stinger missiles.

As Osama's prominence continued to grow in the Islamic world as the main anti-US protagonist, the man himself sought to establish durable relationships within Afghanistan by perhaps marrying a local Pasthun girl. Mullah Mohammad Omar, Emir or the Supreme commander of the Taliban regime, was rumored to have married one of Laden's daughters. The Arab fighters married local Afghan girls. Moreover, he introduced the Afghan Mujahideen to nuances of modern guerrilla warfare. He built up his mujahideen network via Pakistan, which had relaxed visa regulations and allowed liberal inflow of Muslim volunteers from all over the world for training in Afghanistan and Pakistan.

The Muslim countries which Osama bin Laden strongly opposed were Egypt, Algeria, and Turkey for their modernist Islamic approach and Saudi Royal Family which kept the American troops on its soil. In an Interview in the end of 1999 he exhorted Muslims to "rise up and rid Islamic countries of the Americans and Jews". In another declaration during the Kargil operation he identified USA and India as enemies of Islam.

Bin Laden's African chapter

On August 2, 1990, Iraq invaded Kuwait. There was panic in Riyadh as the flow of Iraqi refugees started pouring in to Saudi Arabia. Osama presented a plan for the defence of the country to the royal family. His ten page plan included induction of hardcore Saudi Afghans for the defence of the country. These Saudi Afghans could be used for jihad in Kuwait. Iraqi soldiers would not resist jihadi force. His advice was ignored and American forces landed in Saudi Arabia, which continued to stay put much against the earlier announcements of US Defence Secretary, Dick Cheney who had said that American forces would withdraw the moment they were no longer needed. Meanwhile, 350 reluctant Ulemas (clerics) at Mecca agreed to support the Royal family and the draft agreement between Royal family and the Ulemas only helped in disseminating further angst towards America among the general populace. Intelligent as he was, Osama gained maximum mileage by openly condemning the presence of US and allied troops on the soil of Saudi Arabia, which he considered sacrilegious even though he avoided attacking the house of al-Saud directly. Despite repeated warnings from the Saudi royal family about the forfeiture of contracts and property, Osama continued with his anti-America tirade before slipping to Sudan in 1991 where he found the ground fertile for his movement with ideological and material support from Hassan al-Turabi and Omar Al-Bashir. In Sudan, Turabi and Bashir had captured power by a coup on June 30, 1989.

Sunni Sudan's transformation came in 1989 when military coup installed Hasan-al-Turabi as the country's spiritual leader. This was a significant development and Osama soon developed relationship with Sudanese Islamists and formed training camps in Sudan for promotion of jihad motivated fighting force.

Hasan al Turabi was born in February 1932 at Kassala of eastern Sudan. His merchant father was scholar of Islam. He was anti-imperialist when the country was under the British rule. Turabi received secular education and his father gave him religious educations, classical Arab culture and traditional Arab poetry. He graduated from British run Gordan College in Khartoum in 1955 with a law degree. From 1951 he was a clandestine member of the local branch of the Egyptian Muslim Brotherhood. He became head of the university's Islamic Liberation Movement, an offshoot of the Muslim Brotherhood. From UK he earned Master's degree from London University in 1957. He completed his PhD from Sorbonne in 1964. Fluent in English and French, he had traveled extensively. He established Islamic Charter Front (ICF) and positioned himself as an authority on Political Islam. With the backing of Bashir, Sudan soon became world's centre of Sunni Islamist revivalism.

From 1991 to 1992, there has been evolution of Islamic terrorism, subversion and violence paving way to jihad against the so called Judeo-Christian world order. There was integration of jihadi organizations under the umbrella of Islamist International to operate within the framework of the International Muslims Brotherhood (IBM). Khomeini's dream of unity in Islam was coming true. Since US was supporting regimes serving its purpose, an idea grew that USA need to be targeted first, rest will follow logically. The militant group was known Armed Islamic Movement or International Legion of Islam. Legion since early 1990s was sending its Afghan trained mujahideen all over Asia, Africa, Europe and the US. The support bases were in Sudan, Iran, Afghanistan and Pakistan.

IBM leaders met in London in early August 1989 and decided to set up a leadership group of 19 members at Khartoum under Turabi. The next step Turabi took was to establish Popular International Organization (PIO) with a global plan of action with 33 members from 53 countries. In this, Tehran reportedly offered advanced and secured communication system including electronic jamming equipment. Defectors from army in Egypt came and joined the organization. Few camps were set up for Western Europe operation. Laden was invited to contribute his skill for export of Islamic terrorism. By 1992 Laden grew into a major confidant of Turabi while settling down in Sudan in the garb of expanding his financial and business network. He was promoting both terrorism and business.

On July 5, 1991 Bank of England closed down the Bank of Credit and Commerce International (BCCI) triggering a worldwide financial scandal amidst startling revelations that the bank was laundering money for terrorists funding, deals for purchase of weapons. In 80's it even helped CIA to fund Afghan jihad. After collapse of BCCI, Laden readily agreed the use of his international account and companies for Islamists cause. Some examples of these have been reported by Cooly in his book "Unholy War'.

(a) In 1991 Tehran transferred $30 million to Turabi to assist the IBM controlled banking system. IBM controlled Laden's established Sudanese banks for clandestine transfer of funds.

(b) On the eve of election in Algeria, rich Iranian and gulf sheiks deposited $12 million in the Faysal Islamic bank branch at Khartoum. From Sudan the money was smuggled to assist the Islamic Salvation Front (FIS) in Algeria.

(c) In mid 1992 Iran gave Sudan $30 million for terrorist training. Most of this fund went to bank controlled by Turabi in London to finance international terrorist activities.

(d) Sudan spent money from its budget for terrorist training in Sudan.

(e) $2 million cheque was drawn on Laden's personal accounts in the Faysal Islamic Bank.

(f) Laden capitalized Turabi's the Shamal (North) Islamic Bank in Khartoum after raising $50 million. In lieu of this he (Laden) got ownership of one million acres of land in Korofan in western Sudan, which Laden used for agriculture and to raise further capital.

(g) In 1993/94 Turabi decided on "the establishment of a special fund to finance Islamic jihad in Islamic and African countries". $100 million was placed in the fund. Ibrahim-al-Sansui, an aide of Turabi, was in charge of this fund as found out by the Egyptian Security Service.

(h) In mid 1990s Ayman al-Zawahiri, a close and trusted friend of bin Laden from his days in Afghanistan, created "brotherhood group" of 134 extremely rich Arabs, who have presence in the West and United States. They acted as cover fronts, means of financial support and means of internal communications. Thus, numerous and highly elaborate Islamist networks sustained themselves in the heart of the West *i.e.* Geneva, London and Chicago with visible means of income.

(i) In 1994 the Egyptian security services calculated that the annual amount of funding was estimated to be over one and half billion Egyptian pounds.

(j) Al-Qaeda, the base foundations of bin Laden, sent money in the name of charities reaching up to Bosnia and Albania-Kosovo where mujahideen operated in a big way.

(k) In early 1990s, on Sudan's request, Laden established an infrastructure company called "Al-Hijrah for Construction and Development Ltd." He was aided by his close Sudanese friend Abu-al-Hasan. Some 400 men drawn from Pakistan were employed with this firm. By 1996, while still in Sudan, he had built 23 mujahideen training camps in Sudan.

(l) Khost, near Pakistan border in Afghanistan territory became training base for mujahideen drawn from all over the world. Sudan in 1991 played the same role.

(m) Even in 1991, it is said that 18 Kashmiri militants went for six months training in Sudan under guidance of Turabi and Mustafa Uthman.

(n) The author (Cooly) said that the ISI's vast and highly experienced terrorist support structure tempered by years of assistance to such regional armed struggles as those of Afghan, Kashmiris and Sikhs, was expanding its operations to include support for and sponsorship of global Islamist terrorism. Terrorists trained in Pakistan and Afghanistan became key commanders in Egypt "to support, expedite, incite and facilitate what they consider Islamist Liberation Struggle".

(o) Their targets were Nigeria, Egypt, Tunisia and Jordan.

The Afghan veterans of all nationalities became trainers for locals. Soon they established an "International Jihad Organization". World-wide operations were planned inside this bureau in Peshawar.

(p) Shia Iran and Sunni terrorist organizations established working rapport with each other after a long time. In 1992 Ayman-al-Zawahiri met with Iranians after mediation by Turabi. Iran reportedly agreed to train 800 Egyptian Afghans to escalate jihad in Egypt. This groundwork was made to raise Egyptian Liberation Battalion. In addition another 500 Egyptians were sent to Sudan where Iranian supported Hezbollah had a training centre.

(q) In 1992 the AIM and its International Legion/Brigade of Islam were supporting, training and supplying Islamist terrorists throughout the world directly from centers in Pakistan, Afghanistan and Sudan. Muslims of Algeria, Egypt, Sudan, Yemen, Tunisia, Jordan, Morocco, Lebanon, Saudi Arabia and Palestine joined these forces.

(r) Gradually even Indians, Malaysians joined these camps for training. The first exhibition of terrorist attack was carried out in Mumbai on a large scale by Indians trained in Pakistan.

(s) By mid 1993 the hard-core of the Afghan Arab mujahideen consisted of :

- 800   Egyptians
- 700   Algerian
- 400   Tunisians
- 370   Iraqis
- 300   Yemenis
- 250   Libyans
- 150   Sudanese
- 100   Persian Gulf Arabs
- 70   Europeans

They were sent to forward bases in Iran, Sudan and Yemen under the centralized control of PIO. Bin Laden slowly became dominant as he was providing financial and logistic support earning the respect of Turabi whose main aim was to spread jihad in Africa. Thus began stockpiling of explosives with Islamist militants all over Africa and it was not very late when sporadic action was noticed in some African cities. There were riots in Kenya and Uganda to destabilise local governments to eradicate socio-economic malice as in Somalia and Tanzania.

The first major success was achieved by terrorising the US in abandoning a Muslim land in Somalia which was precipitated by social disorder in the country going through a severe phase of avoidable famine in 1992. There was fratricidal warfare and bin Laden took upon himself the task of providing leadership in terrorist activities in Somalia.

Because of famine in Somalia, in November 1992, US decided to send a large military force to Somalia on a humanitarian mission to ensure delivery of food to starving Somalian people. US marines landed on the beaches of Somalia in early December 1992. Bin Laden, on the other hand, started using his own network for funding the terrorists in Somalia. Tehran and Khartoum decided to turn Somalia into a trap and quagmire for the US forces through a guerrilla war against them. Arms reached Somalia from Pakistan, Iran and Sudan in late 1992. The Islamic World Association and the World Muslim Relief Organization were part of the wide net Saudi supported Islamic proselytization movement comprising underground Islamist elements. Laden soon captured and capitalized on Mohammad Sheikh of Osman's network who had previously transferred money to Somalia. Dr. Ali al-Haj, one of the Turabi's closest friends and confidants, was engaged in training and fighting in Ethiopia, Somalia, Eritrea, Kenya, Uganda and Sudan. Somalia operation was being controlled by Turabi through General Rahim Safari and Turabi's deputy Ali Uthman Taha. One method of funding was through front business organizations and bogus accounts.

Failed attempt to kill Zahir Shah by bin Laden

Osama had reportedly ordered the assassination of ex-King Mohammed Zahir Shah of Afghanistan in 1991. The killer engaged was Paulo Jose De Almeida Santos. He said from his hideout in East Africa that 'the attack was discussed and planned directly with bin Laden'. He met bin Laden thrice before traveling to Rome in November 1991. Santos was converted to Islam in 1989 and posed as a journalist to gain access to the former monarch in his villa in Rome. He took his interview finally saying 'and now I must kill you". To hoodwink he brought a dagger as a present for the former king and tried to stab him through the heart that did not prove fatal as Zahir Khan had kept in his breast a tin of 'Cafi Crhme Cigaros'. Santos then stabbed him several times in the neck before being over powered by Gen Abdul Wali, Zahir's son-in-law. What happened to the case is not known.[24] King Zahir was an opponent of Pakistan and had even opposed to Pakistan's admission as a member of the United Nations. Afghanistan never recognized the Durrand Line as the border between Pakistan and Afghanistan. He was always considered as a threat by the Pakistani establishment. Many prominent Pasthun leaders supporting the king were killed in Pakistan. Majrooh, an Afghan intellectual was killed in Peshawar after he had conducted a survey of the Afghan refugees and found that they overwhelmingly supported the king.[25]

Laden's Somalia operation

As already said, the US Marines landed on the beaches of Somalia in early December 1992 under the glare of flashing cameras. Turabi and Laden rendered help to General Aided who pursued the proclaimed Islamists perception that US intervention was "a conspiracy to prevent Arab and or Muslim control over the Red Sea and the horn of Africa and prelude to a US military strike against Sudan".

A plan was drawn up to strike a couple of hotels in Aden used by US military personnel and facilities at sea and airports. This task was given to Sheikh Tariq al-Fadli with base at Saadh

---

24 HS Rao, *Indian Express* dated 15-04-2002.

25 *The Friday Times*, December 21-27, 2001.

area in northern Yemen. On December 29 bombs were detonated in the Aden Hotel and Golden Moor Hotel in Aden, killing three and wounding five others. However, further damage was avoided as strike team was detected near the fences of the Aden airport while preparing to launch RPG-7 rocket launchers to destroy US planes. Even though the mission was scuttled midway, the operation earned lavish praise for bin Laden.

A lethal ambush was organised on June 5, 1993 in Somalia for killing Pakistani UN Peacekeepers. This was followed by a series of attacks. One of the most important field commanders brought by Zawahiri to Somalia was Ali al-Rashidi, an Egyptian. He was arrested in 1981 after Sadat's assassination. He escaped to Afghanistan in 1986 and joined Ahmad Shah Massud's forces and later joined Laden's forces and participated in jihad operations in various places including Kashmir and soon became one of the most vocal supporters of Laden.

On October 3, 1993, 18 American troops were killed in Mogadishu, Somalia and in a grotesque display of insensitivity the bodies of US servicemen were dragged out and paraded. Boutras Boutras-Ghali, the then UN Secretary General was to visit Somalia. He is a Coptic Christian of Egypt. They are original Christian population in Egypt who had refused to be converted to Islam and naturally they are hated and despised by the orthodox Muslims.

By March 1, 1993 the bulk of US forces were withdrawn out of Somalia and this was considered to be a major triumph by bin Laden against the US and provided him the much needed confidence to take on the US. In several interviews, Laden said that he considered his Somali experience a milestone in his evolution. In March 1997 he told Robert Fisk of the Independent Television: "We believe that God used our holy war in Afghanistan to destroy the Russian army and the Soviet Union .... and now we ask God to use us one more time to do the same to American to a shadow of itself". Seeing the collapse of the American morale he told "the Americans are paper tigers".

Laden's departure from Sudan to Afghanistan

Osama bin Laden was a shrewd operator. He managed to create cells world over with cutout arrangements. A number of bombing incidents remained unrelated to him as the conspirators and perpetrators of these crimes, by omission or commission, did not involve him. They could name those who were in contact with them. In Kanhane's murder case the FBI could reach up to Nosair and few others. In the World Trade Centre truck bombing in 1993 the FBI could reach up to the blind cleric Sheikh Abdul Rehman, who was earlier a CIA sponsored jihadi utilised for recruitment during the Afghan jihad (1979-89) and was ultimately allowed to settle down in America inspite of being on the US watch list.

Osama bin Laden appeared on the FBI's radar screen in 1995 on the basis of scraps of information from the Philippines where Ramzi Yousef failed in his attempts to kill the Pope, Bill Clinton and blast 12 US civil airlines simultaneously. All that could not happen as Yousef was injured while making explosives in his Manila apartment and commotion created there after. He fled to a safe sanctuary in Pakistan. The Saudis were very clear on Osama bin Laden's activities and stripped him of his citizenship in 1994 and froze his assets. Not only that Laden's family was asked to renounce him publicly and an attempt was made on his life in Sudan.[26]

It was a total failure of the FBI and CIA not to have detected Osama bin Laden's invisible hand in Somalian incident in 1993 and New York incidents of Kanhane's murder and the WTC truck blast in 1993. In fact it was only after Ramzi Yousef's arrest in Pakistan that led to bin Laden's emerging as the supreme jihadi leader with worldwide Islamic vision and mission.

The November 1995 pickup trucks with explosives blew up outside a US training mission at Riyadh. It finally settled the issue of bin Laden's involvement. In the blast some Americans and two Indians were killed.[27] The Saudi did not allow the FBI team to assist

---

26 John Miller, Michael Stone, Chris Mitchell, The Cell, Hyperion, New York, 2002, p 163-64.

27 John Miller, Michael Stone, Chris Mitchell, The Cell, Hyperion, New York, 2002, p 149.

the investigation to avoid a backlash. They scanned the profiles of 15,000 jihadis who had participated in Afghan jihad in 1979-89 and zeroed down to four local Saudis. Their confessions were videotaped and subsequently beheaded on 22 April 1995. Their confessions were shown on TV. In their confessions they admitted they were inspired by the tapes and Fatwas (decrees) issued by bin Laden and Al-Qaeda. The USA had perceived him as a financer, but not a hard terrorist with a mission to attack US interests.

In January 1996, President Clinton ordered the CIA and FBI to work together to bring Osama bin Laden to justice. The US strategy was to deal with bin Laden as a criminal and build up a case for prosecution in a Court of Law.[28] Since bin Laden was operating from Sudan teamed up with Hasan al-Turabi, it was decided to put pressure on Sudan. It worked. Sudan decided to hand him over to any responsible authority like Egypt, Saudi Arabia and USA. Fearing a backlash Egypt and Saudi Arabia backed out. The US legal opinion did not anticipate a favourable court verdict in the event of his prosecution in old cases. This forced Sudan with no alternative but to allow him to leave for Afghanistan on 18 May, 1996.[29] The US decision to allow him to land up in Afghanistan was its greatest folly. Perhaps the US thought that Pakistan and the ISI would keep him under control. By 1996 the Taliban established its firm holds in Afghanistan with men and material support of the ISI and Pakistan. After all bin Laden was the test-tube baby of the CIA-ISI combine and he learnt to handle Stinger missiles and other deadly weapons from ISI-CIA combine. Osama arrived in Afghanistan on a visa issued by the government headed by Rabbani.[30]

How funny it looks that the US prosecutors of a southern district court had indicted bin Laden in 1997 for conspiracy to kill American solders in Somalia. In 1996 the view was different. The timidity of the US to deal with bin Laden was fully exposed in 1996 when Sudan was ready to hand him over to US.

---

28 John Miller, Michael Stone, Chris Mitchell, The Cell, Hyperion, New York, 2002, p 150-151.

29 John Miller, Michael Stone, Chris Mitchell, The Cell, Hyperion, New York, 2002, p 152-53.

30 World Affairs, Apr-Jun 2002.

Even in 1997 the US made no effort to extradite him from Afghanistan. The reasons were obvious. The US was negotiating for an oil pipeline project with the Taliban. This project was called UNOCOL oil pipeline project. If the oil pipeline project had been cleared, the US would have even recognized the Taliban regime.

Yossef Bodansky, Director of the US House Task Force on Terrorism and Unconventional Warfare, has a different story behind the exit of bin Laden from Sudan. Sudan agreed on a deal with Saudi Arabia. There was Saudi pressure for deportation of bin Laden in exchange of unstated substantial Saudi financial aid to Sudan. He also speaks of a dispute in Islamic leadership. Turabi and Bashir were using Arab Afghans in the Sudanese civil war when they should have used the strike force of mujahideen against the US and Western interests.

Bin Laden's journey to the Philippines

Yossef Bodansky claims that Osama bin Laden traveled to the Philippines in winter of 1993 as a wealthy Saudi investor eager to help fellow Muslims in the country's southern islands. Many Philippine bureaucrats came in contact with him. The network he built up was handed over to his brother-in-law Mohammed J A Khalifah. Khalifah was detained in San Francisco on immigration charges in December 1994 and subsequently deported. His US visit was significant as it happened after the first World Trade Center attack in 1993. From 1994 Arab Afghans arrived in the Philippines and established operation cells all over the country in large cities. It may be recalled that Ramzi Ahmad Yossef was hovering around the islands of the Philippines. "The US authorities could not even charge Khalifah when they had him" in December 1994.[31]

Before reaching Afghanistan, bin Laden flew out of Khartoum airport and landed in Wadi Saydna airport, a few miles from Khartoum. From there he proceeded to Darfur Province in western Sudan, where Laden had set up a vast terrorist training infrastructure. He ensured transfer of men and material assets to Afghanistan via Pakistan. The transfer of these facilities substantially increased Al-

---

31 Bodonasky, p 114.

Qaeda's capability.[32]

Twin city blast

Bin Laden had the habit of issuing statements before and after each attack on US interest little realizing that such statements could serve as evidence in booking him under the charges of conspiracy. In May 1998, in a press conference in Khost, he said: "We will not settle before the eviction of the American Army from Muslim territories".[33] A few days later in a separate interview to ABC TV he defined his targets and categorically said: "We do not differentiate between those dressed in uniforms and civilians". Bin Laden was a follower of Wahhabi Islam. Wahhabi practice Islam in pure form as was introduced by Prophet Muhammad. Their thrust was to discard non-original rituals and practices. Thus Osama bin Laden too vehemently opposes western civilization.

There were riots in Saudi Arabia when television was introduced in 1965. The Taliban regime too banned television and entertainments. One Arab historian had recorded the ruthless path of Wahhabis in war. He said: "I have seen them hurl themselves on their enemies, utterly fearless of death, not caring how many fall, advancing rank after rank with only one desire - the defeat and annihilation of the enemy. They normally give no quarter, sparing neither boys nor old men".[34] In the light of this, bin Laden's statement that he did not distinguish between military and civilian casualties in jihad has to be understood. This has to be read in the light of 9/11 which happened after three years of this declaration. This statement proved that he knew what was being planned.

Bin Laden's UK visit

Not much is known about bin Laden's UK visit some time perhaps in the early nineties when he was in Sudan. He was said to be the guest of a Middle Eastern Sheikh who owned a mansion in Buckinghamshire green belt. The castle was a virtual fortress, fitted

---

32 Ibid p 186.

33 *Dawn*, 19.08.1998.

34 Bin Laden's uncompromising faith by Neil MacFasquhar, the International Herald Times, 8 October 2001.

with closed circuit television cameras and powerful search lights and a watch tower. This mansion with 10 bed rooms was initially the UK base of Sheikh Khalid bin Mahfauz, 'the scion of the one richest dynasty of Sheikhs of Saudi Arabia'. Bin Laden reportedly spent two or three days in the mansion, relaxing and talking to bin Mahfouz. No body knows what they had discussed.

Evidence surfaced when bin Mahfouz was found using banks in London and America for bin Laden. Mahfouz was also charged in the US for defrauding the Bank of Credit and Commerce International (BCCI) of about $200m. After exposure he returned to Saudi Arabia and lived a retired life in a Saudi military hospital.[35]

Osama bin Laden's expertise in organizing bomb blasts came to notice in a big way when twin trucks bombs were timed to blast two US embassies in Nairobi, Kenya and Dar-es-Salaam, Tanzania on August 7, 1998 resulting in killing of 224 people and wounding more than 5000 people. 12 Americans in these embassies were also killed sending the world into a state of shock. The FBI took up the investigation under the US Laws, which provides them with extra-territorial jurisdiction if the victims are Americans. It may be mentioned that India has yet to develop this type of law of having extra territorial jurisdiction barring cases where the Indians are involved in the commission of offences abroad. In the same way the US law on Money Laundering has been stretched by US courts to have extra territorial applicability in the matter of production of bank documents from a third country. Thus, issuing a notice on the local bank of foreign origin is reason for production of documents lying abroad. After investigation, Osama bin Laden and 16 other associates were indicted by a New York grand jury on charges of plotting these twin embassy attacks and for the first time Osama bin Laden could be directly booked in a specific criminal case in US.

In December 1999 in an interview bin Laden came close to confession when he said that he had supported the attacks of twin US embassies in Africa and knew those who were involved. Bombers were "true men who we respect and hold them in high respect" were his words.

---

35 David Leppard, *Times*, 23.09.2001.

US counter attack

The Khost cruise missile attack by US marines on August 20, 1998 at 10.30 pm did not hit Osama bin-Laden as he had shifted his location just before the attack. The story was that some one from the Pak establishment had alerted bin Laden about the impending missile attack. The truth of the matter may now be known to the Americans. While bin Laden escaped, some Harkat-ul-mujahideen terrorists under training in these camps were killed. It was punitive and preemptive attack as President Clinton declared 'that the terrorist groups led by Osama bin Laden were planning other attacks against the Americans'.[36] Clinton further added that 'the terrorist must have no doubt that in the face of their threat; 'America will protect its citizens'. President Clinton cited three reasons for the attack *viz*, past terrorist attacks against the Americans, planning additional attacks and seeking to acquire chemical and other dangerous weapons.

The cruise missile attack had its rumblings in Islamabad as well. Since the missiles crossed the Pakistan air space some people, prompted by rightist religious leaders, demanded action. As a way out of this embarrassment Pakistan filed a complaint with the United Nation Security Council without pressing for its immediate disposal. This was the only attack launched by Pentagon before the war against terror started in the post September 11 aftermaths. Instead, US had decided to isolate bin Laden by harassing his well known organization called Al-Qaeda and declared a substantial monetary reward of $ 5 million for anyone giving information leading to bin Laden's arrest.

An exaggerated claim made by the then US Defence Secretary Cohen when he said: 'we have taken those actions (missile strike) to reduce the ability of those terrorist organizations to train and equip their misguided followers'. But despite the one time missile attack, terrorist training camps continued to function. One missile strike on 20 August 1998 was merely a warning to Osama to mend his ways. This warning was ignored with contempt.

In June 1999 US banned commercial dealing with Taliban

---

36 *Dawn*, 21.08.1998.

regime for harbouring Osama bin Laden. At the same time the US was allowed a window open for dialogue with Taliban by allowing a Taliban office to operate from the US. Taliban's Abdul Hakeem Mujahid acted as Taliban's unofficial representative to UN. Before the strike, the US asked Taliban to control Osama bin Laden 'if they wished to gain international recognition'. Even after the blast there were tacit negotiations between the USA and the Taliban, a move believed to have been undertaken on the advice of Pakistan. It was in the interest of Pakistan to give patronage and protection to the Taliban regime even at the cost of Afghan unity. Pakistan treated the Taliban controlled Afghanistan as a client state.

A year after the bombing in Africa, posters surfaced in Pakistan urging youths to join bin Laden's movement. Some posters with Laden's signature carried a direct message from him: "I am not afraid of the Americans". He further asserted his right to stay in Afghanistan as he did not believe in political boundaries of nation states. 'The earth belongs to Allah', his messages would often say.

Medeline Albright, US Secretary of State in August 1999 said that Washington would hunt down those responsible for the African embassy bombings. She said: "Today we vow that America will not be intimidated. We will not retreat until every one of those responsible for embassy bombings have been brought to justice". This declaration of intent did not create any effect on bin Laden or Al-Qaeda.

The US State Department stated that Nasser Ahmad Mujahid, Commander-in-Chief of Al-Badr met bin Laden at Darunta in the north-west of Afghanistan and vowed to protect Laden from further US attacks. He said: "we will fight to the last, our mission is martyrdom. We are not afraid of arrest or death. .... America should not compel us, otherwise these hands can reach (President) Clinton's collar". Al Badr was one of the terrorist organizations fighting in Kashmir and elsewhere also.

There was a lot of speculation of another possible US bombing of hideouts of bin Laden in Afghanistan. This became a reason for the Taliban supreme leader Mullah Mohammad Omar to call upon the Muslims of the world to support bin Laden's Islamic movement. "The sole reason" said Mullah Omar "for the United State's hostility towards us is our attachment to the Shariat. (Islamic Law)

The US missile attacks as expected earned widespread condemnation from the Muslim world. Even the Organization of the Islamic Conference (OIC) condemned the attack and a devastating fatwa was issued by the blind jailed cleric in the US Abdel Rehman which was read from mosques all over the world. A part of the fatwa is worth reproducing:

"Destroy them (USA) thoroughly and erase them from face of earth. Ruin their economics, set their companies on fire, turn their conspiracies to powder and dust. Sink their ships, bring their planes down. Slay them in air, on land, on water. And (with the command of Allah) kill them whenever you find them. Catch them and put them in prison. Lie in wait for the man, kill these infidels .... God will support you against them and will cure the afflicted hearts of the faithful and take all anger out of their hearts".[37]

The copies of this 'fatwa' were available in all the prominent madrassas in Pakistan and were in great demand throughout Pakistan which provided the fodder for further motivation to prepare Jihadis for more attacks on US interests.

Several more warnings were administered to USA. Maulana Fazlur Rehman, Emir of Jamait-ul-Ulema-I-Islam (JUI), a close ally of Osama bin Laden, warned USA in a public meeting that the US nationals would not be safe if it attacked Afghanistan in its efforts to capture Osama-bin-Laden. 'We will not handover Osama to the USA even if he is found guilty' said Saeedur Rehman Haqqani, Taliban ambassador in Pakistan on 12 December 1999.[38]

Islamic intolerance of West is fuelled by the seemingly unstoppable spread of westernization through the electronic media. This motivates the terrorists like bin Laden to commit more horrendous, more spectacular strikes only to demonstrate the visibility of radical Islam and its rage against spread of western

---

37 Syed Talat Hussain, *Nation*, 29.08.1998.

38 News, 13.12.1999.

values in the Muslim World. TV footage gave wide publicity of terrorist acts and that induced many to join jihad. Such publicity enhanced the larger than life size image of bin Laden.

The story of bin Laden is the story of events he was part of and the overall dynamics and circumstances within which he strived. It is the story of dedicated zealots driven by extreme hatred. They are ready to endure deprivations and death to force the Islamic World back on to the right path, which means back by few centuries.

On February 2, 1999, George Tenet, the CIA Director, told the Senate: "First, there is not the slightest doubt Osama bin Laden, his worldwide allies, and his sympathizers are planning further attacks against us. Despite progress against his network, bin Laden's organization has contacts virtually worldwide, including the United States – and he has stated unequivocally that all Americans are targets". Bin Laden also knew dangers that he faces. He was always on guard against assassin, commando raids, and air strikes which make him shift from one hideout to another. His forty/fifty commandos always guarded him. This was noted by foreign journalists who interviewed him.

In Unholy Wars, few details of bin Laden have been made available. In May 1998 when the American Television News team managed to establish contact with bin Laden, he said: "We called for the murders of American and Jews". He praised the bombing of World Trade Centre in New York in February 1993 and debacle of US forces sent to Somalia in 1993-94. He also vowed to drive the Saudi Royal family from power and destroy it. The first fact-sheet on Laden was issued by US State Department only in 1994. After 9/11 there was all out efforts to apprehend or kill Osama bin Laden.

Osama bin Laden managed to flee from his hideout in Afghanistan when the US Troops landed in Afghanistan on War on Terror mission. He could not be found in the caves of Tora Bora region. His end came as a surprise after several of hide and seeks game. Bin Laden specific units were created in CIA and FBI. The US has the reputation of being a dangerous enemy focused on the objective. On this it has the ability to have bipartisan approach.

Death of bin Laden

After 9/11 it took almost ten years for CIA to locate and kill bin Laden in Pakistan. The following are the details of this historic encounter:

LOCATION	Laden's compound in Bilal Town, Abbottabad, Pakistan.
Date	May 2, 2011
Participants	President Barrack Obama and six Top executives concerned with bin Laden operation
Deaths	Osama bin Laden with six others
Burial	Osama bin Laden's buried in North Arabian Sea

Osama was killed in Pakistan by the US Navy Seal on 2 May, 2011 at midnight in operation code named Operation Neptune Spear. It was CIA led operation that took off from Afghanistan. His body was taken to Afghanistan for identification and thereafter buried at sea within 24 hours of his death with full Islamic traditions.

Al Qaeda confirmed the death on 6 May, vowing to avenge killing through its website. Pakistan jihadi groups like Tehrik -e-Taliban announced retaliation.

The death of Osama bin ended an era of international hyper terrorism all over the world. The stage is ripe for Lashker-e-Toiba [LeT] to capture the space vacated by Al Qaeda. This reality is being realised by keen watchers and strategic analysts. This fighting outfit is the creation of the ISI of Pakistan confirmed by enough oral and documentary evidence. Pakistan did not lodge a protest to UN for violation of its territory for killing of Osama bin Laden as it did after the Khost missile attack earlier. Did ISI provide protection to bin Laden for almost a decade after 9/11? This question will remain unanswered for a good length of time.

7

Mumbai 26/11 Attack

There was deep anger and anguish about the terrorist attacks in Mumbai on 26 November 2008, which was unprecedented and never happened before. What would have happened if the Lashkar-e-Taiba had landed 100 such daredevil terrorists on 26 November? They have the capability and determination to do so with the support of the ISI.

The well coordinated 10 strikes in Mumbai with grenades and AK-47 rifles by 10 Pakistani terrorist raised the bench mark of brutality and lethality of inhuman killing of nearly 160 people including women and children. It can be called India's 26/11. By sheer courage local police could apprehend one terrorist alive by barricading a road to stop the vehicle where two terrorists were traveling to kill more. The arrested terrorist Ajmal Amir Kasab, hails from Faridkot of Pakistan. Thus, the scope of denial strategy did not work this time. The mastermind of this attack never expected any one to survive as they were trained to die as a fidayeen.

The meticulous planning, money and resources spent were beyond the capacity of any individual organization. It was a very complex operation planned since 2005 when David Coleman Headley was tasked by Sajid Mir of Lashker-e-Taiba to return to USA to change his name from Daood Sayed Gilani to David Coleman Headley to facilitate easy traveling and not easy detection. The first task was the reconnaissance of targets in Mumbai. The selections of targets indicate the political objectives of these attacks. The objectives were to kill Indians, US, British nationals and Jews in tune with 1998 declaration of Al Qaeda and declarations often made by diehard Islamist Hafiz Mohammed Saeed, Emir of Jammat ud Dawa (JuD) previously known as Markaz ul Dawa ul Irshad. This name changing has been the usual practice of all banned organizations in Pakistan when such organizations are listed as terrorist organizations by US or UN. JuD is a part of Islamic Front for Jihad against the Crusaders and Jews of Al Qaeda. Organically all jihadi groups are linked with Al Qaeda by way of interaction, funding, sheltering Al Qaeda operatives and also sharing the Al-Qaeda's world vision of establishment of Islamic Ummah.

The evidence of target selection has already surfaced. Sajid Mir of LeT with deep links with the ISI wanted to use Gilani for operations in India. In 2006 Gilani met Abdur Rehman Hashim 'Pasha Syed, a retired Pakistani army officer and a lashker militant, who put him in touch with Major Iqbal, said to be an ISI officer, who along with Sajid Mir became ISI handlers of Gilani. He made several trips to Mumbai to locate targets. Lashker decided to target the Nariman House, a Jewish community centre. He gathered GPS coordinates for which he received assistance from Pakistan Navy. He stayed in all the hotels selected as targets and video taped all the details of the interior locations of each target.

His last wife complained against Gilani to the officers of US embassy in Islamabad about his activities in Mumbai and the State Department in turn informed all the US agencies concerned. Headley took sadistic pleasure in witnessing the unfolded events on TV from his home in Lahore. Sajid Mir took charge of the control room in Karachi.

Headley was charged for conspiracy to bomb targets in Mumbai in a court in USA. It was reported that Headley's trips to India was financed by the ISI. How did he get visa to visit India? This he could, by obtaining US passport in the false name using mother's surname. In his visa application he gave a false name of his father, using a Christian name. The USA agencies never took seriously the information they had received from his wife from Islamabad. The US court has sentenced Headley for 35 years imprisonment sufficient to keep him 'under lock and key' as said by the judge. Headley avoided death sentence by plea bargain agreement. His testimony proves beyond doubt the links of the ISI in the Mumbai attack. The Indian National Investigation Agency separately interrogated him. As a result he has been charged along with Rana for the Mumbai attack for which he has to be taken into Indian custody. This may not happen as Headley has revealed everything as per plea agreement.

The training for such attacks would involve selection of highly motivated jihadis who would prefer death rather being caught alive. The fidayeen training is nothing but thorough brainwashing like of which was found with LTTE in Sri Lanka. Stories of miracles of martyrs are narrated the same way Abdullah Azzam had done by writing a book on the subject to arouse jihadis for killing themselves for the cause of Allah. Specific mission training is taken care of by experts drawn from the serving or retired men and officers of the Pakistan army and Navy in the Mumbai case. This part of the story has reportedly been narrated by Ajmal Kasab in his confessional statement before a magistrate. 'Kasab in his confession has said one Major General was present during their training and had supervised them. The name of the Major General was not deliberately revealed to the attackers as he occupies a senior position in the army' said the public prosecutor Nikam. He along with several others had gone through a rigorous training schedule at several places in Pakistan. This could not happen without the knowledge of the ISI when ISI have detachment offices in all the districts in Pakistan. Each attacker was a 'killing machine' as described by the prosecutor.

Pakistani response

Initially there was denial. Thanks go to Pakistani press to locate the house of Ajmal Kasab. They identified his village, his background and picture of parental house. Pakistani hand could not be any longer denied. There were leaks from Washington that US had taken a serious view of the matter. Investigators from US, UK and Israel reached Mumbai to participate in the investigation. This was a wise decision from Indian government as there was clear understanding of the involvement of Pakistani state and non state actors in the massacre of Indians and foreigners including Americans.

It was reported that the USA in the event of non-cooperation of Pakistan in the investigation of Mumbai case, might declare Pakistan a state sponsoring terrorism. This was reportedly told by Condoleezza Rice to President Zardari recalling what her predecessor had told Nawaz Sharif in 1992 that Pakistan Army and its intelligence service were involved in the Punjab and J&K terrorism. Nawaz Sharif, to diffuse the situation, shifted Lt Gen Javeed Nasir from the post of DG ISI.

The Washington Post carried a report that Indian and the US investigators identified Yusuf Muzammil, a Lashker leader, as one of the chief conspirators of the Mumbai attack. It was reported that Condoleezza Rice asked Pakistan to turn in Muzammil and other suspects. Rice reportedly told Pakistan that all the details of the living terrorist and training details are known. The US attitude was made clear to Pakistan. This yielded some results as US has a mechanism to deal with such states.

The US is the only sole super power having the capability to enforce its decision on other unwilling powers to deal with terrorism. The US laws have provided a mechanism to deal with state sponsor terrorism. Firstly, they declare such a state 'not cooperating fully'. If the concerned state takes corrective steps, the matter ends there. In case the concerned state does not take action, the state is declared 'not cooperating'. In such a situation the US laws can go in for imposition of sanctions of various kinds. On earlier occasions Pakistan had faced such situations but escaped by taking some cosmetic action like house arrests or handing over some of the terrorists to US on their demand.

In the Mumbai attack case a number of US citizens were killed. The US laws permit registration of a criminal case against the perpetrators of crime independent of the citizenship of the accused. As per press report a case has been registered by the FBI. Thus, the US can invoke provisions under their laws for trial of all the accused of 26/11. In such a situation Pakistan will have no escape route but to go through the process of trial in Pakistan, which is currently in motion in Pakistan.

Pakistan, in view of the international pressure, reluctantly decided to take up the investigation of the case. The case was handed over to FIA (Federal Investigation Agency). Instead, investigating the case speedily, it depended on the evidence collected by India. By October 15, 2013 India handed over the full list of documents asked for by Pakistan. 'Since the planning, training and financing was done in Pakistan, 99 per cent of the evidence would be available in Pakistan' said the Indian home minister. It was the job of FIA to embark on a thorough investigation.

Pakistan identified seven accused including the mastermind Zakiur Rehman Lakhvi. All of them are facing the trial in a court in Rawalpindi. On the basis of press report the trial is proceeding in a very casual manner. The court was constituted in 2009 and five trial court judges were appointed. The present judge has asked for foolproof security. The chief public prosecutor Chaudhury Zulfiqar was killed by militants on May 3, 2013 in Islamabad. The present prosecutor has also asked for foolproof security. In India such securities are normally provided to trial court judges in such sensitive cases. It seems the administration in Pakistan is not keen for earlier finalization of the trial of the case. Even the US president expressed his concerns for the delay in the trial of the case when Nawaz Sharif met him in the month of October, 2013.

Civil Suit in USA

Civil suits were filed in a US court by a wounded American and the heirs of four others who were killed in the Mumbai attacks in a US court claiming damages of $ 75000 from each. The US court issued summons to Hafiz Saeed, ISI chiefs Shuja Pasha and Nadeem Taj and other Pakistani officials and non-officials for complicity in the attack. In the attack more than 160 died and 300 injured.

Pakistan's official stand is to defend the serving and retired ISI chiefs arguing that the attack was carried out by 'non-state actors' from Pakistan. Saeed filed a petition before the Lahore High Court that he too should be defended by Pakistan on the basis of equality of treatment as a citizen. The matter is still pending. Then prime minister of Pakistan Yousaf Raja Gilani said in the National

Assembly that Pak officials could not be subjected to a trial in a US court and efforts were being made to get the case dismissed. Is the same facility available to heirs of the victims of 9/11 attack in India? The subject needs to be discussed by legal luminaries in India.

Let us now bring out Lashker-e-Taiba's (LeT) dangerous character in the public domain. Some misguided strategic analysts including BBC have been naming LeT as a Kashmiri terrorist outfit. This is wholly untrue. It is a Pakistani fighting outfit created by ISI and being used by the ISI to promote terrorism in Kashmir and elsewhere. The Indian Muslims are no fools. The Muslims anger was so profound that city's Muslim Council of Mumbai refused to let the terrorists buried in their graveyards. Saeed's hatred is so pronounced that his agenda include Hindus, Shias, Christians and Jews. In 2000 he said in a Karachi rally that 'there can't be any peace while India remains intact. Cut them, cut them, cut them so much that they kneel before you and ask for mercy.'[1] If Hindus were the intended targets, then how the LeT terrorists who never met a Jew in their life time could torture and kill Rabbi Gavriel Holtzberg and his young pregnant wife Rivka at the Mumbai's obscure Jewish center. Saeed's agenda is clear that his LeT would 'plant the flag of Islam in Washington, Tel Aviv and New Delhi.'[2] JuD's so called charitable work and Dawa are a part of strategy. One is to get donations mainly from rich Arab Pakistanis living abroad. Money on humanitarian works is to win sympathy from Pakistanis. Dawa *i.e.* teaching is to promote jihad in Pakistan and abroad as students are drawn from various countries to his seminaries in Muridke.

So far we have not taken Lashker-e-Taiba's previous Indian attacks very seriously. Our human intelligence assets are inadequate to deal with this and other powerful threats emanating from Jihadi groups operating from Pakistani. People are now demanding a determined response from our side. Lakhs of people assembled in Mumbai demanding action saying 'enough is enough'. This kind of out burst had never been seen before.

Let us face facts. Tariq Ali, a widely known intellectual of

---

1   Patrick French, *New York Times*, 8 December, 2008.

2   Ibid.

Pakistan settled in UK, had described 'Lashker-e-Taiba is the creation of the ISI of Pakistan in 2000'. He had adequate understanding of ground realities of Pakistan. He had bluntly said that the Lashker-e-Taiba 'cannot exist without the patronage of the Pakistan Army.' ISI is part of the army and, therefore, immune from judicial scrutiny.

Origin of Dawat-ul-Irshad now called Jamaat-ud-Dawa

Those who have been closely keeping track of the Lashker-e-Taiba for the last fourteen years have found it to be a dangerous out fit emerging from the Punjabi belt of Pakistan. In January 1999, I wrote an article in the Statesman focusing on Dawat-ul-Irashad the mother organization of Lasker-e-Taiba which is its fighting outfit. The parent body was created in 1987 by three professors of the University of Engineering and Technology of Lahore and some reports suggest that the inspiration came from Osama bin Laden and Abdullah Azzam of The International Islamic University of Islamabad. There were reports that Azzam and Osama had funded this organization. Its headquarters is in Muridke, 30 miles from Lahore. It has area of 200 acres of land under its occupation always guarded by armed Lashkers all the time. The head of the organization is Hafiz Mohammed Saeed, a hard-line Wahabbi Islamist. Saeed had made a brief visit to Afghanistan in 1986 during Afghan Jihad where he met Zaki ur Rehman Lakhvi. Lakhvi had participated in Afghan Jihad and has enough battle experience.[3] Therefore, Zaki ur's name surfacing now in Mumbai case as brain behind is nothing surprising. Zaki ur Rehman Lakhvi has close ties with Afghan mujahideen and his sister is married with an Arab called Abdul Rehman, who was said to be one of the donors for purchase of land in Muridke. He was arrested for his Al Qaeda connections. He followed the policy of controlled 'carefully calibrated' jihad in tune with the international policy. This shows that he is fully controlled by the ISI and military. If Lakhvi is not arrested and handed over for 26/11, it is only because of LeT close connections with these two agencies.

The e-mail messages issued by the terrorist named the group carrying out the attack under the nom de quire 'Deccan Mujahideen' is to give the colour of locals being involved in the Mumbai attack,

---

3   For more details see Herald of January, 1988.

The Pakistan's High Commissioner in London said in an interview with the BBC that the terrorists looked like dark-skinned South Indians and not fair enough like Pakistanis.[4] The ISI game plan has always been to divert attention from Pakistan. The truth is that LeT has been on this agenda ever since its inception. Hafiz Mohammed Saeed on record has said on many occasions that 'Kashmir is a gateway to capture India' and other targets elsewhere.

Political philosophy of Dawat-ul-Irshad

Hafiz Mohammed Saeed originally hailed from undivided Punjab and went to Pakistan during the partition. He is a Gujjar. His mother hailed from Himachal Pradesh of India where he has special focus on Chamba and Kangra districts. His political view is very clear. He had told Pamela Constable, a journalist, that 'revenge is our religious duty. We beat the Russian superpower in Afghanistan. We can beat Indian forces'. Pamela wrote 'that their fervent dreams were to die in Jihad against Indians as they would secure a place in heaven'.[5]

Every year in the first week of November they hold an annual convention. In 1998 convention Hafiz Mohammed Saeed gave a fervent call for Jihad in India, USA and Israel. Even he had the audacity to announce an attack on Indian prime minister's residence. Its annual conventions are attended by former ISI officers and military officers like Gen. Hamid Gul. Retired army officers are tasked to impart military training to Lashkers at different training centers. This can only happen with the full knowledge and support of the government. In the invitation card for 1988 convention a report was attached that boasted that "apart from Pakistan mujahideen, hundreds of mujahideen from other countries like Kashmir, Bosnia, Chechnya, Philippines, Somalia and Europe and America have received training from the camps in Afghanistan and are doing jihad at many fronts of the world. Hundreds of youth are receiving training every day ......The LeT mujahideen, trained in our camps are sounding the death knell for Hindus in India and Jews

---

4   UPI Asia, 22/12/2008.

5   Constable, Pamela, Guns and Yellow Roses, Harper Collins, New Delhi, 1999, p 52.

in Israel……..The whole of Europe is trembling in fear".[6]

Markaz believes in Ahle Hadith which is another name for Wahabbi Islam and Salafi Islam. These schools of Islam believe on establishment of Caliphate. Saeed does not believe in democracy. "Democracy is among the menaces we inherited from an alien government. It is part of the system we are fighting against. Many of our brothers feel that they can work in an Islamic society by working within the system. They are mistaken. It is not possible to work within a democracy and establish an Islamic system. You just dirty your hands by dealing with it. If God gives us a chance, we will try to bring in the pure concept of an Islamic Caliphate."[7]

In 1997 convention, Saeed again said that Markaz should take advantage of the growing public discontent with the political system and widespread corruption. Taking Taliban as a model he called for ending the democratic system in Pakistan. Saeed called for a jihad to turn Pakistan into a pure Islamic state.[8] The notion of the sovereignty of people is anti-Islamic. Only Allah is sovereign, but did not forget to announce that his organization had no immediate plan to do so in Pakistan. In justification he said that there was no Islamic government in the world. He did not muster courage to declare jihad in Pakistan. Theoretically, there was no justification for jihad elsewhere, but the fact was that he is a puppet of the ISI and had to follow their policy of jihad as an instrument of Pakistan's foreign policy objectives. This becomes clear when he said that his main interest was to wage jihad in un-Islamic countries. He knew the fate of Qutab and others in Egypt and Saudi Arabia where hardcore violent Islamist had to face death penalty or long imprisonment.

A year before he addressed the Lahore Press Club in February 1996, Saeed announced that jihad would spread to other parts of India to create three Pakistans in India. To disintegrate India is a cherished dream of the ISI. Saeed is nothing but mouthing the game plan of the ISI. This explains whenever his outfit was banned he was allowed to change the names of the organizations under his control.

---

6   The Jihadi Factroy, Sushant Sareen, p269.

7   *See* Herald,1997 or 1998.

8   *The News*, November 23, 1997.

This has become a joke and everyone knows about this game. Often he was shown under so called 'house arrest' just to hoodwink the international community.

Organizational set up

The Lashker's recruitment offices are located in several places in Pakistan. At one point of time they had nearly 2000 unit offices in Pakistan.[9] These offices were used for recruitment of jihadis and for propaganda. They were also used for fund raising.

They can impart training to thousands of recruits in a year. Even after the first ban of this organization, LeT was running five camps.[10] All the training details are in their websites. One such LeT press release on jihad training runs as follows:

> In our jihad camp we impart training for three weeks in which new comers are introduced to weapons from Kalashnikov up to missiles. Then we train them for three weeks more for Da'wa which is called Suffah Tour. Following this, there comes the Special Tour comprising three months in which they are trained for guerilla war and mine-blast, fighting and firing missiles and rockets. After the completion of guerilla training, a man is enabled to be launched in Kashmir.....After this practice, some of the boys are selected for specialization in making remote control bombs and missiles.....There is no restriction to go for jihad training .....A boy must possess strong muscles and body. Presently boys of eight years of age are mostly taking part in jihad.[11]

Journalists have been reporting of their covert and overt activities. The present Pakistani ambassador in USA had written about these activities and can be used as authentic evidence. He was replaced soon.

Lashkers are recruited after a good deal of screening. Those found fit are given basic training and thereafter selected Lashkers

---

9   *The News*, 20 February, 2000.

10   Jihadi Factroy, p 257.

11   Stern, Jessica, Bulletin of the Atomic Scientists, February 2001, pp42-50.

are given specialized combat training. Again those who are found highly motivated in Jihad are selected for fidayeen attacks. A letter was recovered written in Urdu from the possession of a lashker Jihadi killed in an encounter on Amarnath Yatri in 2001 in Kashmir. In the letter it was written that 'we are fidayeen......In the name of Allah we will continue to kill, be killed, till such time we destroy India and we overcome India'.

A fidayeen is assured of financial assistance to the parents. Such financial assistance is partly provided before they are launched for action. Thus, it shows the financial strength of the Jihadi outfits. This is arranged in a variety of means, like sharing of illegal money earned by organised criminal gangs like Dawood gang. Dawood remains under the protection of the ISI all the time in Pakistan, despite of his being declared as a terrorist by the U N. Dawood is a fugitive of the Mumbai blast cases in which many have been convicted by a court. He is under the Red Alert notice of the Interpol. He is not being handed over to India. The reasons are obvious. If he is handed over he will spill out the real face of the ISI. Because of the Interpol notice, like Amanullah, he is holed up in Pakistan.

In 1999 convention Hafiz Muhammad Saeed and his associates repeated Jihadi utterances. In the annual conventions parents of those killed in action in India and elsewhere are paraded before the gathering by way of honouring them and inducing others to join in Jihad. There is no secrecy about it and this is in the knowledge of the authorities and the ISI, as former and retired army officers participate in the conventions. Gen.(retd) Hamid Gul used to be one of them.

In 1998 Hifiz Muhammad Saeed and Azam Cheema visited Dhaka. Cheema was the launching commander of the Lashker's Indian operations which was widely known to Indian agencies. The duo was in Dhaka to spread Lashkers cells in Bangladesh and tie up with other Jihadi outfits in Bangladesh.

In Dhaka they recruited Abu Nasir, a Bangladeshi, who was tasked to build up a base in Siliguri for anti Indian operations. Nasir was subsequently tasked to blast the American installations in India with the help of a group of Arab terrorists. The Indian agencies foiled that attempt. The US authorities did not perhaps take it seriously as it happened before 9/11.

Hafeez Muhammad (not Saeed) a Pakistani Lashker came to Hyderabad in 1994 and married an Indian girl. He as usual managed to procure Indian identity. His assignment was to recruit Jihadis from Hyderabad, Kurnool, Kannur (Karela), Mewar, Baghpat, Muzaffarnagar, Amroha, Meerut and from the suburbs of Mumbai. These were the target of an ISI spy Mohmmed Sherif caught in Delhi much before Hafeez.

There have been systematic efforts to recruit Indians to build up local Jihad for furtherance of ISI ultimate objective for disintegration of India, a cherished dream of ISI and its sponsored Jihadi outfits. Many locals had reportedly been trained in Afghanistan and Pakistani training camps. It is high time that a data bank is created of such anti national elements for close watch and arrest in the event of their overt and covert activities. I wonder if ever we attempted to undertake such an exercise on sustained basis.

Srinagar airport was attacked by a fidayeen group of Lashker-e Taiba on 16 January 2000. Look at the way the operation was supervised by the Lashker's safe house in Islamabad. A Srinagar support team sent out a wireless message to Islamabad safe house that boys had entered the Srinagar airport. Immediately four bearded Lashkers went to pray. An officer of the rank of a Col used the same frequency on wireless to know the progress. He was told to use the same frequency to know the progress. This not our version but reported by Ghulam Hussain in *Time* of 5 February 2001.

The same story has come to light in the recent 26/11 attack mounted in Mumbai by Lashker-e-Taiba. In *India Today* of December 15, 2008 there is mention of two telephone intercepts. In one intercept, a Pakistani corps commander spoke to his counterpart in Rawalpindi saying 'the Indians have been taught a lesson, now we will see how India will burn.' In another conversion a Lashker-e-Taiba controller Muzaffar spoke to a Lt Colonel of the Pakistan Army in Islamabad on the same subject.

In chapter after chapter it has be shown how Pakistan Army and the ISI have been sponsoring and sustaining international terrorism in name of Islam. These two institutions have never remained under the civilian control of the civilian President or Prime Minister. It may be of interest to study the activities of another anti-Indian outfit operating from Pakistan with the support of the ISI.

Jaish-e-Mohammed (Army of the Prophet)

The creation of this dangerous Jihadi fighting outfit is linked with highjacking of Indian Airline Flight IC 814. The Emir of this dangerous outfit is Maulana Masood Azhar, who is a diehard Sunni fundamentalist. He was arrested in Kashmir along with another Jihadi commander Sajjad Afghani. His mission in Kashmir was to sort out factionalism in Harkat ul Mujhaideen.

His entry into India was unique as he arrived in New Delhi by a flight from Dhaka as a Gujrati born Portugeese national in January 1994. He was born on 10 July 1968 in Bahawalpur, a place where President of Pakistan Zia was killed in a plane crash. It is a part of Punjab province. His father was a teacher in a government school and had 11 children, six sisters and five brothers. The family had a small poultry diary farm to supplement family income. His father was extremely religious with Deobandi leanings.

On prompting of his father's friend he joined the famous Binori madrasa located in Karachi. This mosque is now widely known as the most important jihadi factory where Mullah Omar reportedly met Osama bin Laden. Most of the Taliban leadership was the product of this mosque in Karachi. Here Massod Azhar got infected with jihadi movement the same way the Aligarh Muslim University was infected with 'Muslim India' movement in pre-partition days. Any great movement requires intellectual backing of a reputed institution. The tidal wave of Islamic terrorism has been possible because of Binori and a few other similar Islamic mosques and madrasas in Pakistan.

Azhar was soon drawn to jihad as his principal wanted him to visit Afghanistan in the training course of jihad. The course was under the guidance of Harkat-ul Ansar, subsequently renamed

Harkat-ul-Mujahideen. The training camp was at a place called Yavar in Afghanistan. He being physically weak could not complete the 40 day course in the Harkat camp. But that did not deter him from joining the fight against the Russians. He reportedly got injured. As he failed as a warrior he was made head of the department of motivation of Harkat. He started editing two publications namely Sada'e Mujahideen in Urdu and Sawte Kashmir in Arabic which he had learnt already.

Soon he came close to Maulana Fazlur Rehaman Khalil, head of the political front of Harkat, known as Jamait -e-Ulema Islam(JUI). Khalil's outfit runs several religious schools in Pakistan, which also in a way created Harkat and the Taliban cadres. Azhar was made the general secretary of Harkat as he was found to be an orator of outstanding ability for the cause of jihad. Harkat was notorious for inducting foreign terrorists in Kashmir who were trained earlier in Afghan jihad during 1979 to 1989. Their induction virtually made JKLF redundant. This was also the strategy of Pakistan as they did not like Azadi formulation of JKLF.

Harkat had pan-Islamic vision of Islam and were spreading into other countries. For that Azhar was sent to Lusaka, Zambia, Abu Dhabi, Mongolia, UK, Albania and Nairobi. These visits were significant as the mission was for motivation, recruitment and fund raising. He met many people including Mufti Ismail in Southall in a London mosque.

As said earlier Azhar entered India by a flight and landed in Delhi, stayed in Ashoka Hotel, Janpath Hotel and left for Deoband with others. It is not known what he did in Deoband. He thereafter went to Kashmir by air and met two top commanders of Harkat, Sajjad Afghani and Amjad Bilal in the Lalbazaar area of downtown Srinagar. Azhar there after went to Anantnag to meet Harkat jihadis. His movements would show that he had no fear of being watched by agencies. He, along with Afghani, was caught at Khanbal by accident on 10 February 1994.

As he was a very important functionary of Harkat, Khalil made all efforts to get him released by way of hostage taking of foreigners in India and in Kashmir. In one case of hostage taking Omar Sheikh was caught and his background came to limelight. He was a dropout of The London School of Economics and a British national. As hostage taking did not yield result, a jail break attempt was made resulting in death of Afghani. The IC 814 high jacking resulted in release of Massod Azhar, Omar Sheikh and Mustaq Zargar alias Latrum. All of them met each other in Tihar jail of Delhi. Out of this they got bonded together and a strategic alliance was built up.[12]

Azhar's links with the Taliban, not known much earlier, came to surface when he was embraced and greeted by Mulavi Mohammad Akhtar Usmani, corps commander of the Taliban in Kandahar. This was written by Azahar in an article, 'From Imprisonment To Freedom'.[13] This dramatic release boosted his morale to a high pitch and then and there he decided to lead jihad under his own command and control. The first thing he did was to reach Binori mosque. He received overwhelming welcome and announced jihad against India. In Lahore 100 fully armed jihadis received him. If five people could hijack a plane and get him released, 'they can as well cut India's lifeline too.' This he told to a correspondent of *The Week* on 23 January, 1999.

As he became a hero he needed an independent space for himself. He soon developed differences with Maulana Fazlur Rehaman Khalil and broke away from Harkat-ul-Mujahideen. He created his own jihadi in the name of Jaish-e-Mohammed and operated from Bahawalpur. His cadres were mostly drawn from his previous organization. In no time Jaish was ready for action. He reportedly received money from Osama bin Laden.

The first action of Jaish was in Srinagar in May2000, where a 17 year old boy Afaq Ahmed hailing from Srinagar drove a car with explosives into the Headquarters of the Indian Army in Badamibagh and exploded it. This was the first human bomb used in Kashmir. And that introduced a new phase of terror acts in the valley. In the same year later, Bilal a British national, who was a Jaish activist,

---

12 *see* Azhar's write up in International Mujahid and Muzamil's article published in *Indian Exprees*, 10 December 2008.

13 ibid

similarly drove an explosive loaded Maruti car and exploded it at the gate of corps headquarters. Jaish official publication is Zarbe-e-Momin which incites terrorism and provides information on terrorist acts. Bilal's story was included to inspire others.

Bilal was recruited in 1994 as a teenager in UK. He was recruited by a group called Al Maddad which operated as recruiting agency for UK Muslims living in Birmingham. It was claimed that the agency could recruit 2000 UK citizens for jihad in Chechnya, Bosnia, Kashmir and other hotspots of jihadi terrorism.[14]

Despite 9/11 Jaish ignored Pakistan's 'U' turn on terrorism. It carried out an attack by suicide bombing of the Srinagar Assembly on 1 October, 2001. 38 Persons were killed in this attack. How such attacks could be carried out without the knowledge of the all knowing ISI even after 9/11? The most daring attack was carried out on 13 December 2001, just three months after 9/11. A suicide squad of Jaish terrorists with grenades in backpacks, Kalashnikovs stunned a nation when they attacked Indian Parliament. Indian secularism and pluralism was under attack. The message was clear that nobody was safe in India.

The attack was seen by millions of people in India and abroad on TV. The US-led war on terror was just limited to protect US interest only. The five Jaish terrorists were killed by security forces. They were brave policemen who deserve the country's highest award. The terrorists were 'spraying bullets and lobbing grenades shouting 'Pakistan Painabad' clearly indicating the hand behind the attack. In 24 hours the police arrested two Pakistanis from Hotel Ambassador in Delhi. They were in touch with the militants and the case was cracked. A day before Abdul Ghani Bhatt, a Hurriyat Chairman said in a press conference that, "December 13 will be an important event not only in Kashmir but in US too. How? Wait for 12 hours and you will now-----I trust the events will not disappoint either me or you".[15]

Instead of uniting as a nation, then Congress led opposition,

---

14 *Newsline*, January 2001.

15 Attack on Parliament, K Bhushan and G Katyal, p5.

keeping impending elections in view, took up issue of the POTA (which was an anti-Terrorist Act), that POTA could not prevent this attack. The issue was to keep the vote bank politics alive. They did not realise that because of POTA the case ended in conviction. No law can prevent terrorist acts, it can enable conviction. The PATRIOT ACT of US does that only.

The Delhi Police after three days confirmed that Jaish was behind the attack as they did in Srinagar Assembly attack. Jaish and LeT had jointly carried out this attack conceived and executed by Azhar and Zaki-ur-Rehaman under the ISI direction. Zaki ur Rehaman is a commander of LeT, who has again figured in 26/11 attack in Mumbai. Afzal on interrogation told police that Mohammad who was killed in Parliament attack was one of the hijackers of IC 814.[16] Mohammad killed Rippan Katyal in 1999 hijacking case. The Parliament attack case has ended in conviction of most of the accused in a court of law. In appeal the High Court and the Supreme Court upheld the judgment in favour of state. A study of the Bombay, Coimbatore and the Delhi Parliament cases show that a determined government needs special anti-terrorist act to deal with those who are apprehended for terrorist acts. The ordinary laws can not deal with the prosecution of such cases. The UN resolution 1373 calls upon all the nations to enact anti-terrorist laws in their respective jurisdictions.

The Jaish-e-Mohammed, as said already, was formed in January 2000. Soon there was fight between Jaish and Harkat over Harkat's assets. Most of the Harkat cadre switched over to Jaish. Force was used to capture Harkat's offices, furniture and equipment by Jaish. Three elders were appointed to settle the issue. It was decided that Jaish would be paid Rs 40 lacks for return of offices occupied by Jaish. Jaish returned occupied offices in very bad condition not acceptable to Harkat. Harkat therefore refused to pay the amount of money due to Jaish.

Azhar and Jaish have Sipah-e-Sahaba leanings. Azhar is a diehard Sunni and vehemently anti- Shia. Harkat avoided sectarian linkages. Soon Harkat influence was reduced. Khalil was virtually

---

16 IBID, p 16.

isolated. In this peculiar situation of humiliation and virtual isolation Khalil had to approach Osama bin Laden. Harkat had played a big role in Afghan Jihad and had close relationship with Al- Qaeda and Taliban. It was Harkat which organised hijacking of IC 814 to get Azhar and two others released from Indian jails. Osama bin Laden was equally close to Azhar and his mission of jihad. He donated 12 new double cabin pickups in replacement of those ruined by Jaish.[17]

Many prominent jihadi commanders of Harkat like Mufti Muhammad Asghar, who came to notice for launching jihadis in Kashmir and many others holding high positions in Harkat joined Jaish.[18] Azhar soon started visiting towns and cities of Pakistan for recruitment and fund raising. His cassettes were widely distributed. They contained venoms against India and urged for destruction of India. The cassettes reached India too. These cassettes did serve its purpose by influencing many to join jihad.

Azhar declared that he would raise a liberation force of 5,00,000 for attacks in Kashmir when Musharraf had announced that Pakistani soil will not be used for such activities elsewhere. Joining the war against terrorism was reduced to a farce. The US was not interested as Jaish did nothing against US interest so far. Azhar soon divided the unity of jihadis by his concept of a true jihadi. He said that those who follow 'Muqalids' should unite to fight against Indian forces, and he excluded 'Ghair Muqalids' *i.e.* those who do not follow any of the Imams. This limited the Ummah to a limited section of Muslims.[19]

Azhar and Jaish were favourite to ISI till December, 2003. The attack on Musharraf in December was viewed as the work of Jaish. Another reason was that it become public that Azhar was too close to Osama bin Laden and Al Qaeda.[20] During 2000-2002 thousands of Jaish trained jihdais had gone to Afghanistan under the Taliban regime to fight against the Northern Alliance and after 9/11 against

---

17 *The Friday Times*, 28-29 August 2000.

18 Amir Rana, Jihad Kashmir-WA- Afghanistan, p145 and also see Jihadi Factroy by Sushant Sareen.

19 *News*, February 9, 2000.

20 A to Z of Jihadi organisations, p 22.

the US-led coalition.

In Pakistan Jaish mounted attacks on foreign Christian nationals by way of attack against US-coalition operation in Afghanistan. The northern group of Jaish under Saif, attacked the Protestant International Church in Islamabad on 17 March 2002 followed by attack on the Christian school near Muree on 5 August 2002. Again the Jaish targeted a Christian Hospital in Taxila on 9 August 2002. All these attacks were carried out under the instructions of Mullah Omar.[21] For these attacks Pakistani TV blamed India as a cover to hide its own terrorist groups. This is the normal practice in Pakistan.

The command structure of Jaish is not clear. Maulana Abdul Jabbaris is said to be the supreme commander and a trainer. Much is not known about him. Adil, Saif and Atiqur have surfaced in interrogations. Three Jaish training camps have come to light.

1. Syed Ahemed Shaheed camp is located in Balakot near Mansehra. It could train 2000 terrorists at any given point of time.

2. Khalid Zubair is a madrassa and a training camp. It is located in Mansehra.

3. Madrassa Khalid bin Whalid, Khost, Afghanistan which was used previously by Harkat.

4. Madrassa Mehmood Ghaznavi, Kotli, POK. Jaish in addition has a big office in Bhimbar in POK.

Much is not known now about Azar and his present activities.

---

21 *Herald*, July 2003.

8

The Future of Al Qaeda

The future of Al Qaeda as a philosophy is a widely debated subject. There are reasons for this. After the attack on Afghanistan in October 2001 for ouster of the Taliban regime by the US-led coalition was a success as Al Qaeda was uprooted from Afghanistan. The military action was called operation 'enduring peace'. The success was more due to help rendered by the Northern Alliance which provided foot soldiers to capture grounds held by the Taliban regime. The Al Qaeda leadership was in disarray. Mohammed Atef, the operational head of Al Qaeda, was killed. The rest of the leadership fled to Pakistan, as there was no other place to hide. Pakistan's Federally Administered Area is the best suitable place for regrouping of Al Qaeda and the Taliban forces in this region as Pakistan has the alibi of the area being least administered area. This tribal area is still under the grip of Islamic fundamentalism with a mix of tribal culture of resistance. The reality of the region has been vividly described by Jan Goodwin in her book titled '*The Price of Honour.*' The other reality is that all those involved in 9/11 attacks were not hiding in the tribal area. They were all apprehended in the heartland of Pakistan on the basis of US specific intelligence from Karachi, Faisalabad and around Islamabad.

Almost all prominent Al Qaeda leadership has been neutralised by arrest or by death. Osama bin Laden was said to be suffering from kidney problem. He was reportedly under medical care. One of his associates reportedly visited India for procurement of equipment or medicine. This was not officially confirmed but appeared to be true. All indications were there that he was alive. This must have been in the knowledge of the ISI. The old association could not be snapped so easily. Al Zawahiri, the second most important Al Qaeda leader, is very much alive and active and now assumed the leadership of Al Qaeda after elimination of Osama bin Laden by the US Special Forces.

Al Zawahiri has been very active and has vowed to wage relentless jihad against 'Crusader America and its servant Israel and whoever supports them'. The US announced a reward of $25m on his head after 9/11. One of his wives and two children were killed in 2001 during US strike. Another fruitless US airstrike on a Pakistani village Damdola in 2006 to kill him was found to be untrue. That he is alive is proved by releasing of several video tapes, the latest being in February 2012.

Al Zawahiri appointed his second-in-command Nasser Abdul Karim al-Wuhayshi, leader of Al-Qaeda in the Arabian Peninsula in command of Saudi Arabia, Yemen. He is said to be in his thirties. He is a veteran of the Afghan jihad. He replaces Abu Yahya al-Libi who was from Libya. By this succession the message is clear that Al-Qaeda has the capacity to wage a long war and there is no dearth of leadership.

Khalid al-Habib has since emerged as an important Al-Qaeda operative with important responsibility in south east Afghanistan. He was presumed to have been killed in an air-strike in 2006 which was found to be untrue. Now he is said to be in charge of operations in Afghanistan and FATA region of Pakistan. He hails either from Egypt or Morocco.

Adnan el Shukrijumah, Saudi born, is said to have taken over the role of the alleged mastermind of 9/11 Khalid Sheikh Mohammad. He controls the external operations of Al-Qaeda. He is familiar with the American culture as he had lived there for more than 15 years. His father was a cleric in a mosque in Brooklyn. Some times in the nineties he left for Afghanistan for arms training and participated in jihad in Chechnya. He is said to have attempted plotting a suicide bomb attacks on New York's subway system in 2009. He is said to have been the mastermind of couple of attacks in Europe. He has the distinction of attracting attention of the US which has announced a reward of $5m on his head.

Mustafa Hamid has served as an instructor in tactics in an Al-Qaeda camp in Afghanistan and acted as a link between Iran and Al-Qaeda during the Afghan jihad. He managed to negotiate with Iran and Al-Qaeda for relocation of several senior Al-Qaeda leaders in Iran. He reportedly was held till 2011 in Iran and, thereafter, reached Egypt during the revolution. His present whereabouts are not clear.

Matlur Rehman is a Pakistani jihadi and said to be the architect of the foiled attempt to explode a passenger aircraft in 2006 with fuel liquid bomb. He is reportedly hiding in Pakistan.

Adam Gadahn is a Christian who converted to Islam at a young age. He is a US citizen. He moved to Afghanistan in 1998 and married an Afghan lady. He became close to Abu Zubaydah, who was being groomed as a successor of Atef. He identifies himself as the 'Azzam the American'. In 2006 he had told all Americans to embrace Islam in a video appearance for which he has been charged by the US with treason. A reward of $1m for his capture hangs on his head. He apparently does not hold any important positions in the present Al-Qaeda leadership positions.

The names mentioned above in the present leadership of Al-Qaeda are just illustrative and not exhaustive. The short point that deserves attention is Al-Qaeda is still active in several parts of the world.

The appearance of neo-Taliban in Pakistan's tribal area is sure sign of revival of Al Qaeda. It was firmly under the control of tribal leader of Meshud tribe. There was creeping invasion of neo-Taliban in Swat area under Maulana Fazullah. The Islamic code was being enforced and the government was unable to enforce its writ in these areas. An Islamic state like Pakistan has limited ability to challenge the growth of fundamentalism. Even Zulfikar Ali Bhutto, under pressure, had declared Qadianis as non Muslims. Gen. Zia introduced Hadood Ordinances, which by law enforced male domination. For example a male witness is equal to four women witnesses. For proving rape the victim has to produce four pious male eye witnesses, which by logic, is impossible. The victim then faces a case of adultery by virtue of her own admission of sexual intercourse and is punished for that. The laws introduced by Zia are still intact and no government in Pakistan has the will or determination to amend these features of harsh Islamic laws for fear of a backlash from the fundamentalist forces. Gen. Musharraf initially did try to change the blasphemy law. Due to strong opposition from fundamentalists he had to retreat. Musharraf in his enthusiasm called for adoption of Turkish model governance. Here again he had to retreat. He soon earned the title Gen Retreat. All this would happen if the state is governed by Islamic tenets of one school of thought. By deductive logic no deviation is possible in a state ruled by one religion.

For protection of the ideological frontiers of the state of Pakistan, by virtue of its own declaration, would mean expansion of the idea of imposition of pure Islam of the days of the Prophet. Liberals have no place as would be evident from killing of liberals like President Sadat of Egypt in 1970 and Farag Founda an intellectual in 1972 in Egypt. Founda's crime was that he mocked the extremists, who had declared that men being told not to sit on a bus seat vacated by a woman for at least ten minutes until her body heat was no longer apparent.[1]

The Pakistani leadership lives under the fear of the Army and the ISI. Benazir Bhutto was interviewed by various reporters from time to time and she had been saying this for years. She gave an interview to the author of the book titled '*Deception*' in 2006 in Dubai. She was the only leader who could speak against the army and the ISI. She told that 'these military guys have the capacity to kill. I think that the international community still thinks I am crazy when I say it.'[2] Most of the past and present Pakistani generals and officers were and are under the influence of jihadi culture. The Islam pasand parties of Pakistan are their permanent allies. It is a part of history.

All the jihadi fighting outfits operating from Pakistan are under

---

1   Price of Honour, p11.

2   Adrian Levy and Catherine Scott-Clark, Deception, Pakistan, The United States and The Global Nuclear Conspiracy, Atlantic Books, 2007, p 397.

the control of mullahs. The prominent mullahs remain in touch with the higher officers of the army and the ISI. All these have been discussed elsewhere. The most of the operations of the jihadi are masterminded by the ISI. The 26/11 operation in Mumbai appears to have been carried out by the ISI controlled outfit called Lashker-e-Taiba, which in fact is a creation of the ISI. This is what Tariq Ali had said in 2000. Pakistan despite being attacked by the neo-Taliban and Al Qaeda, has not shown guts to seize this opportunity to apprehend the culprits out of fear of reprisal and ISI's refusal to act. The point to be noted is that Al Qaeda as an idea and Taliban will survive because of Pakistan Army and the ISI. No civilian government can ever control these two agencies. An example of this has happened when President Zardari transferred ISI to Ministry of Interior and this order was withdrawn immediately under the pressure from the Army.

The philosophy of Al Qaeda, given the situation in the Muslim world as being manifested now, will definitely survive. The concept of dar-al-Islam *i.e.* the jurisdiction of Islam and dar-al-Islam inhabited by non-Muslims are non-negotiable. The theoretical formulations of these concepts have been now made action oriented by the emergence of Al Qaeda. The credit for revival of these concepts goes to America as it was America which legitimized jihad as a powerful weapon of war against Soviet Russia, not realizing that the same weapon will be used against them in a virulent manner even before the end of the Afghan Jihad in 1989. Some 25000 foreign trained jihadis fought against the Soviet Russia in Afghan war. Since it was a Mujahideen war, the jihadis got the idea that they too can now challenge any power in the world. This has been called as the 'blowback' effect from Afghan war of 1979-89 and will continue into this century.[3] This prediction has been proved to be true.

All foreign trained jihadis on return to their respective countries created cells of Al Qaeda in their countries and waged local jihad with global aims and ideas. Osama wanted to target Saudi Arabia for a regime change so as to make it a front leader of Islamic jihad. Al Zawahiri wanted a regime change in Egypt to implement the

---

3   Cooly, John K., Unholy War, p 247.

ideas of Hasan al Banna and Syed Qutab to transform Egypt into an ideal Islamic state. They ultimately realised that these regimes can not be dislodged because of harsh treatment they received from these states. Instead, they decided to mount attacks on soft states like USA, Europe, Africa and South and South East Asia. A liberal democracy provides sufficient space even to such virulent ideas to take shapes. UK, France. Germany and other European states became vulnerable and staging places of world wide jihad. Their propaganda machinery operated freely and fugitives from law were allowed to stay on humanitarian grounds. Many of them were facing murder charges in their respective countries and some even were sentenced to death or life imprisonment.

After a severe beating in Afghanistan, the Al Qaeda strategists all over the world were in the mood of reflection and were thinking of a new strategy. It realised that the objective of realizing its goal of world domination would require long time horizon and a new strategy. Muslims of the world have to be united to provide a big and durable platform for consolidation of the Muslim Ummah for an ultimate realization of Caliphate. The attack on US on 9/11 was partly successful by way of demonstration of their commitment to jihad. The attack on Iraq by US-led alliance was an error as that helped Al Qaeda to garner support from Muslims all over the world. The only justification for this unilateral intervention by US was to satisfy the ego of President Bush whose father as President could not overthrow President Saddam Hussein in the previous war to reclaim Kuwait from Saddam. The excuse for this war was on an untenable ground. Saddam was secular and was not tied up with Al Qaeda in any way. Even President Hamid Karzai of Afghanistan was not in favour of this war as it would divert attention from Al Qaeda and Taliban to Iraq. This Iraq war provided a platform for Sunni consolidation and led to attacks on Shias by Al Qaeda Sunni extremists. Sunni character of Al Qaeda was not understood by the US. The Sunnis of Pakistan were behind Al Qaeda and terrorist groups in Pakistan are organically linked to Al Qaeda. The US has now focused on Iran which is a Shia majority state. There was a growing demand in US to attack Iran for its alleged nuclear arsenal capability. The reality is that Iran is a threat to Middle East which is mostly Sunni states. This suited Al Qaeda by way of another diversion for consolidation.

In the future strategic planning of Al Qaeda, new figures have emerged. One of them was called by an assumed name Abu Musab al-Suri, a Syrian said to have written a defining work titled; '*The Call for a Worldwide Islamic Resistance*'. It is said to be a treatise on how 'to bring about the largest number of human and material casualties possible for America and its allies, a plan that involved jihadis obtaining WMDs'.[4] His real name is Mustafa Setmariam Nasar. He had a stint with Al Qaeda's inner council. He graduated from a university in Syria in mechanical engineering in the seventies. He moved to Jordan where he joined the Muslim Brotherhood. By then he became an explosive expert and guerrilla warfare strategist. He then shifted to Spain which every Muslim considers as a lost territory to be reclaimed. By marrying a local he became a citizen of Spain.

As usual with such motivated persons, al-Suri too moved to Afghanistan in 1987 in the midst of the Afghan war to meet the icon of jihad Osama bin Laden. He was not at all impressed by Osama's personality. He found faults with Osama's organizational ability and clear thinking. That impression made him return to Spain again. The real change came when he moved to UK to team up with Abu Qatada, a cleric who was considered as Al Qaeda's point man in Europe and almost openly met all Al Qaeda operatives visiting Europe. His apparent task was to provide spiritual guidance. Two such important operatives who got spiritual guidance from him were Richard Reid, the famous shoe bomber, and Zacarious Moussaoui for participating in 9/11 attack. Abu Qatada is a Palestinian, who had no battle experience. In 1997 during the Taliban regime he moved to Afghanistan as he was identified for the Paris bombing of metros in 1995 July. Many such people wanted in criminal activities elsewhere took refuge in Afghanistan for protection. He joined Al Qaeda camp near Kabul. Here he met another explosive expert called by his assumed name Abu Khatab al- Misri. He was considered Al Qaeda's

---

4   Adrian Levy and Catherine Scott-Clark, Deception, Pakistan, The United States and The Global Nuclear Conspiracy, Atlantic Books, 2007, p 418-9.

Weapon of Mass Destruction chief. Al-Suri was more focused on providing Al Qaeda with materials for 'destruction, calamity and catastrophe'.[5]

Al-Suri by association with die hard Arabs became a strong Salafist. Salaf is an Arabic word which means an ancient one *i.e.* pure Islam of the days of the Prophet. This means discarding all local accretions that happened during the long march of Islam in several countries with local customs. In a way it means slamming of progressive Islam. In South Asia and South East Asia, Islam is not Salafi or Wahhabi which are two sides of the same coin. In Bangladesh for example women wear a type of bangle worn by Hindu wives. Some apply sindur [red powder]on the parting of hair which is a custom of Hindu wives. In Indonesia many Muslims have Sanskrit names. Sukarno is a Sanskrit name. When I asked why it was so, the reply I got in Indonesia was that they have not discarded their past heritage. Converted Muslims in South Asia still retain their Hindu caste surnames like Rana, Saigal, Chauhan in Pakistan. Things are now changing due to Wahhabi or Salafi influence by way of jihadi culture imbibed from Arab jihadis. Abu is now a common first name of every jihadi.

Al-Suri claimed that he had encouraged Osama bin Laden to embrace Salafi Islam. It is said that two again fell out mainly for the reasons of publicity hunger of Osama bin Laden. Osama was not a monk. He wanted his role to be recorded in history as a great fighter for Islamic Ummah and for the cause of Caliphate. Al-Suri went into hiding to write his treatise on the future of the struggle for creation of Dar-al-Islam. He predicted the downfall of Al Qaeda as an organization. 'It will remain a call, a reference, a methodology.'[6] It will be leaderless resistance with cells that would wear down enemy, to prepare for an attack with WMD for final destruction of the US and the West.

After Al-Suri another earthshaking revelation has since

---

5   Adrian Levy and Catherine Scott-Clark, Deception, Pakistan, The United States and The Global Nuclear Conspiracy, Atlantic Books, 2007, pp 418-420.

6   Adrian Levy and Catherine Scott-Clark, Deception, Pakistan, The United States and The Global Nuclear Conspiracy, Atlantic Books, 2007, p 420.

surfaced. A Jordanian journalist Foud Hussein managed to interview two veterans of Afghan Jihad namely Abu Muhammed al-Maqdisi and Abu al-Zarqawi. In 1989 both traveled to Afghanistan to fight the Soviets and joined the Hekmatyar camp. After the war they returned to Jordan to take on the king of Jordan who put them in jail in 1994 till 1996. Out of this interview Hussein produced a book on the future war of Al Qaeda. Both the prisoners were released in 1999. Al-Zarqawi after his failure to blast the Radisson Hotel in Jordan on the millennium eve ultimately left for Afghanistan where he again joined Al Qaeda and soon he separated and went to Herat in Afghanistan to start his own training camp. In November 2001, in the midst of 'operation enduring peace' he left for Iraq. After the end of American's Iraq war in 2003 he and his dedicated group started hitting US targets and subsequently Shias. He felt that the sectarian clashes will arouse the inattentive Sunnis to a danger of a Shia threat. The strategy devised by them came to light when Hussein published his book in 2005.The book was the result of many interviews. Al Qaeda's blueprint of future war was revealed and the final end would happen in 2020 with restoration of Caliphate and jihadis will use nuclear weapons to blast away the world of unbelievers. It is really a chilling account of events to happen in future.

No major attack on US could be mounted so far after 9/11 by Al Qaeda or its splinter groups. Many analysts believe that the US has managed to secure its territory by a variety of stringent measures to protect their homeland. But Osama bin Laden thought otherwise. Osama bin Laden's January 2006 message has gone almost unnoticed. In that message he said: 'As for the delay in carrying similar operations in America, this was not due to failure to breach your security measures. Operations are under preparation, and you will see them on your ground once they are finished.'[7] It was not the style of bin Laden to announce empty declarations and threats. All his past declarations were proved to be real warnings. Osama bin Laden was Allah intoxicated person with a mission to achieve. Right or wrong he was to be taken seriously.

---

7   Mohammad-Mahmoud Ould Mohamedou, Understanding Al Qaeda – The Transformation of War, Pluto Press, 2007, p50.

During the US-led operation in Afghanistan after 9/11 the Al Qaeda leadership realised that it would be futile to engage the US- led troops as that would amount to committing suicide. They relocated in areas safe to them. This was a strategic decision. After all they have a mission and that would require a long period to accomplish. Once bin Laden had said that even after his death hundreds of bin Ladens would emerge to fight for the cause of Islam. The thinking and philosophy of many scholars of Islam are still providing inspiration to many. The period 2000-2004 was utilised for regrouping of Al Qaeda in Pakistan. The structure and functioning style of Al Qaeda has changed. Now because of necessity, the leadership decided for proliferation of mini Al Qaeda groups in several countries connected to mother Al Qaeda in loose manner. Such groups do not require command and control of the central leadership as was the fashion earlier. As aptly said the concept has changed from 'thinking locally and acting globally' to 'thinking globally and acting locally'. Each group of jihadis is now said to be locally self sufficient and action oriented.[8]

This strategy would mean attacking at far off places and make the Americans run to such places in chaotic manner. This will make the US Army war fatigue. This was the strategy in the Vietnam War where the American inducted 5,00,000 troops and suffered 58,000 casualties. This lesson has been well understood by Al Qaeda. This had happened in Iraq under the leadership of Abu Musab al-Zarqawi. He pledged his loyalty to Osama bin Laden and bin Laden made him his deputy in Iraq. His life story was that as a gang leader in Jordan he was in jail along with his Guru al-Maqdisi, seven year senior to him. A journalist Foud Hussein was also in jail for petty political misdemeanors. Three of them became close companions and shared thoughts. That became the subject of a book written by Foud Hussein. Al Maqdisi and al-Zarqawi went to Afghanistan to fight the Soviets. They on return to Jordan took on the king and were subsequently rounded up for that in 1994 and released after two years. Hussein could obtain their views and thinking on the future of jihad and outlines of the future war. His activities in Iraq were another story. Hussein's book is widely read mainly because

---

8   Ibid, p54.

it gives out an Al Qaeda's blueprint of a future war which might wake up in the intelligence community and thinking people at large. The span of Al Qaeda operation will last till 2020. After that there will be restoration of Caliphate, a dream of every jihadi world over. Obviously it would end in a terrific world war with the West, the like of which the world has never seen before. The weapons of this war will be nuclear and nonbelievers would be just blasted away. The stages of this prolonged war are well spelt out.

The first stage is the stage of 'awakening' from 2000 to 2003. This has already happened. During this period the plan is to 'strike the head of the serpent'. This has already happened by way of 9/11 attack. This would force America to act chaotically. This phase has been described as a success by Al Qaeda strategists. The fear of future terror attack has pushed US forces into Iraq. This has been seen as a trap to draw out US forces in the Middle East. Now the Al Qaeda is looking for a war in Iran, a Shia regime for which Al Qaeda has no love. Al Zarqawi killed Shias mercilessly in Iraq. The idea was to divert attention to the US as Shia's misfortune would be placed on the shoulders of the Americans. This luring game has been well played by Al Qaeda. The anti-Shia insurgency was the second stage which has ended in 2006.

Because of heavy restrictions on visa and inflow of Muslim financial capital into West, there will be capital flow into Pakistan, a safe haven for such funds. It is claimed that this has happened. Property boom in Karachi is attributed to it. As visa restrictions are severe, Pakistani middle class will be driven to redirecting some of their wealth to religious schools for jihadi factories to produce more jihadis and there will be no dearth of recruits for jihadi outfits. The Pakistani military and people in higher positions would lean towards Islamist by choice and so would be nuclear scientists. The next target Israel would be drawn into by provoking in border clashes and make Israel war-weary.

The next will be a period of electronic jihad by wide publicity. In this game full use will be made to pass on bomb making lessons. It will also be used to launch a war of ideas. From 2007 and three years after there will be a period of 'Rising and Standing Up'. In this period Syria, Lebanon will be targeted for Sunni unification and for change of regime. 2010 to 2013 would bring about the collapse of 'hated Arab governments.' This will cripple global economy and heighten cyber-terrorism. The US would retreat as its own economy will not be able to fight terrorism world wide. This would also mean weakening of Israel to fight.[9]

Between 2013 and 2016 the resistance to Al Qaeda would be reduced substantially. This phase would be a phase of 'Total Confrontation', a final struggle and fight between 'believers and non-believers' and in this phase the dreaded nuclear weapons, chemical and biological weapons would be used to bring total domination of Islamic forces. By 2020 the whole world would belong to one and half billion Muslims. This is a chilling account of a future, supposedly planned by Al Qaeda strategists. As a blueprint it is fine. It is not disclosed from where the nuclear weapons would come in hands of Al Qaeda. Perhaps this has been kept vague. The obvious source would appear to be Pakistan. Therefore, next task at the penultimate stage would be to capture power in Pakistan some time in the future. Already neo-Taliban has already emerged in Pakistan as a force to reckon with. The Pakistan establishment has no will to fight against terrorism. In fact the Al Qaeda and neo-Taliban have already seized a big chunk of area under its control. It is reaching out into Sindh, Punjab, and Baluchistan in a planned and systematic manner.

Osama bin Laden is on record to have announced the threat of use of nuclear weapon even after 9/11 from a safe heaven in Pakistan or Afghanistan border that 'if America uses chemical or nuclear weapons against us, then we may retort with chemical and nuclear weapons as a deterrent'.[10] This was also published on 10 November 2001 in *Dawn*, a respectable newspaper in Pakistan. This was endorsed by another Islamic scholar Sheikh Nasser bin Hamid al Fahad stating clearly that civilian casualties would be acceptable

---

9   Adrian Levy and Catherine Scott-Clark, Deception, Pakistan, The United States and The Global Nuclear Conspiracy, Atlantic Books, 2007, p 418-428.

10   Understanding of Al Qaeda, Mohammad-Mahmoud Ould Mohamedou, Pluto Press, 2007, p 56.

to defeat mighty enemy. He added that in jihad this was legitimate.[11] In this war against infidels killing of some Muslims would be unavoidable said al-Zarqawi as reported in CNN Arabic. Com, 18 May 2005. By this logic thousands of Muslims will be killed in the final war against the enemies of Islam. This is a serious question that needs to be debated by educated Muslims all over the world. Their views must be known to all. If they remain silent it would mean acceptance of this view of collateral damage in the event of a 'final confrontation'.

This dangerous view was shared with concern by Muslims like Anwar Sheikh. He was from Pakistan and was a devout Muslim. He saw the madness during the partition days. In fact, he killed three innocent Sikhs for which he later regretted. He shifted to UK and studied the Koran, the Hadith in light of new understanding and carried out 'a campaign against the mullahs and politicians, who use Islam as a cloak to justify their grisly deeds.[12] Anwar questioned the validity of Revelation in Koran. The daily Awaz of London carried a headline, 'Anwar Shaikh of Cardiff is a renegade and deserves to be killed.' Apostate is a crime in Islam where a non-believer is punished with death.[13] He attacked the concept of so-called Islamic paradise, where scores of hours wait for a jihadi killed in war. This promise was beyond his understanding. No one could produce a book to counter his arguments 'as the house they have built for themselves is on weak foundation'.[14] He was genuinely worried about the future of the world because 'with nuclear weapons they could destroy every thing in the name of religion. They might, you know.'[15]

This fear is genuine if one goes into the past of ISI and Osama bin Laden nexus with nuclear concerns of the world. The ISI knew that two nuclear scientists of eminence were in close touch with bin

---

11 Ibid.

12 Tariq Ali, The Clash of Fundamentalisms, Crusades, Jihads And Modernity, Verso, London, p157.

13 Ibid, p159.

14 Ibid, p164.

15 Ibid. p165.

Laden. They are Sultan Bashiruddin Mahmood and Choudhry Abdul Majeed. They met Osama bin Laden in Afghanistan. Mahmood was the same person who had raised his hand when Bhutto asked whether Islamic bomb can be produced in two years in Multan meeting held in 1972. Mahmood subsequently became a follower of pro-Taliban cleric Dr. Israr Ahmed. He reportedly published a short pamphlet called 'mechanics of doomsday and life after death' saying that catastrophes were inevitable in countries that were inflicted with moral decay and described the 1998 nuclear test as the 'property of whole Ummah.[16] Osama bin Laden told the scientists in August 2001 that he had procured enriched uranium from the Islamic Movement of Uzbekistan and wanted their help to turn them into bombs. This meeting was reportedly attended by Gen. Hamid Gul. The US did not realise the danger that looms ahead.[17]

Ould Mohamedou, a US based Islamic scholar, focused on the two messages of truce offered by Osama bin Laden. Osama's method of communication is from a position of strength arising from the strength of call of jihad. He made his first offer on 12 November 2002 *i.e.* after 14 months of 9/11 attack. He said that the road to safety begins by ending the aggression. Reciprocal treatment is part of justice. He cited all killings after 9/11 as part of reciprocal killings of Western targets. He narrated attacks in Palestine, Afghanistan and Iraq as the reasons for counter attacks by Al Qaeda. He said that 'the door of reconciliation is open for three months from the date of announcing of this statement'. The basic element of the so called offer to end this war is the vacation of foreign forces from Muslim areas including Palestine.

The second offer was made on 15 April in 2004. He again stressed on 'reciprocal treatment is part of justice and the one who starts injustice bears greater blame'. 'The reconciliation will start with the departure of its last soldier from our country. Again he threatens that 'stop spilling our blood in order to save yours'. On 29 October 2004 message was to convince the US people that Sweden was never

---

16 Adrian Levy and Catherine Scott-Clark, Deception, Pakistan, The United States and The Global Nuclear Conspiracy, Atlantic Books, 2007, p310.

17 Adrian Levy and Catherine Scott-Clark, Deception, Pakistan, The United States and The Global Nuclear Conspiracy, Atlantic Books, 2007, p311.

attacked as it remained neutral. In this message he explained why 9/11 happened. He repeated the theory that 'oppression and tyranny of the American/Israeli coalition against our people in Palestine and Lebanon was unbearable'. He said that the Mujahideen bled Russia for ten years, until it went bankrupt and was forced to withdraw in defeat. 'So we are continuing this policy in bleeding America to the point of bankruptcy'. On 19 January 2006 bin Laden said jihad was continuing as also the ranks jihadis. He said that truce will rebuild Afghanistan and Iraq. This amounts to saying vacation of troops from these places for Al Qaeda to operate again. There is a threat in this message. 'If you win it, [war] you should read history. We are a nation that does not tolerate injustice and seeks revenge forever.' Again on perpetual war, he said 'refraining from performing jihad, which is sanctioned by our religion, is an appalling sin. The best way of death for us is under the shadows of swords'. Therefore, the core issue is jihad. Jihad is the instrument for subjugation of dar al-Herb into dar al-Islam. In Islam there is no concept of permanent peace treaty. Osama bin Laden has nowhere promised a peaceful interfaith coexistence concept which is the demand of this century.

From the Afghan Jihad experience, the author of the *'Bear Trap'* has said that for a long war the 'guerrilla forces cannot survive without adequate bases to which they can withdraw from time to time to rest and refit. They need means with to fight, they need re-supply, they need to train and they need intelligence. Pakistan provided all these to Mujahideen'.[18] Therefore, the future of Al Qaeda will depend on availability of a safe sanctuary. There is no other place in the world than Pakistan and Afghanistan for regrouping of Al Qaeda as a core organization. How did Pakistan behave after 9/11? Is Pakistan serious and capable to fight neo-Taliban and Al Qaeda? Why Pakistan failed to capture Osama bin Laden? Al Zahawiri who is in Pakistan is yet to be accounted for. Let us view what was Pakistan's track record of its war on terror.

Musharraf's war on terror

Gen. Musharraf by temperament and training was an adept army commando. He could quickly change his tactic depending upon the

---

18   Yousaf and Mark Adkin, The Bear Trap, Jung Publications, 1992, p 49.

situation he would face. Before 9/11 he was pleading for acceptance of the Taliban regime as a reality. He in fact was helping the Taliban regime in every possible way. Pakistan army and ISI were in Afghanistan to help and sustain the Taliban regime. Army generals were guiding annual attacks on northern positions. These are matters of record. He made a 'u' turn immediately after 9/11. He joined the US-led coalition of war on terror. He explained that he did so to save Pakistan. Thus it was fear and not a genuine change of heart.

The story of change of heart has been well recapitulated by the authors of the book 'Deception.' Gen. Ahmed, the ISI chief was in Washington on 9/11 on invitation to meet the CIA chief George Tenet to know where Pakistan stood in the matter interdicting Al Qaeda and Osama bin Laden. 'It was like asking bin Laden to find out Al Zawahiri.' At the time of attack Ahmed was having breakfast with two senators who had earlier visited Islamabad to discuss the same subject with Gen. Musharraf. Musharraf then had said that he could do nothing. The same answer was given by Ahmad to senators 'when the New York descended into chaos.'

Next day *i.e.* on 12 September Armitage gave a dressing down to Ahmed and asked him a straight question: 'Are you with us or against us.' This was said as Pakistan was a great supporter of Taliban and bin Laden and maintained diplomatic relations with the Taliban. This as said aptly 'was a black and white choice with no grey.'[19] At night Colin Powel called Musharraf on phone and he repeated the same question *i.e.* 'Are you with us or against us.'

Two days later Gen. Ahmed returned to Pakistan. Musharraf discussed the matter with the ISI chief and other generals. Most of them were against giving aid to US. But Musharraf knew the consequences of non cooperation with the USA. Pakistan would have been clubbed with Afghanistan in the impending war on terror. Therefore, Musharraf kept on harping on the security of Pakistan in all his television addresses to the nation. At the same time he did not forget to draw attention to 'the charter of Medina' to secure Islam and that the peace treaties in Islam are temporary and tactical.

---

19 Adrian Levy and Catherine Scott-Clark, Deception, Pakistan, The United States and The Global Nuclear Conspiracy, Atlantic Books, 2007, p 312.

What Musharraf said about the charter of Medina needs to be quoted to understand its implications in terms of a long term peace with non-believers. 'The Holy Prophet signed the charter of Medina with his Jewish adversaries. This treaty remained effective for six years. Three battles were fought with non-believers of Mecca during this period-like the battle of Badr, Uhad and Khandaq. The Muslims emerged victorious in these battles with the non-believers of Mecca because the Jews had signed a treaty with the Muslims. The Holy Prophet signed the treaty with the non-believers with the Meccans who had been imposing wars on Islam,' The Holy Prophet, because of protest of non-believers, did not sign as Mohammad Rasool Allah. He told his followers that the rational thinking demanded that. Then Musharraf said that his action will pass the test of time. He thus justified 'U' turn policy by joining the US-led coalition. It is, therefore, clear that his decision was tactical and not because of his change of heart.

After 9/11 India's Parliament was attacked by Lashker-e-Taiba with Jaish-e-Mohammed on 13 December 2001. Pakistan denied its involvement but condemned the attack, a standard practice in Pakistani establishment. Only some Jihadi leaders were kept under house arrest. After a month of the attack Musharraf under US pressure addressed the Nation on 13 January 2002 and said that he received a list of 20 fugitives from India living in Pakistan. He said 'there is no question of handing over any Pakistani. This will never be done. If we are given evidence against those people, we will take action against them in Pakistan under own laws. As far as non-Pakistanis are concerned, we have not given asylum to anyone which was blatant lie. Any one falling under this category will be proceeded against whenever one is found.' Thus, he made it clear that all the twenty are safe in Pakistan. This was a clear violation of UN convention on hijacking and bombing.

Musharraf did try his best to delay the attack on Afghanistan and when the operation was on he pleaded for ceasefire in the name of Ramzan. The real reason was to take out Pakistani troops from Kunduz as the Northern Alliance had already advanced to that area.

The next step he took was amusing. He made a demand during

operation enduring peace that the Northern Alliance should not enter Kabul. This would have meant slowing down of progress of the war. This too was unacceptable to US- led coalition. All these are matters of record.

On 13 December 2001, when Indian Parliament was attacked by Pakistani terrorists, the Indian nation stood up united and demanded action. The aim of this attack was to enter Parliament and kill politicians of all hues. This did not succeed as police and security staff managed to close the doors and fired on the terrorists, killing all of them. As usual, the Pakistan government denied the involvement of any Pakistani in the attack. The nation was outraged. The government had no other alternative but to mobilize its troops on the borders. As the-US led War on Terror was in progress, the international pressure was mounted to defuse the situation. This was another attempt by Pakistan to slow down pressure on the Taliban regime and disintegration of Al-Qaeda. The previous attack of Srinagar Assembly in October 2001 was again timed to divert attention from the Afghanistan to India. Parliament attack was taken seriously by the international community. Diplomatic pressure on Musharraf yielded some results. In January he announced on TV how he would combat terrorism. He said "no individual, organization or party will be allowed to break the law of the land" and promised registration of all religious schools, regulate their curriculum and prevent them being used by extremists. After bombings in London on 7 July 2005 that linked Shehzad Taweer, who had stayed for months in a madarssa run by a Lashker-e-Taiba in Lahore, he made another declaration of registration of religious schools. That move never took off. Lashker-e-Taiba and its parent body were spared again.

Jaish-e-Mohammed was banned in July 2002 and Maulana Azar Masood was put under so-called house arrest, a peculiar Pakistani method to hoodwink the international world. He was soon freed and he renamed his outfit called Khuddam-ul-Islam. The same trick was seen in the case of the parent body of Lashker-e-Taiba now called Jamaat-ud-Dawa after the release of Hafiz Mohammed Saeed from his so called house arrest. The US took notice of this drama and brought this to the attention of Musharraf.[20]

Maulana Azam Tariq of Sipah-e-Sahaba was arrested in January 2002 and released after being elected to National Assembly while in jail. This happened after he pledged his support to Musharraf.[21] He was a die-hard Sunni Muslim. The patron chief of Sahaba was Ramzi Yousef, a most wanted terrorist for first attack of World Trade Centre in 1993 in New York. Yousef was behind the conspiracy to organise an Ariel attack in USA. He was arrested on US intelligence in Pakistan in January 2002. He was handed over to US without extradition proceedings. This happened in number of cases. In case of India it has become a standard procedure in Pakistan to demand for proofs even when the principal case ended in convictions. Dawood Ibrahim case falls under this category.

There is a tidal wave of a new movement called neo-Taliban of Pakistan. Zakir Hussain, a journalist, took the risk of visiting Miranshah located in North Waziristhan. What he wrote was alarming. What he found was 'a scene of hell'. A line of bullet ridden bodies strung from electric poles......a severed body with currency notes shoved into the mouth ....a dead dog thrown on the mutilated bodies in a crowed bazaar. 'This is the fate of criminals and those who disobey God, thundered a long bearded mullah, as he hit one of the bodies with the butt of rifle'.[22]

President Bush's only visit to Pakistan was in March 2006. He was aware of the ground realities by his delayed visit, when Musharraf was a dear friend of his. The Air Force One flew in to Pakistan at night to reduce a night attack from those who had US supplied Stinger missiles. They are Mujahideen's trained to fight in Afghan war. Gen Asalm Beg and Gen Javed Nasir refused to return the surplus Stinger missiles back to US. In 1999 Pakistan had used Stinger missiles against Indian Air Force. US Black Hawks hovered around the air space of Pakistan for safety of US President.

---

20 Adrian Levy and Catherine Scott-Clark, Deception, Pakistan, The United States and The Global Nuclear Conspiracy, Atlantic Books, 2007, p 432.

21 Adrian Levy and Catherine Scott-Clark, Deception, Pakistan, The United States and The Global Nuclear Conspiracy, Atlantic Books, 2007, p 436.

22 Terror in Miranshah-Zahid Hussain, *Newsline*, April 2006.

Before the Islamabad visit Bush was in Kabul where Hamid Karzai presented a dossier of evidence to show how the Pak providing elements of military and ISI assistance and were arming the Taliban and Al-Qaeda. Karzai reportedly provided location hideouts of bin Laden and Mullah Omar. Not only this a few days before his Islamabad visit David Foy of the US consulate and three others were killed when an explosive packed vehicle rammed into Foy's car in the secured zone of the US consulate in Karachi.

Despite the alarming situation Bush said: "Musharraf understands the stakes, he understands the responsibility, the need to make sure the strategy to defeat the enemy". He said: the best way to vanquish Al-Qaeda was to share good intelligence, to locate them and then be prepared to bring them to justice. He said that best way to defeat terrorism was to replace the ideology of hate to ideology of hope. 'Together we will win' was his war cry.[23]

Musharraf told Bush that 80,000 of his troops were in the western border to fight terrorists and claimed that just four days before, 25 foreign terrorists were killed when an eye witness account was that those killed were children, women and teenage students.[24]

Musharraf described President Karzai's report as rubbish. The events and happenings did not warrant such a view. All knowledgeable people have noticed the revival of Al Qaeda, Taliban, neo Taliban in Pakistan, ferocity of attacks being carried out by Lashker-e-Taiba, Jaish-e-Mohammed and other Sunni armed groups which are posing serious threats to world. Let us quote experts on the subject. The director of MI5 made an unusual public statement before an invited audience in London almost warning that 'resilient networks' of terror in Britain and capabilities elsewhere in Europe were being 'directed by al-Qaeda in Pakistan.' She further told al Qaedas were serious and growing.[25] Such observations were based on facts. The same

23 Adrian Levy and Catherine Scott-Clark, Deception, Pakistan, The United States and The Global Nuclear Conspiracy, Atlantic Books, 2007, p 429.

24 Adrian Levy and Catherine Scott-Clark, Deception, Pakistan, The United States and The Global Nuclear Conspiracy, Atlantic Books, 2007, p 431.

25 Adrian Levy and Catherine Scott-Clark, Deception, Pakistan, The United States and The Global Nuclear Conspiracy, Atlantic Books, 2007, p 431.

was told by the British Prime Minister in Delhi in a press conference on 14 December 2008. He also said that the Lashker-e-Taiba was behind the attack on 26 November 2008 in Mumbai.

Bruce Riedel, former director of US National Security Council, who served under Clinton and Bush administration, expressed the same view. 'Between 2002 and 2004, they were on survival mode and creating new bases of operations in Pakistan, especially around Quetta and Balucisthan.' This revival happened during Musharraf regime. He, as head of the state, was a part of this revival. All his public posture was for the consumption of the international community and for obtaining US aid. The same trick was adopted by Gen Zia during the Afghan jihad. Most of US military aids were used for Pakistan army to enhance its strength to obtain parity with India.

Musharraf peace deals with extremist groups in Pakistan were to provide them space to expand their capabilities and safe space to al-Qaeda and Taliban and neo-Taliban. From the very beginning he was a reluctant partner of the war on terror coalition. Most of his trusted generals were involved in promoting and sustaining al-Qaeda and Taliban.

Musharaff's rubbishing of President Karzai's report was nothing but a lie. A so-called jihadi commander was killed in Helmand province in Afghanistan in 2007. British press has now revealed that the jihadi commander was a senior level officer of the Pakistan army. This could be found from ID card on him.[26]

Khaled Ahmed, a reputed journalist of Pakistan, writes in March 2000 that in Pakistan Huntington's is accepted. As a result there is perception that as long as America lived, the security of Islamic world is at risk and a prominent philanthropist Hakim Saeed gave a typical security discourse. He claimed he seen in a dream which forecast an Islamic alliance with yellow races and that combination will conquer the Christian world. Huntington's tentative imagination had become a reality in Pakistan and elsewhere in the Islamic world.[27]

---

26 *The Times of India*,25 December, 2008.

27 Khaled Ahmed , *The Friday Times*, April-March, 2000.

The cat is out of bag now. Baitullah Mashud, who was said to be behind the assassination of Benazir Bhutto, had offered to give his men and material support to Pakistan army in the event of a war between India and Pakistan. He was the Emir of a neo-Taliban outfit called Tehrik-e-Taliban of FATA. Same offer was made by Maulana Fazullah, Emir of Tehreek-e-Nafaz-e-Shariat-e-Mohammad who was virtually controlling the Swat region. Thus, the foreign experts feel that such statements confirms Pakistan's suspected links with neo-Taliban which is nothing but to support Taliban in Afghanistan. Even it was reported that after the Mumbai attack a Pak corps commander told a journalist that the military fighting the Taliban was because of misunderstandings which could be removed through dialogues.[28]

The future blueprint of Al Qaeda, as discussed already, can be implemented if the ideological frontiers of Pakistan can be stretched by toppling the Karzi government in Afghanistan. By resorting to covert action this has been happening in Afghanistan and Pakistan's ISI is again raising the level of Mujahideen war. The foreigners in Pakistan are also being attacked for creating a fear psychosis. All attack cases have not been solved by the Pakistani police. The police in Pakistan are not incapable. It is just due to lack of political will to bring the culprits to justice. Not a single important political murder case has ever been solved in Pakistan. Grounds are being created for another coup in Pakistan as that would create a space for jihadis to wage the final 'confrontation', which may take another ten years.

The strategy will be to capture Pasthun areas of Afghanistan for re-emergence of Al Qaeda in Afghanistan. For this to happen there will be attacks on foreign forces in Afghanistan to cripple their fighting ability and morale. This had happened during the Afghan jihad in 1979-89. The unfolding of events happening in Afghanistan and Pakistan are indicative of such a situation emerging again. Only 'divine intervention' can prevent the ultimate 'confrontation'. The author of 'the Islamic Threat, Myth or Real', John Esposito writes 'resurgent Islam promises to be the most powerful ideological force at work in the world over the next several decades'. The policy

---

28 *The Times of India*, 25 December, 2008.

formulations of every free country should be realistic or else the world will face a terrible situation of ultimate self destruction.

Appendix-1

Directors of ISI

1. Colonel Syed Shahid Hamid 1948-1950.

2. Maj Gen Robert Cawthome 1950-1959.

3. Brig. Riaz Hussain, 1959-1966.

4. Maj Gen (then Brig.) Mohammad Akbar Khan, 1966-1971.

5. Lt Gen (then Maj Gen) Ghulam Jilani Khan, 1971-1978.

6. Lt Gen Muhammad Riaz, 1978-1980.

7. Lt Gen Akhtar Abdur Rahman, 1980 – March 1987.

8. Lt Gen Hamid Gul, March 1987- May 1989.

9. Lt Gen (Retd.) Shamsur Rahman Kallu, May 1989-August 1990.

10. Lt Gen Asad Durrani, August 1990 – March 1992.

11. Lt Gen Javed Naris, March 1992-May 1993.

12. Lt Gen Javed Ashraf Qazi, May 1993-1995.

13. Lt Gen (then Maj Gen) Nasim Rana, 1995 – Oct 1998.

14. Lt Gen Ziauddin Butt, October 1998-October 1999.

15. Lt Gen Ehsan ul Haq, October 2001-October 2004.

16. Lt Gen Ashfaq Parvez Kayani, October 2004 – October 2007.

17. Lt Gen Nadeem Taj, October 2007 – September 2008.

18. Lt Gen Ahmad Shuja Pasha, September 2008-2012.

19. Lt Gen Zaheerul Islam 2012- till date (present chief).

Appendix-2

United Nations Security Council Resolution 1368, 12 September 2001 (adopted unanimously)

The Security Council,

Reaffirming the principles and purposes of the Charter of the United Nations, Determined to combat by all means threats to international peace and security caused by terrorist acts,

Recognizing the inherent right of individual or collective self-dence in accordance with the Charter,

1. Unequivocally condemns in the strongest terms the horrifying terrorist attacks which took place on 11 September 2001 in New York, Washington (DC) and Pennsylvania and regards such acts, like any act of international terrorism, as a threat to international peace and security;

2. Expresses its deepest sympathy and condolences to the victims and their families and to the People and Government of the United States of America;

3. Calls on all States to work together urgently to bring to justice the perpetrators, organisers and sponsors of these terrorist attacks and stresses that those responsible for aiding, supporting or harbouring the perpetrators, organisers and sponsors of these acts will be held accountable;

4. Calls also on the international community to redouble their efforts to prevent and suppress terrorist acts including by increased cooperation and full implementation of the relevant international anti-terrorist conventions and Security Council resolution, in particular resolution 1269 of 19 October 1999;

5. Expresses its readiness to take all necessary steps to respond to the terrorist attacks of 11 September 2001, and to combat all forms of terrorism, in accordance with its responsibilities under the Charter of the United Nations;

6. Decides to remain seized of the matter.

Appendix-3

United Nations Security Council Resolution 1373, 28 September 2001 (adopted unanimously)

The Security Council,

Reaffirming its resolutions 1269 (1999) of 19 October 1999 and 1368 (2001) of 12 September 2001,

Reaffirming also its unequivocal condemnation of the terrorist attacks which took place in New York, Washington, DC, and Pennsylvania on 11 September 2001, and expressing its determination to prevent all such acts,

Reaffirming further that such acts, like any act of international terrorism, constitute a threat to international peace and security. Reaffirming the inherent right of individual or collective self-defence as recognized by the Charter of the United Nations as reiterated in resolution 1368 (2001),

Reaffirming the need to combat by all means, in accordance with the Charter of the United Nations, threats to international peace and security caused by terrorist acts,

Deeply concerned by the increase, in various regions of the world, of acts of terrorism motivated by intolerance or extremism,

Calling on States to work together urgently to prevent and suppress terrorist acts, including through increased cooperation and full implementation of the relevant international conventions relating to terrorism,

Recognizing the need for States to complement international cooperation by taking additional measures to prevent and suppress, in their territories through all lawful means, the financing and preparation of any acts of terrorism,

Reaffirming the principle established by the General Assembly in its declaration of October 1970 (resolution 2625 (XXV)) and reiterated by the Security Council in its resolution 1189 (1998) of 13 August 1998, namely that every State has the duty to refrain from organizing, instigating, assisting or participating in terrorist acts in another state or acquiescing in organised activities within its territory directed towards the commission of such acts,

Acting under Chapter VII of the Charter of the United Nations,

1. Decides that all States shall:

(a) Prevent and suppress the financing of terrorist acts;

(b) Criminalize the wilful provision or collection, by any means, directly or indirectly, of funds by their nationals or in their territories with the intention that the funds should be used, or in the knowledge that they are to be used, in order to carry out terrorist acts;

(c) Freeze without delay funds and other financial assets or economic resources of persons who commit, or attempt to commit, terrorist acts or participate in or facilitate the commission of terrorist acts; of entities owned or controlled directly or indirectly by such persons; and of persons and entities acting on behalf of, or at the direction of such persons and entities, including funds derived or generated from property owned or controlled directly or indirectly by such persons and associated persons and entities;

(d) Prohibit their nationals or any persons and entities within their territories from making any funds, financial assets or economic resources or financial or other related services available, directly or indirectly, for the benefit of persons who commit or attempt to commit or facilitate or participate in the commission of terrorist acts, of entities owned or controlled, directly or indirectly, by such persons and of persons and entities acting on behalf of or at the direction of such persons;

2.   Decides also that all States shall:

(a) Refrain from providing any form of support, active or passive, to entities or persons involved in terrorist acts, including by suppressing recruitment of members of terrorist groups and eliminating the supply of weapons to terrorists;

(b) Take the necessary steps to prevent the commission of terrorist acts, including by provision of early warning to other States by exchange of information;

(c) Deny safe haven to those who finance, plan, support, or commit terrorist acts, or provide safe havens;

(d) Prevent those who finance, plan, facilitate or commit terrorist acts from using their respective territories for those purposes against other States or their citizens;

(e) Ensure that any person who participates in the financing, planning, preparation or perpetration of terrorist acts or in supporting terrorist acts is brought to justice and ensure that, in addition to any other measures against them, such terrorist acts are established as serious criminal offences in domestic laws and regulations and that the punishment duly reflects the seriousness of such terrorist acts;

(f) Afford one another the greatest measure of assistance in connection with criminal investigations or criminal proceedings relating to the financing or support of terrorist acts; including assistance in obtaining evidence in their possession necessary for the proceedings;

(g) Prevent the movement of terrorists or terrorist groups by effective border controls and controls on issuance of identity papers and travel documents, and through measures for preventing counterfeiting, forgery or fraudulent use of identity papers and travel documents;

3. Calls upon all States to:

(a) Find ways of intensifying and accelerating the exchange of operational information, especially regarding actions or movements of terrorist persons or networks; forged or falsified travel documents; traffic in arms, explosives or sensitive materials; use of communications technologies by terrorist groups; and the threat posed by the possession of weapons of mass destruction by terrorist groups;

(b) Exchange information in accordance with international and domestic law and cooperate on administrative and judicial matters to prevent the commission of terrorist acts;

(c) Cooperate, particularly through bilateral and multilateral arrangements and agreements, to prevent and suppress terrorist attacks and take action against perpetrators of such acts;

(d) Become parties as soon as possible to the relevant international conventions and protocols relating to terrorism, including the International Convention for the Suppression of the Financing of Terrorism of 9 December 1999;

(e) Increase cooperation and fully implement the relevant international conventions and protocols relating to terrorism and Security Council resolutions 1269 (1999) and 1368 (2001);

(f) Take appropriate measures in conformity with the relevant provisions of national and international law, including international standards of human rights, before granting refugee status, for the purpose of ensuring that the asylum seeker has not planned, facilitated or participated in the commission of terrorist acts;

(g) Ensure, in conformity with international law, that refugee status is not abused by the perpetrators, organisers or facilitators of terrorist acts, and that claims of political motivation are not recognized as grounds for refusing requests for the extradition of alleged terrorists;

4. Notes with concern the close connection between international terrorism and transnational organised crime, illicit drugs, money-laundering, illegal arms-trafficking, and illegal movement of nuclear, chemical, biological and other potentially deadly materials, and in this regard emphasizes the need to enhance coordination of efforts on national, sub-regional, regional and international levels in order to strengthen a global response to this serious challenge and threat to international security;

5. Declares that acts, methods, and practices of terrorism are contrary to the purposes and principles of the United Nations and that knowingly financing, planning and inciting terrorist acts are also contrary to the purposes and principles of the United Nations;

6. Decides to establish, in accordance with rule 28 of its provisional rules of procedure, a Committee of the Security Council, consisting of all the members of the Council, to monitor implementation of this resolution, with the assistance of appropriate expertise, and calls upon all States to report to the Committee, no later than 90 days from the date of adoption of this resolution and thereafter according to a timetable to be proposed by the Committee, on the steps they have taken to implement this resolution;

7. Directs the Committee to delineate its tasks, submit a work programme within 30 days of the adoption of this resolution, and to consider the support it requires, in consultation, with the Secretary General;

8. Expresses its determination to take all necessary steps in order to ensure the full implementation of tj1is resolution, in accordance with its responsibilities under the Charter;

9. Decides to remain seized of this matter.

List Of Muslim Lands Conquered By Non-Muslims

1757-1919

Year of Conquest	Land
1757	Ili (China)
1759	Kashgar (China)
1760	Tarim Basin (China)
1764	Bengal (Britain)
1777	Balam-Bangan, Indonesia (Holland)
1783	Crimea (Russia)
1785	Pattani (Thailand)
	Arakan (Burma)
1786	Penang, Malaysia (Britain)
1798	Egypt (France)
1799	Syria (France)
1800	Parts of Malaysia (Britain)
1801	Georgia (Russia)
1803-28	Azerbaijan, Russia
1804	Armenia (Russia)
1808	Western Java (Holland)
1820	Bahrain; Qatar; United Arab Emirates (Britain)
1830	Manchanagara, Indonesia (Holland)
1830-46	Algerian Coast (France)
1834-59	Caucasus (Russia)
1839	Central Sumatra, Indonesia (Holland)

	Aden, South Yemen (Britain)
1841	Sarawak (Sir James Brooke, a Briton)
1843	Sind (Britain)
1849	Kashmir and Punjab, (Britain) Pans of Guinea (France)
1893	Uganda (Britain)
1896-98	Northern Sudan (Britain)
1898-1903	Southern Niger (France)
1899	Kuwait (Britain)
1900-14	Southern Algeria (France)
1903	Macedonia (Russia and Austria)
1906	Wadai, Chad (France)
1908	Crete (Greece)
1909	Northern Malay Peninsula (Britain)
1911-28	Libya (Italy)
1912	Dodecanese (Italy)
1913	Southern Philippines (United States) Central Thrace (Bulgaria)
1914	All Malaysia (Britain)
1917	Palestine (Britain)
1918	Lebanon; Syria (France)
1919	Parts of Turkey (Italy, Greece, and France) Iraq

(Countries in the parentheses are the respective conquering powers).

Original Source: Pipes, Daniel, "In the Path of God", Basic Books, New York, 1980 and reproduced in 'Pakistan Resolution to Pakistan'

Fatwa

Jihad needs scriptural support to make it an effective instrument of relentless war against the infidels. Only well versed scholars of Islam can issue Fatwa. A fatwa was issued by Dr Hasan al-Turabi, a Sudanese scholar of Islam, in summer 1995 as precedent setting legal religious texts for legislating relations between Muslims and non-Muslims in areas where the infidels were not willing to be simply subdued by the Muslim forces and in areas contested by Mujhahideen'.[1]

Before that a Fatwa was issued by the Islamic Religious Conference held at AI-Obaeid, Sudan, on April 23, 1993. In this Fatwa rebel Muslims who are fighting against the (Muslim) states are hereby declared apostates from Islam, and non-Muslims are hereby declared Kaffirs (infidels).

Warning Muslims who do not kill in name of Jihad, the Fatwa declared – those Muslims who .... try to question or doubt the Islamic justifiability of Jihad are hereby classified as 'hypocrites', who are no longer Muslims, and also 'apostates' from the religion of Islam; and they 'will be condemned permanently to the fire of hell.'[2]

Another key document in the light of a judgment decree issued earlier by Sayyid Muhammad Qutab, who was renowned scholar in Egypt in 1995. In that Qutab had dealt with the relationship between the believer and the modem secular state. He identified a secular state as 'Jahiliyyah' *i.e* barbarity or ignorance. There must be fight against such states by the Muslims as part of their obligation. This was renewed by the Islamic leadership in Khartoum to take up Jihad against Jahaliyyah where large Muslim communities live under non-Muslim regimes. "It is not the function of Islam to compromise with the concepts of Jahiliyyah which are current in the world or to

---

1   John Cooley, bin Laden, The Man Who Declared War on America, Prima Publishing, 1999.

2   ibid, p 110.

coexist in the same land together with a Jahili system. Jahiliyyah is deviation from the worship of one Allah and the way of life prescribed by Allah".[3]

Thus Qutab saw no alternative to an all out armed struggle-a Jihad to free believers from servitude to the Jahiliyyah. Said Qutab: "The foremost duty of Islam is to depose Jahiliyyah from the leadership of man." This view was concurred by Hasan allTurabi. If you examine this concept in the light of secular states where Muslims form a substantial numbers there will religious war. No scholar of Islam has challenged this dangerous concept. Thus, there is apprehension in such secular states.

An organization called "World Front For Jihad Against Jews and Crusaders" was formed on February 20, 1998 by bin Laden's Al Qaeda. The key signatories were Osama bin Laden, Dr Ayman al-Zawahiri, Rifai Ahmed Taha (Abu Vasser), Sheikh Mir Hamzah, secretary of the Jamait-ul-Ulema-e-Pakistan (JUIP), Fazlur Rehman khalil, leader of the Harkat ul-Mujahideen of Pakistan, and Sheikh Abdul Salam Muhammad, Emir of the Jihad movement in Bangladesh.[4]

The principal targets chosen were the American and their allies, the objective being to liberate the al-Aqsa mosque in Jerusalem and the Holy Mosque in Mecca from their grip.

A series of Fatwas were issued by London's office of Azzam organization in 1998 calling the Muslims to follow a text of dua, *i.e.* prayer to answer the call of Islam. The text was to be read in the mosques during Friday prayers. The mosques were told to do three things – participate in Jihad, contribute in support of Jihad, and pray for the success of Jihad. A long list of missions to be achieved was also added to make the Jihad a worldwide movement. Apart from general attacks of interest of Kaffir nations, attacks on Israel, Russians, foreign forces in the Gulf countries and 'Hindu forces in Kashmir.'

In 1998 Sheikh Omar Abdtir Rehaman's Fatwa on war against

---

3   ibid, p 111-112.

4   Bodonosky, p 223.

America was widely distributed in Pakistan after the US missile strike in Khost on 20.8.1998. He said: "Destroy them(US) thoroughly and erase them from the face of earth. Ruin their economies, set their companies on fire, turn their conspiracies to powder and dust. Sink their ships, bring their planes down. Slay them in the air, on land, on water. And (with the command of Allah) kill them wherever you find them ... Kill these infidels.[5]

---

5   Nation, a Pakistan daily, 29.8.1998.

Bibliography

1. Adrian Levy and Catherine Scott-Clark. Deception, Pakistan, The United States and The Global Nuclear Weapons Conspiracy, Atlantic Books, 2007.

2. Ahmed, Samina. The (Un) holy Nexus? , Newsline, Karachi: vol.10, September 1998, pp31-34.

3. Abdul Bari Atwan. The Secret History of Al Qaeda, Saqi Books, London: 2006.

4. Akhar S. Ahmad. Post modernism and Islam, Penguin Books, 1993.

5. Akhar S. Ahmad. Jinnah, Pakistan and Islamic Identity, Oxford University Press.

6. Ali, Tariq. The Fundamentalisms, Crusades, Jihad and Modernity, Verso, London: 2002.

7. Ali, Tariq. Can Pakistan Survive? The Death of a State, Penguin Books, 1983.

8. Arif, K. M. Gen. Working with Zia, Oxford, Pakistan; 1995.

9. Ayubi, Nazih N. Political Islam: Religion and Politics in the Arab World, Routledge, London: 1991.

10. Aziz Al-Azmeh. Islam and Modernities, Verso, London.

11. Bassam Tibi. The Challenge of Fundamentalism: Political Islam and the New World Order, University of California Press, Barkely; 1998, pp.54-55.

12. Bruce James. Arab Volunteers of the Afghan War, Jane's Intelligence Review, Vol. 7, no 4.

13. Burke Jason. The True Story of Racidal Islam, Penguin Books, 2004.

14. Jason Burke. Al Qaeda, Casting a Shadow of Terror. I.B. Tauris, 2003, p 72.

15. Chagla M.C. Roses in December, Bhartiya Vidhya Bhawan.

16. Constable Pamela. Guns and Yellow Roses, Harper Collins, New Delhi.

17. Constable Pamela. International Herald, November 6, 2000.

18. Cooly, John K. Unholy War: Afghanistan, America and International Terrorism, Pluto Press, 2012.

19. Datta, S K and Rajeev Sharma. Pakistan: From Jinnah to Jihad, UPBS Publishers' Distributors, Delhi; 2003.

20. Durrani, Tehmina. My Feudal Lord, Bantam Press, UK; 1994.

21. Eason Ahrari M. China, Pakistan, and the Taliban syndrome, *Asian survey* vol xl no 4, July/August, 2000.

22. Esposito, John L. Islam and Politics, Syracuse University Press, New York; 1984.

23. Gauhar Altaf. Ayub Khan- Pakistan's First Military Ruler, United Press, Dhaka.

24. Goodwin, Jan. The Price of Honour, Little Brown and Company, UK: 1994.

25. Harris Proctor. J (ed) Islam and International Relations, Pall Mall Press, London: 1965.

26. Haqqani Husain. Pakistan: From Mosque to Military, Carnegie Endowment for International Peace, Washington, 2005.

27. Husband, Mark. Warriors of the Prophet; The struggle for Islam, Westview Press, 1998.

28. Ignatius, David. Qaeda Agents in the West Wait Quietly for

Orders, *International Herald Tribune*, November 19, 2001.

29. Jansen, Godfrey. The Afghans-an Islamic Time Bomb, Middle East International, 20 November, 1992.

30. Johannes, J.G. The Neglected Duty, The Creed of Sadat's Assassins, and Islamic Resurgence in the Middle East, Macmillan, New York; 1986.

31. Joshi V T. Pakistan to Benazir, Konark Publishing, New Delhi.

32. Juergensmeyer, Mark. Terror in the God: The Global Rise of Religious Violence, University of Calfornia Press, 2000.

33. Kamal, Matinduddin. The Taliban phenomenon. Lancer Publications and Distributors, New Delhi, 2000.

34. Kaplan Robert D. The Atlantic Monthly, 2000.

35. Khalilzad Zalmay. Anarchy in Afghanistan, Journal International Affairs, Summer 1997.

36. Khan Illyas M. The ISI Taliban Nexus, The Herald, November, 2000.

37. Khan Mazhar Ali. Pakistan: The Barren Years 1975-1992, Oxford University Press, New York; 1998.

38. Laqueur, Walter.The Age of Terrorism, Little Brown, London; 1987.

39. Lawrence, Bruce B. Shattering the Myth, Princeton University Press, New Jersey; 1998.

40. Lewis Bernad. The Return of Islam.

41. License to Kill; Osama bin Laden's Declaration of Jihad, Foreign Affairs vol.77, no.6 (November/December1998) pp.14-19.

42. Malik, Brig. S.K. The Quranic Concept of War, Himalayan Books, New Delhi, 1986.

43. Maudud, S Abdul. A' la, Rights of Non-Muslims in Islamic

State, Islamic Publications, Lahore.

44. McGrath Allen. Destruction of Pakistan's Democracy, Oxford University Press.

45. Mendelson, Sarah E. Changing Course Ideas, Politics and Soviet Withdrawal from Afghanistan.

46. Miller John C. Michael Stone, Chris Mitchell. The Cell: Inside the 9/11 Plot, and Why the FBI and CIA Failed to Stop It. New York: 2002.

47. Mohammad-Mahmoud, Ould Mohamedou. Understanding Al Qaeda, Pluto Press, 2007

48. Nayyar, K.K., Admiral. (Ed.) Pakistan At Crossroads, Rupa and Co, New Delhi; 2003.

49. Nasar, Serman. Background on Al Qaeda's Arrested Strategist, Stephen Ulph, published in the Jameston Foundation's terrorism Focus' vol 3, issue 12, 28 March 2006 or on line http;/www.jamestown.org/terrorism/news/article.Php?articleid=2369941

50. On the Abyss, Pakistan After the Coup, Harper Collins, 2000.

51. Proctor, J. Harris. (ed.), Islam and International Relations, , Pall Mall Press, London, 1965.

52. Qutb, Sayyid. Islam and Universal Peace, Indianpolis; American Trust Publications, 1993.

53. Qutb, Sayyid. The Religion of Islam, Holy Koran Publishing, Kuwait; 1988.

54. Rahnema, Ali. (ed.) Pioneers of Islamic Revival, Zed Books, 1995.

55. Ranstorp, Magnus. Terrorism in the Name of Religion, Journal of International Affairs, vol. 50, no. 1, summer 1996. pp. 49-55.

56. Rashid, Ahmed. Taliban: Militant Islam, Oil and Fundamentalism in Central Asia.

57. Rehman, Fazlur Islam. Weildenfeld and Nicolson, London: 1966, pp. 23-24.

58. Roy, Oliver. The Failure of Political Islam, I.B. Tauris, London; 1994.

59. Roy, Oliver. The lessons of the Soviet Afghan War, International Institute for Strategic Studies, Summer 1991, p 36.

60. Sharma, Rajeev. (ed.) Pakistan Trap, UBS Publishers' Distributors, Delhi, 2001.

61. Shah, Mehatab Ali. The Foreign Policy of Pakistan, IB Tauris, London: 1997.

62. Sherwani, Latif Ahmed. (ed) Pakistan Resolution to Pakistan 1940-1947: A Selection of Documents, Daya Publishing House, Delhi; 1985.

63. Sivan, Emmanuel. Radical Islam: Medieval Theology and Modern Politics, New Haven, Yale University Press, 1991.

64. Sivan E. and M. Friedman. (eds), Religious Radicalism and Politics in Middle East, New York State University, 1990.

65. Stern, Jessica. Pakistan's Jihad Culture, Foreign Affairs, Vol. 79, no 6, November/December 2000.

66. The Call for Worldwide Islamic Resistance.

67. The Jihad Fixation-Agenda, Strategy, Porentents, A Woodsmith Compilation, Wordsmith Compilation, Delhi; 2001.

68. Yousaf and Mark Adkin. The Bear Trap, Jung Publications, 1992..

69. Woodward, Bob. The Veil, The Secret Wars of CIA, 1981-87, Simon & Schuster; 2005.

70. Woodward, Bob. The Commander, Simon and Schuster, New York: 1991

Index

www.ingramcontent.com/pod-product-compliance
Lightning Source LLC
Chambersburg PA
CBHW071836270326
41929CB00013B/2016

* 9 7 8 9 3 8 4 4 6 4 2 7 1 *